HOW TO WIN YOUR TAX AUDIT

An Insider's Guide to Successfully Negotiating with the IRS

Chronicled from the files of the nation's most successful and respected taxpayers' rights advocate

Daniel J. Pilla

WINNING Publications, Inc.
215 W. Myrtle Street
Stillwater, MN 55082
800-346-6829
www.taxhelponline.com

Cover and contents design: Sandi Holmgren – www.holmgrendesign.com

First edition: December 2014

Printed in the United States of America

ISBN: 978-1-884367-09-0 90000

Notice from the Author and Publisher

This book is designed to present the author's findings and opinions based on research, analysis and experience with the subject matter covered. This information is not provided for purposes of rendering legal, accounting or other professional advice. It is intended purely for educational purposes. In publishing this book, neither the author nor the publisher is engaged in rendering legal, accounting or other professional service. If legal advice or other professional assistance is required, the services of a competent professional should be sought.

Because the United States currently functions under an evolutionary legal system, the reader bears the burden of assuring that the principles of law stated in this work are current and binding at the time of any intended use or application. Caution: The law in this country is subject to change arbitrarily and without notice.

TABLE OF CONTENTS

Abbreviations

The following abbreviations are used throughout the text.

ACS	Automated Collection Site
AO	Appeals Officer
ASED	Assessment Statute of Limitations
BLS	Bureau of Labor Statistics
BMF	Business Master File
CADE 2	Customer Account Database
CBO	Congressional Budget Office
CI	Criminal Investigation function
CIP	Compliance Initiative Project
CPI	Consumer Price Index
CSED	Collection Statute of Limitations
DIF	Discriminant Income Function
DLN	Document Locator Number
EIN	Employer Identification Number
FBAR	Report of Foreign Bank and Financial Accounts
FOIA	Freedom of Information Act
GAO	Government Accountability Office, formerly General Accounting Office
IA	Installment Agreement
IDR	Information Document Request
IMF	Individual Master File
IRC	Internal Revenue Code
IRM	Internal Revenue Manual
IRMF	Information Returns Master File
LLC	Limited Liability Company
MSSP	Market Segment Specialization Program
NOD	Notice of Deficiency (audit cases) Notice of Determination (collection cases)
NTA	National Taxpayer Advocate
NRP	National Research Project
OIC	Offer in Compromise
OVDP	Offshore Voluntary Disclosure Program
PLE	Personal Living Expenses
POA	Power of Attorney
PPACA	Patient Protection and Affordable Care Act
QB	QuickBooks
RA	Revenue Agent (tax examiner/auditor)
RAL	Refund Anticipation Loan
RAR	Revenue Agent's Report
Rev. Reg.	Revenue Regulation
RO	Revenue Officer
SA	Special Agent
SFR	Substitute for Return
SSA	Social Security Administration
SSN	Social Security Number
TC	Transaction Code
TCMP	Taxpayer Compliance Measurement Program
T&E	Travel and Entertainment
TIGTA	Treasury Inspector General for Tax Administration
TIN	Taxpayer Identification Number

DEDICATION

To Jeannie

My life partner, business partner and best friend

Put on the whole armor of God, that you may be
able to stand against the wiles of the devil.
For we are not contending against flesh and blood,
but against the principalities, against the powers,
against the world rules of this present darkness,
against the spiritual hosts of wickedness
in the heavenly places. Therefore, take
the whole armor of God, that you may be
able to withstand the evil day,
and having done all, to stand.

- Ephesians 6:11-13

There is no crueler tyranny than that
which is perpetrated under the shield
of law and in the name of justice.

- Montesquieu, 1742

PART ONE

THE IRS'S GAME
OF
CAT AND MOUSE

"The right of the people to be secure in their persons, houses, papers, and effects, against unreasonable searches and seizures, shall not be violated, and no Warrants shall issue, but upon probable cause, supported by Oath or affirmation, and particularly describing the place to be searched, and the persons or things to be seized."

**AMENDMENT FOUR
UNITED STATES CONSTITUTION**

CHAPTER ONE

THE
STORY LINE

THE MAN SAT PATIENTLY IN HIS CAR, WATCHING carefully. He parked a safe distance away from the front door of the house but would be sure to notice if anybody came out. He didn't particularly like the waiting, the hours of doing nothing. But hey, it's part of the job.

Suddenly, there was some action. The door opened and out stepped the subject of his curiosity. A tall, middle-aged man walked down the front steps and climbed into his car. He was dressed very casually and carried a cooler.

"This could be it," thought the man. "Here we go!" He started his car and slowly followed the subject.

He was kind of new at this sort of thing. His heart was pounding. He wasn't sure how close to follow. Would he be spotted? But if he dropped back too far, he'd lose him. "Can't let that happen," he thought. "I've been waiting too long for this. Damn! They make it look so easy in the movies."

The subject twisted and turned through traffic, oblivious to his tail. He then headed south, toward the river. The scenic drive along the banks led to the marina. He pulled in and stopped near one of the many piers.

The man followed carefully, but stopped well back of the subject's car. He looked out at row after row of beautiful boats. Even the smaller ones seemed incredible. "How can people afford these things?" he wondered, more than just a bit rhetorically.

As the subject walked down one of the docks, the man thought, "I've got him now."

The subject stopped at one of the larger boats, fiddled with lines, hoses and cords then fired the engines.

The man watched through binoculars as the subject cruised deliberately away from the marina. As the boat turned into the main channel, he mumbled out loud, "Man, that thing musta cost a fortune."

To be sure, he *would* find out.

What is This All About?

Is this a drug investigation? Is the subject suspected of smuggling? Is the boat part of a cache of illegal booty obtained through illegal underworld activity?

What about the investigator? He must be a police officer, right? Maybe a Drug Enforcement Administration agent. Perhaps he is an FBI agent tailing a local Mafia kingpin.

In fact, the investigation is about none of those things. The subject is not suspected of dealing drugs. He is not suspected of any illegal activity.

He owns a small business in town and has a spotless record. He and his wife have owned the boat for years. Bought it used. It is their only luxury, really. He is involved with the Chamber of Commerce, is active in his church and coaches Little League every summer. His wife volunteers at the homeless center twice a week and has been the church Sunday school director for going on five years.

What about the investigator? He is not a DEA agent, nor does he work for the FBI. He is not even a local police officer. He is an Internal Revenue agent. That is right. IRS.

He is involved in what *he* would call a routine tax audit. The subject is not suspected of owing any taxes, necessarily, but the IRS agent is curious about his lifestyle because the subject lives in a more affluent area of town and has a large boat registered to his name. The IRS agent is engaged in what the IRS calls an *"economic reality"* audit.

You Must be Kidding!

No, I am not kidding. The scenario outlined above is fictional, but at one level or another, such investigations are routine. You see, some years ago, the IRS introduced an audit program known as the economic reality audit. It is premised on the notion that every American cheats on his tax return, but not by overstating deductions. Rather, they cheat by underreporting income. In order to verify that the income reported on a tax return is correct, the IRS conducts what could amount to a full-scale investigation of the assets and lifestyles of those selected for audit.

There you have it. The IRS believes you are a tax cheat. It believes you earned income you did not report. It uses its audit program to ferret out that income and collect the tax, interest and penalties it is convinced you most certainly owe.

How Did We Get to this Point?

This scenario evidences a radical departure from our system of constitutional limited government where express rights are reserved to the people. One would expect such behavior only from communist China and the former Soviet Union. Inarguably, these measures are a departure from our unique system in which the citizen is to be protected from such invasions through a Constitution limiting the power of the federal government and by a Bill of Rights clearly delineating the liberties enjoyed by our citizens.

The departure was originally occasioned and is now exacerbated by the introduction of what I believe to be the grandest public policy *mistake* of the twentieth century, that being the establishment of an income tax in 1913 through the 16th Amendment.

The income tax was the first legislative move imparting to the federal government any claim to direct contact with and enforcement power over each individual citizen. Enforcing a law that revolves around what you earn, how you earn it and how you spend it purports to birth the need of the federal government to know every aspect of your private life. As the IRS states in its own words, "where there is information, there is compliance." IRS Strategic Plan, 2014-2017, Publication 3744, June 2014, pg 34.

In 1913, the IRS began as an obscure federal agency. The impact of the tax law at that time was felt by just 1 percent of the population, our nation's very richest. But with the passage of both time and legislation, the IRS and the reach of the tax law have found their way into the living rooms of every American family and the offices of every business. Now, virtually all of us, even many *underaged children*, must contend with the IRS for one reason or another, at one time or another.

Moreover, every decision you make in your personal life has tax consequences. For example, if you get married or divorced, there are tax consequences. If you save money or take money from savings, there are tax consequences. Sending children to college, paying for medical care, taking an underprivileged child into your home, taking money from retirement accounts – all have tax consequences. If you start a business, sell a business or even simply get a new job – there are tax consequences to that also. Even when you die, there are tax consequences. There is just no aspect of your life that is not touched by the federal tax law. It follows then, that there is no area of your life free from the prying eyes of IRS auditors.

With the increase in the size, scope and financial burdens of the tax law comes another phenomenon: tax avoidance. As the income tax saps more of the emoluments of American productivity, the desire to avoid the tax grows in proportion. We have reached a point where saving a dollar in taxes carries more benefit than earning a dollar of income. This reality has created a sophisticated game of financial cat and mouse between citizens and the IRS. The IRS perceives citizens' actions as cheating—pure and simple. But citizens often count them as necessary just to survive.

An integral part of this game is the tax audit in general and the economic reality audit in particular. The economic reality audit is the ultimate inquisition into one's financial affairs. On paper, it is designed to outflank any creative accounting maneuvers, use of loopholes, legal gyrations or other devices used by sagacious citizens and tax professionals. In practice, however, it has become the means by which the IRS assesses what I call "phantom income" against citizens who in fact do not cheat on their tax returns, but simply find themselves unable to prove a negative when it comes to the IRS's insistence that they earned income they did not report.The intrusive economic reality audit is certainly not the first of the aggressive acts contrived by the IRS to apprehend the allegedly non-compliant. It is but one in a long train of moves designed to achieve omnipotence and ubiquity for an agency with an insatiable appetite for information about you and your financial affairs, for without such information, the IRS perceives it cannot win the battle to administer and enforce the tax law. This is precisely why the IRS's 2014-2017 Strategic Plan makes the collection of data "from third-party reporting or through taxpayer self-disclosure" a paramount objective.

It is also why every American needs to know how to protect himself from this attack.

CHAPTER TWO

THE IRS MOVES CLOSER TO "BIG BROTHER"

IN 1984, THE IRS RELEASED A FIVE-YEAR STRATEGIC Plan that put forth a number of startling proposals. This plan was the subject of my first book, *The Naked Truth* (WINNING Publications 1986). Not the least of those proposals was the idea of moving to a paperless tax return filing system in which citizens submit their returns electronically and the IRS processes the return without handling any paper. While seemingly fantastic at the time, the idea is no longer so far-fetched. In 2013, Americans filed over 241 million personal and business tax returns. Of those, 82.5 percent of the 146 million personal returns and 40.2 percent of business returns were filed electronically. See: IRS, "Management's Discussion and Analysis, Fiscal Year 2013," pg 2. The IRS continues to push to achieve its goal of having 80 percent of all tax returns filed electronically.

Another idea floated in the 1984 Strategic Plan was the notion that the IRS's computers would evolve to the point where citizens could actually be taken out of the return filing process entirely. That is, the IRS would have prior access to the data needed to prepare the return and compute the tax. The citizen would simply get a statement showing what was done and either a kind "thank you" note for paying (assuming wage withholding and estimated payments covered the tab) or a stern bill asking for payment.

But that idea must truly be crazy. After all, the common perception is that the IRS's computer systems are archaic and even after years of work and billions of dollars in expensive upgrades and software developments, they still operate in the stone ages. As it turns out, that is not quite true either. As stated, those computer systems processed 241 million business and personal tax returns in 2013 and over 2 billion (that's with a *B*) information returns, including Forms W-2 and 1099. In its 2014-2017 Strategic Plan, the IRS brags that it "takes pride in our ability to administer the Tax Code each filing season, and the strength of our IT systems and applications are a strong asset in doing so." IRS, Strategic Plan 2014-2017, pg 20.

The agency's systems are developed to the point that former IRS Commissioner Douglas Shulman again floated the idea that the IRS should put itself on the front-end of the returns preparation and submission chain, not the back end. Shulman floated this in his speech to the National Press Club in Washington on April 6, 2011, when he discussed "a potential new structure of tax administration, a structure of opportunity, and a fundamentally different way to run our tax system." See: Prepared Remarks of IRS Commissioner Doug Shulman at the National Press Club, IR-2011-38, April 6,

2011. All quotes in this chapter are to that document unless otherwise indicated. See: www.irs.gov/uac/Prepared-Remarks-of-IRS-Commissioner-Doug-Shulman-at-the-National-Press-Club-1.

Shulman referred to his vision as an "up-front tax system." He went on to describe a system under which the IRS was the initial repository of all the information a citizen needed to prepare his tax return. Here is what he said:

> The vision is relatively straightforward. The IRS would get all information returns from third parties (W2s, 1099s, etc) *before* individual taxpayers filed their returns. Taxpayers or their professional return preparers could then access that information, via the Web, and download it into their returns, using commercial tax software. Taxpayers would then add any self-reported and supplemental information to their returns, and file the returns with us. We would embed this core third-party information into our pre-screening filters, and would immediately reject any return that did not match up with our records. That's right; we reject the return and ask you to fix it *before* we process it. We would then have more accurate returns and deal with many more problems up-front. We could shift resources to spend more money getting it right in the first place, and do less back-end auditing.

Before you suggest that such a thing is impossible, Shulman added:

> I will tell you that we could not have even thought about this a few years back, before we were on a solid path to complete our core customer account database, which we call CADE 2.

But the fact is, the IRS did think about it and laid the foundation for this very thing with the creation of electronic filing. Recall that electronic filing began in the early 1990s as a voluntary program but became mandatory with the IRS Restructuring and Reform Act of 1998. And given the changes the IRS made to its data processing systems, this idea is now not only feasible, but in the eyes of former Commissioner Shulman, worthy of earnest pursuit. He went on to talk about how this will be possible, as the IRS:

- Establishes the ability to "match in real-time" information returns with tax returns,
- Works to revise "information return filing dates" so the data gets to the IRS faster,
- "Pushes information returns" into the system faster, and
- Gains access to more "third-party information."

In 1994, the IRS took a major step toward developing what Shulman now calls a "front-end tax system." At that time, the IRS announced intentions to create a system of recordkeeping that would allow real-time access to the nation's public and private databases, including

commercial sources, state and local agencies, construction contract information, license information from state and local agencies, currency and banking reports

(CBRS), data regarding assets and financial transactions from state and local agencies, and information on significant financial transactions from reviews of periodicals and newspapers and other media sources. See: IRS, "Notice of Proposed Amendment to Privacy Act System of Records," *Federal Register 59*, No. 243, December 20, 1994.

The same notice goes on to describe exactly who would be the target of the proposed invasion. The people covered under the aggressive electronic surveillance system are described as

> any individual who has business and/or financial activities. These may be grouped by industry, occupation, or financial transactions included in commercial databases, or in information provided by state and local licensing agencies.

There is no description more broad or all encompassing than "any individual who has business and/or financial activities." In practical effect, this is no limitation whatsoever since every American, including a growing number of minor children, engage in "business and/or financial activities" at some level.

In describing the benefits of Shulman's "front-end tax system," Elizabeth Tucker, IRS deputy commissioner for operations and support, stated, "Imagine if we at the IRS already had the W-2s, the 1099s, the property tax information, *whatever is necessary*, before the returns come in." (Emphasis added; Tucker's remarks were made at an August 15, 2011 conference of tax pros in St. Louis, MO.)

Shuman refers to this vision as a "shift in the tax structure." In fact, it is a restatement (in more refined terms) of what the IRS called for decades ago. I describe it as the ubiquitous IRS and exposed it in detail in my 1997 book, *IRS, Taxes and the Beast*. It is really a reflection of an insatiable drive by the agency to know every detail of your private life and to have computer access to "all third party information" to pull it off.

And it is not just former Commissioner Shulman with this vision. These same goals are essentially restated in the IRS's 2014-2017 Strategic Plan. There, the IRS talks about the need to increase the use of third-party information and to move "the matching process closer to the time of taxpayer return filing." The overall goal is to "increase data transparency." 2014-2017 Strategic Plan, pg 32.

To use deputy commissioner Tucker's words, "imagine" if the IRS had real-time access to "whatever is necessary" – access to all private and public databases in the nation. Imagine if the IRS was able to know everything you do, and when and how you do it. Imagine if the IRS had so much personal data that it did not even need your tax return. The agency could just send you a bill with a note saying, "Here's what we did." In the words of the IRS, the agency is becoming more "data-driven" to better track citizens and all their financial activities. 2014-2017 Strategic Plan, pg 30.

How is that for tax simplification?

I imagine such a system to be rife with errors, duplication and abuse. Consider the IRS's history of incorrectly answering questions, issuing erroneous notices and making incorrect audit decisions. As I have documented extensively over the past twenty-plus years, the track record in all these areas is deplorable. So what makes anybody believe that the IRS will assimilate information from potentially tens of billions of data points more accurately than it does the two billion data points it handles today?

And that assumes that the data provided to the IRS by third parties is accurate to begin with. The facts indicate that this is not a very safe assumption. According to the Treasury Inspector General for Tax Administration (TIGTA), of the nearly 2 *billion* information returns submitted to the IRS in 2007 alone, almost 31.7 million had incorrect or incomplete data. See: TIGTA, Ref. No. 2011-30-019, "Targeted Compliance Efforts May Reduce the Number of Inaccurate Information Returns," (February 15, 2011).

Note that as of 2013, nearly 2.1 billion information returns filed annually with the IRS. As such, third-party information returns can be unreliable and puts the taxpayer at a decided disadvantage since the IRS relies heavily on this data, then tries to force the taxpayer into the position of having to prove a negative. I address this issue in more detail in chapters 6 and 10.

It is these very facts that led the National Taxpayer Advocate to report that, "Longstanding IRS matching programs illustrate how third-party data are often unreliable when used as the sole basis to conclude that the taxpayer's return is wrong." She concludes that, "even the most reliable third-party data—data from information returns—may be a weak basis on which to conclude that a taxpayer's return is wrong." National Taxpayer Advocate, 2011 Annual Report to Congress, pg 20.

Shulman's vision is not unique by any means. Long before he took office as commissioner in 2008, the IRS was pushing for more laws requiring the filing of more information returns. Ever since I have been paying attention, the IRS has cried out to Congress for more third-party reporting laws. These laws are the manifestation of the IRS's goal to know everything about you. It is to the point where the IRS now has an "advisory committee," known as the Information Reporting Program Advisory Committee, that reports to the IRS on new information reporting ideas.

Here are a few examples of their work. As of 2012, three new information return requirements became effective. The first applies to credit card sales for businesses. Credit card processing companies are now required to file reports with the IRS showing the gross amount of payments made to businesses through their credit card sales. At the same time, securities companies are required to report basis information on most securities purchased in 2012 and thereafter. And finally, offshore banks that have entered into reporting agreements with the U.S. Treasury must file Forms 1099 to report interest, dividends and capital gain income of U.S. citizens to the same extent that U.S. banks must file such reports. For more on offshore financial issues, see chapter 19, under the heading, *How to Handle Undisclosed Offshore Income and Assets*.

On the table now are further proposals to require:

- Life insurance companies to report private insurance account information,
- Increased reporting on government payments to private businesses for goods and services sold to the government,

- Information reporting on expense payments relating to rental property, and not surprisingly,

- Increased penalties for not complying with information reporting rules.

Note that none of the above has anything to do with the vast information reporting required by the Patient Protection and Affordable Care Act (PPACA-Obamacare), which is an entirely different subject and which carries its own substantial information reporting requirements. For more on this, see my special report, *Implementing National Health Care*, available at my website, www.taxhelponline.com.

For years, the IRS pushed Congress for broader requirements to file 1099 Forms reporting more business transactions. In fact, one such requirement would have imposed on businesses the duty to file information returns on their transactions with other businesses, even corporations, if $600 or more was paid to a corporation in a given year. Under the law, all the payments your business makes to say, your phone company, mortgage company or the landlord of your business property, and purchases you make for office supplies, and so on down the endless list of third parties the typical business trades with, would require a Form 1099 every year.

This would have caused an explosion in the number of such forms filed annually. As I said, this provision was on the table for years and Congress finally worked up the nerve to pass it as part of the PPACA in 2010.

After passage of the Act, there was outrage from all quarters, including within the very Congress that passed the bill. The cry went out that this requirement would put tremendous burdens on businesses to file billions more information returns each year. For my part in this fight, I wrote an article, published in the April 2010 issue of my newsletter *Pilla Talks Taxes*, entitled "1,883,000,000 And It's Still Not Enough." That was the number of information returns filed with the IRS just in 2008 alone. My article was distributed to all federal lawmakers and other policymakers across the nation.

Owing to this and to pressure from other sources, the very Congress that passed Obamacare was suddenly concerned about the impact the law would have on the paperwork burden of small businesses. I predicted that there would be at least a four-fold increase in the number of 1099s filed each year if the legislation were to go into effect. I might well have been kidding myself with that prediction. At the time the law was passed, the IRS received nearly 2 billion information returns annually. At that, such returns *do not* report payments by businesses to corporations. A typical business might have fifteen or twenty corporate trading partners, each of which get paid $600 or more per year. So it is easy to see how extensive this reporting requirement would have been.

The combined impact of the pressure I and other organizations put on Congress led to the repeal of the 1099 reporting requirements. The law was repealed on April 14, 2011, by the "Comprehensive 1099 Taxpayer Protection and Repayment of Exchange Subsidy Overpayments Act of 2011." The amazing part of all this is that the very Congress that enacted the provision in the first place seemed to have no idea what the consequence would be of its action.

President Obama took the heat for the provision since it was part of his healthcare act but in all fairness, it was not his baby. As I stated, the IRS pushed for that legislation for years and only happened to find willing stooges in Obama's Congress. But as Shulman's vision takes shape, such reporting is only the beginning of the blizzard of information returns that will be filed with the IRS annually.

Why Change the Tax System?

Shulman argued that the changes he proposed are necessary to bring about a system that reduces the burden on taxpayers and is more efficient to operate. He said, for example, the information returns "are real timesavers for taxpayers." By extension, if an individual taxpayer had every detail of his life reported to the IRS by third parties, that individual has no reporting he must do on his own. What Shulman does not discuss, however, is the burden it puts on third-party filers to create and file the forms. We know from experience with the 1099 provision in Obamacare that the public does not want to cope with more reporting burdens.

Shulman describes the benefits of his system as follows:

> The vision I'm articulating is a potential win-win for honest taxpayers and our government. It streamlines the tax return process for the vast majority of people who play by the rules and want to get it right. It also minimizes interactions with the IRS, which is what most taxpayers want.

This comment seems to indicate that perhaps the IRS's brain trust got religion and wants to make life easier for people. I doubt it. The real issue here is this, as Shulman himself points out: "Of course, these information returns foster voluntary compliance, since they are filed with the IRS." And as the IRS puts it in the 2014-2017 Strategic Plan, "where there is information, there is compliance." Ibid., pg 34. Said another way, as long as the IRS has your financial information from third parties, the agency is in a better position to separate you from your money.

That is the real problem for the IRS, and it is a growing problem. There are more people in trouble with the IRS now than at any time in the past two decades. The economic problems the nation has suffered since 2008 bring into high relief the problems people struggle with when forced to make a choice between paying their taxes and feeding their families. And despite all the lip service the IRS paid in the recent past to helping financially strapped taxpayers, the fact is, the agency continues to issue a staggering number of wage levies, bank levies and tax liens. From 2008 through 2013, the IRS filed more than 5.182 *million* federal tax liens and executed more than 18.014 *million* third-party levies. Data source: *IRS Databook*, Table 16, Publication 55B, for the years indicated.

In short, the agency just wants the money.

Ironically, during that same period, the IRS's total outstanding accounts receivable— the amount of taxes assessed but not collected— *jumped* from $278 billion in 2008 to $356 billion in 2011. And by September 2013, receivables reached $374 billion. See: IRS, "Management's Discussion and Analysis" of financial statements for the year indicated.

So, no, the IRS did not get religion and decide to do you a favor. It is not stricken with grief because of the burdens the system places on individuals and businesses. The IRS must consider changing the system because the system is becoming increasingly unenforceable. The fact is, given the context of our income tax system, the IRS simply needs to either: 1) rely on people to personally report all the details of their daily financial lives, or 2) have the machinery in place to spy on people sufficiently to be able to gather it without your help.

We have reached the point where the IRS is rapidly turning to the latter mechanism. Despite the fallout from the Obama 1099 debacle, the IRS continues to press for evermore information reporting laws. This creates a previously unimaginable invasion of privacy that comes with the IRS knowing everything you do, when and how you do it, along with incredible burdens of time, recordkeeping and compliance that come with a nearly universal duty to spy on your neighbors in the name of enforcing the income tax.

CHAPTER THREE

PREVENTING CONTACTS WITH THIRD PARTIES

IN CHAPTER 2, I TALKED ABOUT THE HIGH-TECH IRS that is turning more and more to twenty-first century tools to spy on Americans. In the opening chapter, I presented a hypothetical (but very real) scenario in which the IRS uses old-fashioned gumshoeing to track down the location and type of assets held by the tax audit target. What actually happens in a modern tax audit is a healthy mix of both strategies.

As the IRS gets increasingly high-tech, it uses those tools to their fullest potential. On the other hand, there is no substitute for visual confirmation of the items in question. As such, in any audit scenario, it is very possible (and often probable) that a revenue agent (RA) conducting an audit will not only make field visits to physically inspect certain aspects of one's business or lifestyle, but may also contact third parties in the process.

It would certainly not be very helpful to your business or personal reputation if the IRS sent a letter to your business associates, customers, clients, suppliers, or somehow contacted your co-workers or even relatives, friends or neighbors, explaining that you are under a tax audit and asking for certain information. The conclusion many people may likely come to is that you must be in "in trouble" with the IRS and they may want to keep their distance—both personally and professionally.

But as the IRS gets more aggressive with its audits, third-party contacts are increasingly more likely. And while it is certainly true that the mere fact you are being audited does not mean you are in any kind of trouble with the IRS, the majority of people do not believe that. This is why it is so important to understand what the agency can and cannot do when it comes to contacting third parties.

How the IRS Discovers Potential Third-Party Contacts

One of the first steps the IRS takes in any audit scenario is to obtain what is known as a Custom Comprehensive Report on the target of the audit. This is essentially a background report produced by any number of private businesses and sold to subscribers. For a fee, the IRS obtains a report based upon the name, SSN and known address of the taxpayer. The report provides at least the following information:

- Summary details that include the subject's current verified physical address, age, date of birth, etc.,

- Whether any liens or judgments, including whether any Uniform Commercial Code filings are in place,

- A legal history showing criminal records, bankruptcy filings and sexual offender information, if any,

- All licenses and permits, including driver's licenses, FAA pilot's licenses, professional licenses, concealed weapons permits, hunting and fishing licenses, etc.,

- Vehicle registrations including cars, RVs, aircraft, boats and other watercraft (which is how the agent in chapter 1 discovered that the audit target owned a boat),

- Voter registration information,

- Real estate ownership facts, including current and past ownership data and home addresses, and

- A phone number analysis produced by querying nearly 100 billion phone numbers, including unlisted and unpublished landlines and unlisted cell phone numbers.

If you think this is appalling—and invasive—that is not even the worst part. The report also provides information on the subject's current employer, the people who work with him, non-business associates, relatives and even neighbors.

You might ask, "How can this be legal?" The simple answer is that this is all public information. The commercial providers amass the data by painstakingly gathering it from a myriad of public databases that report information. Just for example, anybody can access county real estate records and find out who owns a specific parcel of property, what the tax base is, how long that person owned it, etc. In fact, the more people live their lives on line and through social media sites, the easier it is for the IRS or any other government agency to find out details they otherwise might have no way to know.

But even beyond that, the tax code gives the IRS broad power to gather information in the name of enforcing the tax law that is not readily available from public databases. Code section 7601 reads:

> The Secretary shall, to the extent he deems it practicable, cause officers or employees of the Treasury Department to proceed, from time to time, through each internal revenue district and inquire after and concerning all persons therein who may be liable to pay any internal revenue tax, and all persons owning or having the care and management of any objects with respect to which any tax is imposed.

Very clearly, this grants the legal authority for the IRS to go on a literal fishing expedition to gather information for tax law enforcement. Note that there is no requirement that a person subject to an inquiry actually *owe* a tax. Rather, the purpose of this broad authority is merely to "*inquire* after and concerning all persons who *may* be liable" to pay any tax.

The purposes for which the IRS is authorized to contact third parties includes:

1. Determining the correctness of a return – i.e., the standard audit process;

2. Making a return when none was filed – this process arises in the case of tax return non-filers;

3. Determining the liability of any person for any tax – this too describes the audit process very broadly and generally; and

4. Collecting any tax liability – this arises after it is determined that a tax is owed but is not paid.

The IRS may contact any of the following individuals:

1. The person liable for the tax or required to perform the act in question, such as filing a required return,

2. An officer or employee of such person,

3. Any person having possession, custody, or care of any records relating to the business of such person, or

4. "Any other person the Secretary may deem proper." Code section 7602(a)(2).

And, if during the process of inquiring after a person who may be liable, the IRS is somehow stonewalled, the agency has broad authority to use its administrative summons power to force a party—including the taxpayer himself—to disclose documents and information relevant to the inquiry. I discuss the summons power more specifically later in this chapter.

The IRS Must Tell You Before Making Third-Party Contacts

Before the IRS can make any contact with third parties, code section 7602(c) requires that the agency first tell you of its intention to do so. The IRS does this with Letter 3164B, a very short letter an agent mails shortly after the audit commences, even before any exchanges occur between the auditor and the taxpayer. The key phrase of the letter states:

> We are writing to tell you that we may contact other persons. If we do contact other persons, we will generally need to tell them limited information, such as your name.

The letter asks for no action on your part and apparently gives you no options with regard to the potential contacts. Please note that the letter does not say that IRS *will* contact third parties, only that it *may*. This is important because the letter generally causes the uninformed citizen to immediately panic. "Why would they contact third parties when they haven't even asked me for anything yet?" The answer is the IRS has not necessary decided to contact third parties or whom it will contact. By law, the agency must tell you about potential contacts beforehand and this is how they do it.

Whom Will They Contact?

Earlier we addressed the question of how the IRS finds potential third parties to contact. Now the question is, whom will they contact? While it seems there is no limit to whom the IRS may contact, the fact is that its third-party contacts will by necessity be limited and therefore, you can control them. Let us examine exactly who the agency is likely to contact and why.

In an audit situation, the agent is most likely to contact your bank to obtain account information. It might also seek information from credit card companies, mortgage companies, personal loan companies, securities dealers and brokerage firms, investment management firms, insurance companies, real estate title companies, your employer and any person or company that pays you in the course of its business. For small business people, the IRS may contact any of your trading partners, such as customers, clients, suppliers, contractors, etc. The bottom line is that anybody you do business with may be subject to contact by the IRS to obtain the details of their transactions with you.

The third-party contacts made in an audit are almost always pointed at ascertaining your correct income. The IRS will spend very little if any time seeking information from third parties regarding the payment of your deductible expenses. The reason is that you have the burden of proof on all deduction issues. If you do not provide proof of your deductions, the IRS's remedy generally is to simply disallow the deduction. The agency does not need information from third parties to sustain such an action. But as discussed in more detail in chapters 10 and 11, it must support any claim that you had income you did not report on your return.

When Can the IRS Make Third-Party Contacts?

The IRS will contact third parties only if the agency cannot get the information it needs from you. It cannot make third-party contacts solely for the purposes of disrupting your business or harassing you. As a general rule, the IRS cannot take actions against a citizen the natural consequences of which are to "harass, oppress, or abuse any person." Code section 6304(b). Moreover, the IRS cannot contact any third party unless it has first told you that it may do so, and hence, the use of Letter 3164B. Code section 7602(c)(1).

So the key to keeping the agency from going to third parties is to make sure that the RA you are dealing with knows that you will provide all the information you are legally responsible to provide and will do so in a timely manner.

It is also a firm rule that when the taxpayer has a valid Power of Attorney on file with the IRS, the IRS cannot contact either the taxpayer or third parties without going through the representative first. Code section 7521(c). The only exception to this is if the representative deliberately delays or impedes the progress of the case. See chapter 8 under the heading, *Assistance of Professional Counsel.*

Responding to Letter 3164B

If you receive Letter 3164B, the first and most important thing to understand is, as I stated earlier, the IRS is not automatically going to rush out and blab to everybody the fact that you are under audit. As stated, the agency usually makes third-party contacts only if it cannot get the information from you that it needs to resolve your case. Therefore, you should immediately respond in writing to Letter 3164B with a letter that makes the following key points:

- That you understand your duty to provide information regarding the accuracy of your tax return,

- That you will in fact provide whatever information is legally necessary to address the questions raised in the audit,

- That you expect the IRS to make all requests for information in writing to you in the first instance, before going to any third parties, and to give you a reasonable time to provide the requested information,

- That you do not authorize the IRS to make any third-party contacts whatsoever, and

- That contacting third parties without first giving you the opportunity to provide the needed information will have a serious negative impact on your business or personal affairs and will be regarded by you as conduct the natural consequence of which is to harass, oppress, or abuse you.

If you intend to retain counsel to help with your audit, your letter should state that fact clearly and explain that once a Power of Attorney is filed with the IRS, you expect the agent to deal with counsel and not pursue third parties to obtain any information.

Send this letter to the agent who signed Letter 3164B. Mail it using certified mail with return receipt requested. Keep a copy of the letter for your files along with the Postal Service receipts for certified mail. If you do retain counsel, provide counsel with a copy of the letter and receipts for certified mail.

The IRS's Summons Authority

If the auditor does not obtain the information requested in a timely manner, expect the agent to use his summons authority to secure the missing data. A summons is an administrative tool that works somewhat like a subpoena. The key difference is while a subpoena is issued as part of a judicial process, the summons requires no court case to be in effect before it can be used. A summons can be used by the IRS in the administrative process and carries almost the same weight as a subpoena, but without the inconvenience having to be issued under the authority of a court.

The IRS's summons authority is found in code section 7602, which affords the IRS the authority to summons "any person" in connection with

. . .ascertaining the correctness of any return, making a return where none has been made, determining the liability of any person for any internal revenue tax or the liability at law or in equity of any transferee or fiduciary of any person in respect of any internal revenue tax, or collecting any such liability.

"Any person" can be the taxpayer himself or any of the many persons and institutions described above, including his tax return preparer, attorney or accountant. The summons is the chief means the IRS uses to contact third parties. The summons authority extends to obtaining both the testimony of such persons and to obtaining "any books, papers, records, or other data which *may be relevant* or material to such inquiry" (emphasis added).

The "may be relevant" language is the key to the broad sweep of the law. For example, it is not necessary for the IRS to prove—or even allege—that there is a mistake, discrepancy or even so much as a *potential* error in the return. The law allows the IRS to issue a summons for the purposes of "determining the correctness of any return." Therefore, to justify its summons, it is sufficient for the agency to claim that it merely wants to verify whether a return is correct. If this seems very broad, that is because *it is* very broad. And the courts have consistently applied it as such. See: *United States v. Euge*, 444 U.S. 707 (1980); *United States v. Norwest*, 116 F.3d 1227 (8th Cir. 1997).

In *United States v. Arthur Young*, 465 U.S. 805 (1984), the Supreme Court directly addressed the "may be relevant" language. The Court pointed out that the definition of the term "relevant" is far broader than that applied to the Federal Rules of Evidence. It held that the term includes any "items of even *potential* relevance to an ongoing investigation" (emphasis in original). The reason justifying such a broad sweep, according to the Court, is that "the Service can hardly be expected to know whether such data will in fact be relevant until is procured and scrutinized." In this context, the Court held that code section 7602 is actually "a tool of discovery" available in any examination.

While the IRS does not need court approval to issue a summons, the summons is not self-enforcing. That is, if a person refuses to provide the information sought by the summons, the IRS cannot unilaterally impose sanctions, fines or any other penalty for such refusal. Rather, the IRS must file a petition in federal court to have the summons enforced. This is known as a summons enforcement proceeding.

In the course of that proceeding, the IRS must prove to the court that its summons meets all the legal requirements necessary for enforcement. In the leading case of *United States v. Powell*, 279 U.S. 48 (1964), the Supreme Court established four elements the IRS must prove to get a summons enforced. These are often referred to as the *Powell* elements. They are:

1. The summons was issued in connection with a legitimate examination or investigation,

2. The records sought may be relevant to that examination or investigation,

3. The information reflected in the records is not already in the IRS's possession, and

4. All required administrative steps were followed in issuing the summons.

The IRS's burden to prove these issues is "slight." An affidavit from a revenue agent attesting to these facts is usually all it takes. *United States v. Samuels, Kramer and Co.*,

712 F.2d 1342, 1345 (9th Cir. 1983). The widely accepted standard used by the courts to determine whether summoned information "may be relevant" is whether it "might throw light upon the correctness of the return." *See United States v. Wyatt*, 637 F.2d 293 (5th Cir. 1981); *United States v. Turner*, 480 F.2d 272 (7th Cir. 1973); *United States v. Ryan*, 455 F.2d 728 (9th Cir. 1972); *United States v. Egenberg*, 443 F.2d 512 (3d Cir. 1971); *Foster v. United States*, 265 F.2d 183 (2d Cir. 1959). Thus, the vast majority of summons enforcement proceedings result in a judge ordering the summoned person to produce the information sought or face a contempt of court charge for failure to obey the order.

Finding Out Whom the IRS Contacted

Code section 7602(c)(2) provides that the IRS must "periodically provide" you with a record of all persons the agency contacted. According to Rev. Reg. section 301.7602.2(e)(1), the list must be provided at least annually. Because I have *never* seen the IRS voluntarily provide such a list, the better approach is to simply request it in writing from your agent. He has an affirmative duty to do so unless one of the exceptions applies.

Code section 7602(c)(3) provides the exceptions to the third-party contact rules. They are as follows:

1. Contacts authorized by the citizen – If you specifically state in writing that the IRS is allowed to contact a specific person or organization, the agency may do so without further notice or warning to you;

2. When IRS determines that notice to you will "jeopardize collection" or cause "reprisal" against the person contacted – This exception may come into play if the IRS can establish that you are hiding or destroying records or may attempt to prevent third parties from communicating with the IRS or otherwise may pressure the third party into not cooperating; and

3. Criminal investigations – if there is a pending criminal investigation (which is a rare occurrence). Code section 7602(c)(3).

In any of the above three situations, the IRS does not have to notify you prior to any third-party contact and does not have to tell you who was contacted. But each of these exceptions is very rare and not likely to apply in the garden-variety audit.

Thus, I recommend you contact the agent handling your audit to find out if he made any third-party contacts. If he did, you can then determine what if any remedial action you should take to mitigate whatever negative impact might grow from those contacts. For example, if a particular customer suddenly just stopped dealing with you for no apparent reason, you can address the issue and perhaps soothe his fears about your being "in tax trouble."

By following these procedures, you can save yourself embarrassment and the potential loss of business and your personal reputation.

CHAPTER FOUR

DEBUNKING
TAX AUDIT MYTHS

ONE OF THE MOST TRAUMATIC FINANCIAL experiences imaginable for most Americans is the idea of an IRS audit. Why are so many Americans terrified of an audit? Is it because they cheat on their tax returns? Not Likely.

Despite what the IRS believes, most Americans do their level best to comply with the tax laws by conscientiously struggling through the thousands of pages of mind-numbing forms and instructions the IRS produces every year. The National Taxpayer Advocate once referred to the American taxpayers' job of "understanding and complying with the tax laws" as "nearly impossible." NTA 2004 Annual Report to Congress, vol. 1, pg 2.

In fact, according to research produced by the NTA, Americans spend about 6.1 billion hours each year complying with the filing requirements of the Internal Revenue Code. If tax law compliance were an industry, it would be one of the largest in America. To eat up that many hours "would require the equivalent of more than three million full time workers." National Taxpayer Advocate, 2010 Annual Report to Congress, vol. 1, pg 3. Moreover, the GAO notes that 98 percent of all tax revenue is paid to the IRS through wage withholding and estimated payments—*without* the need of IRS enforcement action. GAO: IRS Modernization, Continued Progress Necessary for Improving Service to Taxpayers, GAO-03-1791, May 20, 2003, pg 19.

Citizens are generally afraid of an audit for at least two reasons. First, most citizens do not understand the audit process, nor do they understand their rights in an audit or their rights to challenge tax audit decisions. And it is not just a matter of lacking information about the procedure. Citizens harbor *misinformation* about the procedure. Americans believe the IRS selects tax returns for examination because the agency found an error. When a letter bringing the news of an audit hits the mailbox, the average citizen reacts as though he just heard from the draft board. He immediately thinks the worst, believing he made a serious mistake and has "been caught." The mind races from thoughts of what the error may be, to its likely financial cost and even to the question, "Am I going to jail?" From the start, he adopts a defensive posture premised on the mistaken notion that he did something wrong and now must pay.

The second problem also stems from misinformation. The public is under the impression that the tax auditor wields the power of financial life and death and citizens have no right to stop or challenge auditors. People believe a tax auditor can disallow deductions at will, effectively increasing a person's tax bill. People believe the auditor has the authority to use the IRS's potent weapons of lien, levy and seizure. Even worse, people fathom that an auditor can put them in jail. These perceived powers, coupled with the belief that a mistake was made in the first place, makes it difficult or impossible for the uninformed person to survive the audit process.

These facts explain why the IRS has such tremendous success in assessing additional revenue through the audit process. In 2013 alone, the IRS produced more than $37 billion in additional assessments through the examination of all classes of tax returns. This does not include the penalties and interest that go along with these assessments, which often double or triple a tax bill.

Of the total additional assessments, $14.05 billion is attributable to the audit of individual income tax returns. In 2013, the average taxpayer going through a face-to-face examination faced an additional tax assessment of $16,255 and the average taxpayer going through a correspondence audit faced an additional assessment of $7,917. Add the interest and penalties to these amounts and the total liability more than doubles. Of all the returns examined through the face-to-face process during 2013, 91 percent were found to owe additional taxes. Just 9 percent were given a clean bill of health. For correspondence exams, only 12 percent of audit victims got out unscathed. IRS 2013 Data Book, Publication 55B, March 2014, pgs 22-24.

That means on average, if selected for a face-to-face examination, you have about a 90 percent chance of getting hit with a tax bill of over sixteen grand, before penalties and interest. No wonder people are afraid.

These facts teach us that it is fundamentally necessary for you to understand the basics of the tax audit process if you are to survive the ordeal. Let us start by debunking the two myths identified earlier. The first relates to how returns are selected for audit. A tax return is not necessarily targeted because it contains an error. It is true that certain correspondence from the IRS is generated by errors in a return, either real or imagined. In a face-to-face confrontation, however, most returns are selected by nothing more than a computer analysis of the claims in a return. As I explain later in this chapter, the IRS's computers compare entries in your return with known averages. If any line of your return is out of sync with those averages, the difference is scored. The higher the score, the more likely the return is to be audited.

That is not to say that a difference in your entries versus the known averages means your return is somehow wrong. On the contrary, averages are nothing more than a balanced high and low for a given category. It only means that an individual whose scores are sufficiently in excess of (or in some cases, below) the averages may be called upon to prove his claims. Assuming you understand this and are able to prove that the claims in your return are correct, you will owe nothing at the end of your audit.

The second myth relates to the power of the tax auditor. Too many people succumb to pressure from the IRS to accept what they know or believe are improper audit results because they wrongfully believe the agent has the power to make their life miserable. What else can explain an examination change rate of 91 percent when it comes to face-to-face audits?

Let us start by realizing that a tax auditor has no power to put people in jail. Revenue agents—IRS employees who conduct face-to-face tax audits—are examiners only, working within the IRS's Examination function. Their sole task is to determine the "correct tax liability." They are not the arbiters of whether criminal tax laws were violated. In fact, the investigation of possible tax crimes is not even within the scope of their jurisdiction. Such investigations are handled only by Special Agents, working under the authority of the IRS's Criminal Investigation unit.

Nor do auditors have the authority to enforce collection through the tools of lien, levy and seizure. Those tools are within the sole province of the Collection function and are carried out by Revenue Officers or through the IRS's Automated Collection Site (ACS) via computer-generated notices. Before any such weapon may be fired at a citizen, there must first be a valid "assessment" of tax in place. An assessment arises after the tax has been determined, either by the citizen signing a tax return or through administrative procedures, such as an audit. Once an assessment is in place, the case is transferred to the Collection function (and thus, out of the hands of a tax auditor) for the physical process of collecting the tax. And only after several collection notices are mailed, including a Final Notice, Notice of Intent to Levy and Notice of Your Right to a Hearing, IRS Letter 1058, is the agency legally allowed to levy or seize any income or assets. All of this happens well *after* the audit process is over. For more details on the collection process and how to handle collection notices, see my *Tax Amnesty Package.*

Tax auditors do not even possess the power to change your return, i.e., disallow deductions, without your consent. Rather, tax auditors merely recommend that certain deductions be disallowed or other changes be made, such as adding alleged unreported income. If accepted, these recommendations lead to the assessment described above. However, you must agree to both the recommendations and the assessment before the auditor's report becomes binding. Should you refuse, various rights of appeal are available. When used fully and properly, these rights ensure you will never pay taxes you do not owe. These rights are discussed in chapter 13.

What is a Tax Audit?

Even the most basic element of a tax audit is often misunderstood. That is, what is a tax audit? Many look upon the audit as a form of punishment in and of itself. To some extent that may be true, given the amount of time and effort needed to complete the task and the amount of money typically owed when it is done. However, the true premise is much different.

The tax audit is nothing more or less than the process by which the IRS ascertains the correctness of your tax return. Going into an audit, the IRS has no clue whether, for example, your claimed deduction of $5,000 in charitable contributions is correct. The fact that your return may have been selected for audit on the basis of this claim does not signal an error. It says only that the IRS questions the claim and now calls on you to verify it.

Each tax return contains two general categories of claims. The return states an amount of income you claim was earned during the year and any reductions to income that operate to lower the tax. Such reductions might include—alone or in combination—

personal dependent exemptions, a standard deduction or itemized deductions, business expense deductions, capital losses, operating losses, one or more tax credits, etc. The IRS has the authority to require you to prove all such claims.

The economic reality audit and a growing number of business audits focus on the income issue. As stated earlier, the IRS is of the opinion that most of the perceived cheating occurs with regard to income, not deductions. For example, in recent report to Congress, the GAO explains that taxpayers operating small businesses as S corporations and partnerships misreported their income by roughly $91 billion per year for the years 2006 through 2009. See: PARTNERSHIPS AND S CORPORATIONS: IRS Needs to Improve Information to Address Tax Noncompliance, GAO-14-453, May 2014.

And while Congress further narrows the scope of deductions allowable for individuals in the first place, it broadens the dragnet by which income is gathered. Therefore, the more fruitful approach for the IRS is fast becoming to challenge your income, not your deductions. This is precisely why the Treasury Inspector General for Tax Administration continues to push the IRS to spend more time on income audits. See: National Research Program Audits of Individuals are Closely Monitored, but the Quality of Tests for Unreported Income is a Concern, TIGTA, 2011-30-102, September 2011.

While the stated purpose of the tax audit is to ascertain the correctness of your return, the IRS looks at the audit as a revenue enhancement tool. Stated another way, it uses the audit as a means to "get the money." My years of experience dealing with IRS audits have taught many sobering lessons. The most troubling is the fact that the IRS cares little about whether or not your return is correct. Rather, its intention is to "get the money" regardless.

Tax auditors use carefully orchestrated and well-rehearsed tactics to persuade citizens to part with money they do not owe. In July 1995, I presented testimony to the House subcommittee on IRS Oversight, Committee on Ways and Means, concerning these problems. In my testimony, I identified specific, deliberate acts tax auditors use to bluff and intimidate citizens into accepting audit results that are just plain wrong. I identified nine specific duplicitous tactics used to accomplish that goal. Quoting directly from my testimony, they are:

1. Where examiners wrongfully claim a citizen has insufficient proof to support an otherwise legitimate deduction and therefore disallow the deduction;

2. Where examiners wrongfully give an incorrect statement of the law to a citizen regarding a particular tax deduction or tax treatment of an item, leading to the disallowance of such item;

3. Where amounts of money transferred from one of the citizen's bank accounts to another (transactions known as re-deposits) are double and triple counted by examiners, and therefore a citizen is said to have earned income he did not report on his return;

4. Where tax examiners falsely claim that citizens have no, or limited, appeal rights from the decision of tax examiners, and therefore have no choice but to accept audit results that are clearly in error;

Calvin Sandburg
UNIV - B.C. - ENVIRONMENTAL LAW

5. Where tax examiners falsely claim that citizens will suffer other or greater penalties if they pursue their right of appeal, and therefore accept audit results that are clearly in error;

6. Where tax examiners explain to citizens that the avenue of appeal is lengthy, costly, time consuming and the IRS wins its cases anyway, and all the while additional interest and penalties stack up;

7. Where, in certain unusual but nevertheless prevalent cases, tax examiners claim a citizen can go to jail if he does not sign and accept audit results that are clearly wrong;

8. Where, as very commonly happens, tax examiners threaten citizens with lien, levy and seizure of bank accounts and property if they refuse to sign and accept audit results that are clearly wrong; and

9. Probably the single most common reason erroneous audit assessments arise is that most citizens are simply unaware of their right to appeal. Upon completion of a tax audit, the IRS mails to the citizen a so-called 30-day letter. The letter contains the Revenue Agent's Report (RAR) that details the proposed changes. Citizens commonly mistake the RAR for a bill, which it is not. They do not understand that it is merely a proposed change, which they can appeal. But with a lack of understanding of the appeal right or process and generally a lack of funds to hire a professional, many do nothing. This leads to the issuance of a Notice of Deficiency, which requires the filing of a petition in the Tax Court within ninety days. If a petition is not filed, the tax claimed by the IRS becomes assessed without further action necessary on the part of the IRS. In effect, the citizen loses his tax audit case by default. Daniel J. Pilla, Testimony before the subcommittee on IRS Oversight, House committee on Ways and Means, "Taxpayer Compliance Measurement Program," Serial 104-30, July 18, 1995, pg 146.

As I explained to the subcommittee, the above is not an exhaustive list of the things that commonly happen to honest citizens during the course of face-to-face examinations. They are, however, a few of the more common examples of what takes place on a daily basis. This happens chiefly because people do not know their rights and this has not changed since I gave that testimony to Congress nearly twenty years ago. See chapters 14 and 15 for more discussion on IRS bluffs and how to counter them.

Scattered throughout the length and breadth of the tax code are several provisions that create dozens of important rights and protections for taxpayers. The problem is they are not presented in any systematic or cohesive manner so that one can turn to a certain code section to find a comprehensive list of taxpayers' rights. Because of this, the National Taxpayer Advocate (NTA) writes that, "Most taxpayers have no idea what their rights are and therefore often cannot take advantage of them." In a survey of taxpayers conducted for the NTA, it was discovered that "less than half said they believed they have any rights before the IRS, and only 11 percent said they knew what those rights were." NTA's 2013 Annual Report to Congress, pg 5.

Now let us add the fact that auditors are poorly trained in the constantly changing tax law. In testimony to the same congressional subcommittee I testified to, but in an earlier hearing, Lynda D. Willis, then the associate director of tax policy at the General Accounting Office (now referred to as the Government Accountability Office—still the "GAO") described many problems businesses face in complying with the tax laws. She described the results of a survey the GAO conducted to determine the compliance burden faced by small businesses. Among other things, she said:

> The complexity of the code has a direct impact on IRS's ability to administer the code. The volume and complexity of information in the code make if difficult for IRS to ensure that its tax auditors are knowledgeable about the tax code and that their knowledge is current. Some business officials and tax experts said that IRS auditors lack sufficient knowledge about federal tax requirements, and in their opinion this deficiency has caused IRS audits to take more time than they otherwise might. GAO, "Tax System Burden, Tax Compliance Burden Faced by Business Taxpayers," GAO/T-GGD-95-42, December 9, 1994, page 3.

As is the case with taxpayers' rights, the problems caused by a complicated tax law have not improved in the twenty years since that testimony. It is now worse than ever. Former IRS Commissioner Charles Rossotti once addressed this issue in explaining why the IRS's telephone assisters cannot provide accurate tax law information to citizens calling in for help, sometimes even with the most basic of questions. Commissioner Rossotti stated,

> Fundamentally, we are attempting the *impossible*. We are expecting employees and our managers to be trained in areas that are far too broad to *ever succeed*, and our manuals and training courses are, therefore, *unmanageable in scope and complexity*. Charles O. Rossotti, "Comments on Customer Service Employee Feedback Report," Internal Revenue Service, May 25, 2000; emphasis added.

Very simply, Commissioner Rossotti conceded that the job of providing accurate information about the tax law to the public *cannot be done* given the scope, breadth, complexity and fluidity of the tax code. But even that remark was made in 2000. Look what happened to the tax law since then.

In her 2012 Annual Report to Congress, the NTA wrote that between 2001 and 2012, there were "approximately 4,680 changes to the tax code, an average of more than one a day." This includes an estimated 579 changes in 2010 alone. NTA, 2012 Annual Report to Congress, pg 6. It is no wonder that the National Taxpayer Advocate regularly reports that tax law complexity is perennially one of the most serious problems citizens face in their efforts to comply with the law. She estimates that the code now approaches nearly four million words. Interestingly, in 2010, she estimated the number of words to be 2.1 million. See: NTA's 2010 Annual Report to Congress, pg. 4.

At the January 2010 meeting of the New York State Bar Association's Taxation Section, former IRS Commissioner Shulman summarized just how bad the issue of complexity has become. He stated, "We have gone from complexity to perplexity."

Due to our massively complicated and constantly changing tax code, most audit results are simply dead wrong. This leads to the assessment of thousands of dollars in taxes, penalties, interest that are simply not owed.

How Returns are Selected for Audit

Let us now turn our attention to the question every citizen asks: "How are returns selected for audit?" Let us start by identifying the two general types of tax audits: the correspondence audit and the face-to-face audit. As their titles imply, the former is conducted through letter writing, while the latter takes place "in person." Let us address each in turn.

The correspondence audit. The IRS's computers scrutinize every tax return filed. The computers perform a number of review and comparison tasks leading to millions of notices demanding increased taxes and penalties. The notices explain that the IRS reviewed the return and found an error. It declares that you owe additional tax and penalties and it demands payment.

Computers review returns for mathematical correctness, to determine whether all necessary supporting schedules are included, and to determine whether entries are properly carried from one form or schedule to another. The computers also compare all information returns filed, such as Forms W-2 and 1099, with tax returns. This crosschecking is designed to ensure that all income is reported and that citizens required to file do in fact file.

Over the past decade, as pointed out by the NTA in her 2011 Annual Report to Congress, "the IRS has significantly increased its use of automated procedures for second-guessing returns (or the taxpayer's decision not to file) in a wide range of areas." She lists the following examples of how the use of the automated correspondence process has exploded:

- The Electronic Fraud Detection System selected 1,054,704 returns in 2011 – an increase of 72 percent over the prior year;

- The math error program processed 10.6 million math errors and issued 8.4 million math error notices in 2010 – 170 percent more than in 2003;

- The Automated Underreporter (AUR) matching program closed 4,336,000 cases in 2010 – 277 percent more than in 2003;

- The Automated Substitute for Return (ASFR) program made 1,150,573 assessments in 2011 – 896 percent more than in 2003; and

- The Correspondence Examination program, which uses automation more than the IRS's other audit programs, closed 1,238,632 examinations of individual returns in 2010 – 13 percent more than the prior year and 93 percent more than 2003. See: NTA, 2011 Annual Report to Congress, pgs 18-19.

For decades, I have pointed out that the IRS's letters and notices often are unclear or incomplete, providing little detail or using confusing language to explain what citizens need to do. In many cases, the letters are dead wrong. For example, a 1994 GAO examination of the IRS's correspondence process found serious problems throughout the system. The GAO looked at forty-seven of the IRS's most common notices. It found that thirty-one of them—66 percent of those examined—used unspecific language, unclear references, inconsistent terminology, illogical presentation of material, and provided insufficient information and guidance. GAO, "IRS Notices Can be Improved," GAO/GGD-95-6, December, 1994, pg 8.

I have spoken about this publicly for years and even provided testimony to Congress regarding the IRS's errant computer notice program. My repeated complaints about this serious problem forced Congress to at least partially address it. With the passage of the Taxpayers' Bill of Rights Act 2 in 1996, Congress amended code section 7522. The law requires that notices mailed to citizens set forth "the basis for" any tax, interest or penalty demanded. However, Congress failed to put any teeth in the law. In fact, the opposite is true. The law states that the lack of an adequate description "shall not invalidate such notice." Code section 7522(a). As a result, in 1997, shortly after the law was passed, in my book *IRS, Taxes and the Beast*, I predicted that this measure simply would not end the IRS's practices of sending bogus bills to the public. As the following evidence indicates, I was right.

In her 2002 Annual Report to Congress, the NTA stated that "many taxpayers remain confused about explanations of adjustments, which are difficult to follow within the notice and do not correlate to specific line numbers on [tax] returns." See: NTA, 2002 Annual Report to Congress, pg 27.

Despite these problems, the IRS continued to expand its computer notice program, as evidenced by the data presented above. The NTA stated that redesigning and correcting computer notices should be "a priority" for the IRS, but clearly it has failed to do so. The NTA's 2011 Annual Report shows that this remains a major problem. The notices remain "difficult to understand." Various NTA surveys show that:

- About 43 percent of people do not understand that the correspondence process is in fact an audit,

- About 40 percent did not know what the IRS was questioning about their tax returns, and

- Only about half the people questioned believe they knew what they had to do to respond to the audit letter. See: NTA, 2011 Annual Report to Congress, pg 21.

Some IRS notices provide no information regarding the alleged errors. I have come to refer to these notices as "arbitrary notices." They merely claim that a mistake was made and demand payment. Because people are unaware of how to handle these letters and are intimidated by the IRS, most end up just paying the bill.

If there is just one reason to understand your rights as a citizen, this is it: the IRS issues tens of millions of computer notices each year and the high error rates are well documented. Any citizen, however honest and forthright he is, can be victimized by such errors. But it is simply not enough to be honest. You must prove you are honest. You must be prepared to back your honesty with action. Your action must take the form of proper and timely responses to IRS attacks.

My book, *The IRS Problem Solver,* is dedicated to dealing with correspondence audits. I examine the most common correspondence audit notices, including claims that you failed to file a tax return, and I show you exactly how to respond to those notices.

The face-to-face audit. The IRS conducts face-to-face audits of approximately 1 to 2 percent of the returns filed in a given year. The decision to conduct a face-to-face examination is based upon several selection criteria. However, the most common is the so-called Discriminate Income Function (DIF) system. Nearly one-third of all returns audited are selected through the DIF scoring process.

The DIF is a sophisticated computer program that compares every line of your return with national and regional statistical averages for a person in your same income category and profession. If any line of your return is out of balance with those averages, the difference is scored. The higher the DIF score, the more likely you are to be selected for examination. That is not to say your return is wrong simply because an entry happens to be out of sync with averages. It simply means that from a statistical analytical viewpoint, the farther away from the average an entry happens to be, the more likely it is to be incorrect. Therefore, the IRS uses that analysis as a means of targeting returns that, at least statistically, have more potential for change, thus increasing the tax liability. Said another way, the IRS uses a sophisticated "profiling" strategy to select returns for audit.

Historically, the DIF scores were built through a research audit program known as the Taxpayer Compliance Measurement Program (TCMP). The TCMP audit was a grueling line-by-line examination of your return. In a TCMP audit, you were asked to prove your name, address, marital status, and so on, throughout the *entire* return. The results of TCMP audits were then assimilated into the DIF parameters. TCMP audit victims were selected on a purely random basis, without regard to any particular claim whatsoever. Essentially, the names were drawn out of a hat.

In 1995, the IRS proposed the most far-reaching TCMP audit ever conducted to that point. The agency was to spend $240 million and three years examining 153,000 individual and small business tax returns. This would have been the largest universe of returns ever examined in any single TCMP sweep. However, Congress stopped the audits by defunding them because of testimony I presented to the Ways and Means IRS Oversight subcommittee. In that testimony, I proved to Congress that because of the significant error rates in audits generally, TCMP audit results were simply unreliable. To use bad data as the means by which to subject millions of citizens to face-to-face audits was, I argued, unreasonable.

But the IRS did not leave the issue alone. Rather than trying to persuade Congress that TCMP audits were not the monster I made them out to be, the agency later just changed the name of its research audits, narrowed the focus a bit and reduced the universe of audit targets. The audit project now goes by the more innocuous name of National Research Project (NRP). Over the past ten or so years, the IRS has operated numerous NRP audit projects—some with as few as 6,000 targets and others with as many as 13,000 at a time—on small business sole proprietors, small business corporations, small business partnerships and individuals. One NRP study done in the mid-2000s targeted 39,000 business tax returns over a three-year period and focused exclusively on the income side of the ledger.

While the typical NRP audit does not always involve the same exhaustive line-by-line scrutiny (though it certainly can) that TCMP audits once did, the selection process remains entirely random. And just like the TCMP audits of old, the results are used to build, modify and update the DIF scores, which in turn are used to target millions of citizens for face-to-face audits. I discuss NRP audits further in chapter 15.

While DIF scores continue to be the more widely used audit selection process, the IRS also uses other selection tools. Common audit selection criteria focus on the general nature of the tax return and its specific claims. Claims within a return that fall under a specific classification can be selected for audit merely because the return includes such an item. These are referred to as Compliance Initiative Projects (CIP). For example, for decades, the IRS has targeted certain so-called tax shelter investments. Any tax return possessing tax shelter attributes is subject to review. Other CIP classes include:

1. Employment tax enforcement. This project attacks small businesses to ensure that all Social Security and hospital taxes are assessed on the wages or salaries paid to workers. The IRS also scrutinizes a business's use of independent contractors, the payment of fringe benefits to employees, distributions of cash or property to owners and the payment of reasonable compensation to officers and shareholders performing services.

2. Personal and employment tax return non-filers. There are millions of non-filers and the IRS spends a great deal of resources chasing them down as best it can. Each year, the IRS develops new programs and strategies for identifying non-filers and squeezing the missing returns—and then the money—from them.

3. "Flow-through" entities. A flow-through entity is one which itself does not pay taxes. Rather, the owners or shareholders of the entity pay the tax. The chief examples of flow-through entities are subchapter S corporations, partnerships and limited liability companies (LLC). These entities merely report gross business income and expenses. The profit (or loss) then "flows through" to the owners or shareholders and in turn is reported on the owners' respective tax returns as a net income number. As such, the entity does not pay income tax, the owner does. The IRS targets flow-through entities to ensure they are reporting all income.

4. Offshore assets and bank accounts. Since 2001, the IRS has been on fire over the idea of capturing the tax due from assets held and income generated offshore. U.S. citizens are taxed on their worldwide income and while it is not illegal to own an offshore bank account or derive income from any legitimate offshore endeavor, it is illegal to not report that income on your tax return and pay the U.S. income tax due. The IRS has managed to tear down the veil of secrecy that once separated many offshore financial institutions from the U.S. government's prying eyes. Moreover, the IRS managed to glean

mountains of information from the approximately 40,000 people who to date have stepped forward to utilize the IRS's Offshore Voluntary Disclosure Program (OVDP) to avoid the confiscatory penalties associated with failure to report these assets and pay the taxes. That data is now being "mined" to find other citizens who have not stepped forward. I discuss the OVDP in chapter 19.

5. Penalties under the Patient Protection and Affordable Care Act (PPACA). The PPACA ("Obamacare") contains substantial penalties for individuals who fail to purchase health insurance for themselves and families, and for businesses that fail to provide "affordable health insurance" to their employees. While the IRS claims that it will not screen tax returns for the purposes of enforcing these penalties, I do not believe it. I fully expect these issues to find their way onto the IRS's audit plate soon enough.

6. Multi-level marketing. For years, the IRS has targeted multi-level marketers, such as those involved with Amway, Shaklee and the dozens of other companies that use independent, home-based business operators to market their products. The IRS often claims most such distributors are not engaged in a legitimate business. Rather, it contends their endeavors are merely "hobbies" undertaken for the benefit of pursuing lavish travel and opulent entertainment. The agency attacks the business expenses claimed by these citizens, including their home office deductions, long distance telephone charges and so on. I discuss this issue in chapter 12.

When the agency's computer screening mechanism identifies one or more of the above areas of curiosity, the chances of a face-to-face audit grow significantly.

Now that we have debunked the basic misconceptions about the tax audit process, let us move to the next level. We shall examine the specific manner in which the IRS attacks a return during the course of a typical face-to-face audit.

PART TWO

THE IRS
ON
THE PROWL

"The Core Competency Training for newly hired Revenue Agents (i.e., auditors or examiners) includes a 575-page participant guide, but only six paragraphs mention discussing taxpayer rights and the audit process with taxpayers."

NATIONAL TAXPAYER ADVOCATE
2013 ANNUAL REPORT TO CONGRESS

CHAPTER FIVE

HOW THE IRS ATTACKS A TAX RETURN

NOW THAT WE DEBUNKED THE KEY MYTHS ABOUT the audit process, it is time to address some basic truths concerning it. We know the IRS attacks returns on two general grounds. The first is the question of income and the second is the question of reductions to income, most notably deductions, dependent exemptions and credits. The IRS may claim you earned income but failed to report it or it may disallow one or more of your deductions for various reasons. Through either or both of these tactics, the IRS acts to increase your taxable income.

To win a tax audit, it is important to understand this great truth about the process: *You have the burden of proof* as to the items claimed in your return. You must prove you reported all income. You must prove your deductions are not only accurate in terms of the amount claimed, but that the deduction is allowed by law in the year claimed. As a general rule, the IRS *never* has to prove you made a mistake. Rather, you have to prove you filed correctly. (There are a few exceptions, which I address in chapters 10 and 11.)

This is particularly true with regard to deductions. In 1943, the Supreme Court used a phrase that has since become commonplace with courts addressing the question. In the case of *Interstate Transit Lines v. Commissioner,* 319 U. S. 590, 593 (1943), the Court stated that "an income tax deduction is a matter of legislative grace and that the burden of clearly showing the right to the claimed deduction is on the taxpayer." If you cannot prove the deduction is justified, it will be disallowed.

If you do not fully understand this, it is 100 percent predicable that you will lose your audit and will end up owing the IRS more money—over $16,000 on average. On the other hand, when you know exactly how the IRS is likely to attack your return and precisely how to defend it, your success is just as predictable.

How the IRS Attacks a Tax Return

With nearly 4 million words in the tax code, not even counting the millions more found in the regulations, we can safely say there are countless *possible* ways the IRS could attack a return. The scope depends solely on the actual claims in your return. If, for example, you did not claim a deduction for charitable contributions, you cannot expect trouble regarding your charitable giving.

But for all the code's breadth and complexity, for all of the millions of audits raising countless potential tax law questions, you might be amazed to know that there are just a handful that arise year after year. In each of the annual reports to Congress released by the National Taxpayer Advocate, the NTA identifies the most litigated issues during that year. On that list we usually find:

- Gross income,

- Business expense deductions,

- Depreciation of business equipment,

- Office in home deductions,

- Charitable deductions,

- Family status issues involving dependent exemptions, and

- Penalties.

While most of these issues involve businesses, there is one overriding issue pointed squarely at both businesses and individuals, and that is the question of gross income. Therefore, it is critical that you understand how the IRS attacks income and how to prove your income is reported correctly.

Another item that makes the list nearly every year is the question of business expense deductions, including home office issues and the depreciation of business equipment. Code section 162 allows a deduction for any "ordinary and necessary" expense incurred for the purposes of "earning income." As a business, whether a small corporation or a sole proprietor, you are entitled to deduct any expense you incur that is necessary to generate income.

The list of such deductions is broad and variable, depending upon the nature of the business. What is ordinary and necessary for one business may not be for another. What generates income for one business may not for another. This very broad brush is what accounts for the fact that the IRS disallows these deductions with staggering regularity.

- In one analysis limited to section 162 business deductions, the GAO found six recurring themes in the IRS's practice of disallowing these deductions. They are:

- Inadequate documentation – citizens either did not provide documentation or the documentation provided was (or was alleged to be) inadequate to prove the expense;

- Unreasonable compensation – closely held corporations deduct more than is "reasonable" for an officer's salary, or conversely, fail to pay adequate compensation to corporate officers or shareholders performing services for the corporation;

- Not a trade or business – IRS claims the citizen is not involved in a business for profit, but rather is engaged in a hobby activity for which expenses are non-deductible;

- Personal expenses – IRS claims the expense (which might have been fully documented) was not business related, but rather constituted a non-deductible personal expense;

- Capital expenditures – IRS alleges that the claimed expenses are capital in nature and must be depreciated rather than fully deducted in the year incurred; and

- Miscellaneous – This category involves a number of general areas. See: GAO, "Recurring Issues in Tax Disputes Over Business Expense Deductions," GAO/GGD-95-232, September, 1995.

Of all business taxpayers, sole proprietors face the highest risk that the IRS will in some way tamper with their returns. Of the cases reviewed by the GAO, 51 percent involved sole proprietors. Just two of the six issues identified posed the most problems for sole proprietors. First is the question of documenting deductions. Two-thirds of all disputes with the IRS grow from inadequate (or allegedly inadequate) documentation. Next is the hobby versus business question. Twenty-one percent of cases involve a claim by the IRS that the business is not legitimate, but rather is a hobby engaged in merely for personal pleasure or recreation. If you are to survive an audit as a sole proprietor, you better know how to document your deductions and prove your business is legitimate. I discuss it in chapter 12.

Small business corporations are also attacked on the basis of documentation, but to a lesser extent. However, two other major problems present themselves for corporations. First is the question of reasonable compensation in the case of regular corporations (that is, not subchapter S corporations). Since regular corporations are entitled to deduct salaries but not dividends paid to shareholders, the IRS is wont to claim that officers' salaries are "unreasonably high." By reducing the salary, it decreases the corresponding deduction, and hence increases the corporation's income tax liability.

On the other side of the coin, we have subchapter S corporations. As I explained earlier, subchapter S corporations do not pay taxes. Rather, the company's profit flows through to the owners and is taxed on their personal tax returns. But many subchapter S corporations pay no salary to their owners, though often the owners are the only persons performing services for the corporation. In that case, the IRS takes the position that the corporation must pay a "reasonable salary" to the corporate officers (or shareholders) who perform services for the company. Why? Because those salaries are subject to the full scope of employment taxes, while the flow-through profits are subject only to the income tax. In short, the IRS gets more money when the officers and shareholders of subchapter S corporations are treated as employees.

The second issue for corporations (both regular and subchapter S corporations) involves the payment of personal expenses to corporate officers or shareholders. Seventeen percent of all small corporation cases involve a claim that one or more expenses were in fact non-deductible personal expenses paid on behalf of the corporation's shareholders.

Because the IRS is so aggressive with businesses, for years it has operated the Market Segment Specialization Program (MSSP). MSSP is to businesses what the economic reality audit is to individuals. It is designed to examine and evaluate every single aspect of how a business operates.

For example, one MSSP project focuses on gasoline retailers. Let us say the marketplace is Philadelphia. The IRS selects for audit a number of gas retailers within that area, perhaps dozens or more. To build a profile of how gas retailers operate, it audits every element of the business. The audit includes not only an examination of income, expenses, assets and liabilities, but delves deeply into the industry itself. Auditors may contact manufacturers, wholesalers, distributors, trade associations and others directly or indirectly connected with the business.

The results of these dragnet audits lead to the production of MSSP handbooks. The handbook is a working model for the audit of such a business in other areas of the nation. To date, the IRS has issued ninety-nine MSSP handbooks. The manuals cover, for example, the following businesses:

- Attorneys,
- Ministers,
- The wine industry,
- Gasoline retailers,
- Alaskan commercial fishing,
- Construction,
- Bars and restaurants,
- Beauty and barber shops,
- Auto body and repair,
- Grain farmers,
- Sports franchises,
- Taxicabs,
- Pizza restaurants,
- Bed and breakfasts,
- The trucking industry,
- Mobile food vendors, and
- The entertainment industry.

An essential element of preparation for any business under audit is to consult the MSSP manual (if one exists) for that business. There you will find the IRS's battle plan for the audit of your business.

One Problem with the Tax Code

One has to wonder why so many people face problems with inadequate records. At least part of the problem can be traced to the lack of clear guidance or specific definitions as to exactly what constitutes adequate records in the first place. Amazingly, the Internal Revenue Code does not define "records" or "recordkeeping" generally, nor does it generally specify what type of records a person is to keep with respect to proving income. Only in a very few instances does the code define what records a person must have to support a particular deduction. For example, code section 274(d) defines clearly what documents a person must offer to support a deduction for business travel and entertainment expense deductions. I discuss this in detail in chapter 6.

The general recordkeeping requirements are provided in code section 6001, which reads in relevant part:

> Every person liable for any tax imposed by this title, or for the collection thereof, shall keep such records, render such statements, make such returns, and comply with such rules and regulations as the Secretary may from time to time prescribe.

Rev. Reg. section 31.6001-1(a), Form of Records, states as follows:

> The records required by the regulations in this part shall be kept accurately, but no particular form is required for keeping the records. Such forms and systems of accounting shall be used as will enable the district director to ascertain whether liability for tax is incurred and, if so, the amount thereof.

The IRS clearly does not mandate that a person keep records in one way or another, merely that his records be accurate and allow the IRS to determine his correct tax liability. Rev. Reg. sections 1.6001-1(a) and (b) are entirely consistent with this conclusion. They provide:

> (a) In General. Except as provided in paragraph (b) of this section, any person subject to tax under Subtitle A of the Code (including a qualified State individual income tax which is treated pursuant to section 6361(a) as if it were imposed by Chapter 1 of Subtitle A), or any person required to file a return of information with respect to income, shall keep such permanent books of account or records, including inventories, as are sufficient to establish the amount of gross income, deductions, credits, or other matters required to be shown by such person in any return of such tax or information.

> (b) Farmers And Wage-Earners. Individuals deriving gross income from the business of farming, and individuals whose gross income includes salaries, wages, or similar compensation for personal services rendered, are required with respect to such income to keep such records as will enable the district director to determine the correct amount of income subject to the tax. It is not necessary, however, that with respect to such income individuals keep the books of account or records required by paragraph (a) of this section. * * *

Based on the above, this is the recordkeeping formula—the records must be permanent, accurate and allow the IRS to determine your correct tax liability. It is as simple as that. In the simplest of cases, this could be just a bank account with the monthly bank statements showing income deposited and checks showing payments made. Provided it is established as a matter of fact that all income earned was deposited to the account and all expenses were paid out of the account, what more is needed?

Moreover, under code section 446(a), a citizen is required to compute his income using "a method of accounting on the basis of which the taxpayer regularly computes his income in keeping his books." And since there is so little guidance as to exactly what "books" one must keep, each citizen and business may have, and often does have, an entirely different method of keeping track of income and expenses for tax purposes. Add to this the great "discretion" the IRS has under 446(b), and the potential for abuse is staggering. Code section 446(b) reads:

> (b) If no method of accounting has been regularly used by the taxpayer, or if the method used does not clearly reflect income, the computation of taxable income shall be made under such method as, in the *opinion of the Secretary*, does clearly reflect income. (Emphasis added.)

As I have already demonstrated, it is the "opinion of the Secretary" that most individuals earned income they did not report on their tax returns. "In the opinion of the Secretary," then, their income should be "adjusted" under such method "as does clearly reflect income." To translate, the IRS adds taxable income, and hence, tax liability, in almost every audit situation.

But as we shall see later, only when your records do not exist or do not clearly reflect income can the IRS step in and do it their way. For most citizens under audit, and especially most businesses, non-existent records are not usually the problem. Certainly there are often deficiencies in recordkeeping but not to the level that would justify the IRS trashing the system and reconstructing from the ground up.

How the IRS Attacks Income

The IRS uses several techniques for flushing out evidence of unreported income. Let us examine seven of the most common methods.

1. The Bank Deposits Method. The audit process always involves the IRS reviewing one's bank records. Expect the agent to request all personal and business bank records, including duplicate deposit slips, monthly bank statements, canceled checks and loan documents for a given year. The IRS will likely also request any financial statements or loan applications that you submitted to a bank or other lender.

Most people believe their bank transactions are sacred and private. Nothing could be further from the truth. The IRS has ready access to your bank records with its administrative summons power, which I talked about in chapter 3. Your bank records can be obtained with or without your cooperation, and no, you do not have a constitutional right to privacy regarding your bank records. In the case of *United States v. Miller,* the Supreme Court determined that a person essentially waives his right of privacy with respect to any matter shared with a bank, or for that matter, any third party. When you voluntarily choose to do business with a bank, "the depositor takes the risk, in revealing his affairs to another, that the information will be conveyed by that person to the Government." *Miller,* 425 U.S. 435, at 443 (1976).

So much for your Fourth Amendment rights.

But believing bank accounts are private, people nevertheless deposit to their accounts money or receipts that may not be reported on a tax return and which in fact, are not even necessarily taxable income. This creates a discrepancy between the income on the tax return versus the "apparent" income shown from the bank deposits. Let me illustrate.

Suppose you work for a corporation that issues a Form W-2, *Wage and Tax Statement*, at the end of the year. That statement, which is also filed with the IRS, reports total wages earned during the year. When you prepare your return, you overlook the fact that you sold your old riding lawn mower to your neighbor. That money, along with all of the other garage sale proceeds, was deposited to your bank account along with a paycheck one month.

During your audit, the examiner adds the deposits to the account, taken from the duplicate deposit slips and monthly statements you provide. He finds, for example, that $1,200 more appeared in the bank account than was reported as income on your tax return. The difference is determined to be unreported income.

Only in the case of criminals is the failure to report income a deliberate act. Most people just do not believe that every dime coming into their possession must be reported to the government. And in fact, not every dime is required to be reported. Even for those people who are highly conscientious about reporting everything, truthfully, who remembers to write down *every dime*? Yet, the IRS believes these "underreporters" are intentionally hiding income and when the new tax liability is computed, penalties are naturally included.

Another common tactic for auditors is to double count re-deposits. This happens routinely when a person has more than one bank account. Most people never see it coming. This is how it works.

Suppose you earn W-2 wages of $40,000 and deposit all your paychecks to a checking account. Suppose further you run a small business on the side, which needs operating capital from time to time. To fund the business, you write checks from your personal account and deposit them to your business account. Of course, all your business income is deposited to the business account as well.

When the business tax return is prepared, the income figures are taken from the income journal. The journal is your daily logbook reflecting income from all sources. The log may be nothing more than your deposit records of business receipts. If there is a separate journal, it does not show the deposits from your personal account because, simply, that is not income to the business. However, these deposits do show up in the business bank statements.

When the auditor reviews the business account statements, he adds all deposits, assuming they are income. If you re-deposited $2,500 from your personal account to your business account, those deposits are picked up as income. The result is the auditor assumes you have $2,500 more income than reported on your business return.

However simple this may sound and however simple it may be to prove the matter, take note of something very important. Tax auditors do this *all the time*. They do it *knowing* it is wrong and they do it *knowing* they will get away with it a fair percentage of the time. Recall that I reported this as one of the IRS's common improper audit tactics when I testified before Congress. I have never seen a business audit in which re-deposits were not a large part of the alleged unreported income determined by the auditor.

2. Information Returns. As I discuss at length in chapter 2, information returns are a steadily growing source of data for the IRS—and the agency wants more. The most common information return is Form W-2, *Wage and Tax Statement*, which is filed by employers reporting wages paid to and taxes withheld from their employees. Form 1099 covers a wide range of non-employee payments. For example, 1099-R reports royalty income, 1099-INT reports interest income. Form 1099-MISC is used to report non-specific payments, such as those made to independent contractors.

The law requires that a W-2 be filed for every employee reporting the first dollar of wages. A Form 1099 is generally required when payments made in the course of business are at least $600 for the year. However, the threshold is lower for certain other payments.

As I explained earlier, IRS computers crosscheck information returns with tax returns. They look for unreported income. Suppose, for example, the IRS shows two Forms W-2 that report total wages of $35,000. However, the tax return reports income of just $20,000 from one source. This discrepancy leads to the assumption that you had income you did not report.

The IRS handles through correspondence most (but not all) of the under-reporter cases turned up this way. Correspondence audits are discussed at length in my book, *The IRS Problem Solver*.

3. Net Worth Increases. A less common method of adding income is the "Net Worth Increase" method. Under this system, the IRS makes a determination of any substantial increase in one's net worth (the value of his assets less liabilities) during a particular year. A year-end net worth is established then compared with the net worth that existed at the beginning of the same year. The difference is calculated. The difference is compared to the income shown on the tax return. The IRS then asks itself whether the after-tax income reported was sufficient to account for the net worth increase. If not, the agency claims that additional income must have been earned to account for the higher net worth.

Let me illustrate. Suppose on January 1, 2015, you have a $75,000 mortgage on your home. The home is worth $100,000. If the home is your only asset and the mortgage is your only liability, your net worth is $25,000. Let us further suppose that by December 31, 2015, your home mortgage is paid in full. Without any debt on the home, your net worth, assuming no other assets or liabilities, is now $100,000. Your net worth *increased* by $75,000 in one year.

Now let us suppose that your 2015 tax return reports wage income of $50,000. Based on all deductions and exemptions shown in the return, let us further suppose your after-tax income (the money left after paying federal, state and social security taxes) is $33,000. This is the money available to spend on all personal living expenses, recreation, investments, charitable contributions, etc.

As anyone can plainly see—and *so would the IRS*—it is impossible to have paid off a $75,000 mortgage *and* all other living expenses with just $33,000. Obviously, the government quickly concludes that you had unreported income.

This example is exaggerated and simplified in that *all* assets and liabilities must be taken into consideration before any increases can be assumed. The IRS also must consider borrowing, gifts, inheritances and the sale of other assets that might account for the additional cash. Furthermore, the IRS must *correctly* establish the net worth at the beginning of the year in question before it can say the net worth *increased* by the end of the year.

4. Cash Expenditures. Code section 6050I requires all cash transactions in excess of $10,000 to be reported to the IRS. The law stipulates that if any person engaged in "a trade or business receives more than $10,000 in cash in one transaction (or two or more related transactions)," that person must provide to the IRS a Form 8300, *Report of Cash Payments Over $10,000 Received in Business*. The form gives the payer's name, social security number and the date and nature of the transaction.

The IRS uses this information to make evaluations of unreported income in much the same way it does with net worth assessments. Using the same example as above, suppose, rather than paying off the house, information reveals you purchased expensive furs and diamonds during the course of the year. While these are not "title" assets such as an automobile or house, they are just as easily traceable through the reporting requirements of code section 6050I and Form 8300 if you used cash to purchase them.

In addition, the IRS regularly uses Form 4822, S*tatement of Annual Estimated Personal and Family Living Expenses*, to determine income. The form, discussed in detail in Part III, asks the citizen to list all personal expenses paid during the year, either by check or with cash. If the expenses seem to exceed available after-tax income, the IRS assumes you earned income you did not report and increases your tax accordingly.

5. Bureau of Labor Statistics. The Bureau of Labor publishes statistics of the average earnings of persons throughout the United States. The statistics cover individuals in virtually every walk of life. They also take into account the level of disposable income necessary to exist in a given community in the United States.

In the absence of other information, the IRS makes estimates of income based upon Bureau of Labor Statistics (BLS) if one fails to file a tax return. Using one's employment or profession and geographic location as a starting point, the IRS refers to BLS publications to ascertain the income you "must have earned" in order to live. The statistics consider whether you are a homeowner, whether you are married, whether you have children and other factors either known or readily ascertainable.

Despite the fact that they are really not much more than guesses, BLS estimates stand up unless the citizen can demonstrate the figures are incorrect based on the facts of his case.

6. Consumer Price Index Estimates. The Consumer Price Index (CPI) marks

increases in the cost of living in the United States from year to year. Moreover, like the BLS tables, these figures are broken into specific geographic locations. A person in St. Louis, for example, may not be faced with the same cost of living increases as, say, a person in San Francisco. The differences are reflected in the particular CPI tables.

CPI tables provide the IRS with a fruitful source of information upon which to base a tax assessment in the absence of more accurate data or when a person fails to file a tax return. To use CPI tables, the IRS pulls the last tax return available for the taxpayer, determines his gross income from that return, and merely increases it year to year by multiplying the appropriate CPI ratio to the last known income figure. Let me illustrate.

Suppose your last tax return, filed in 2005, discloses income of $38,000. Suppose also that you live in Atlanta. Further suppose that the CPI for Atlanta increased each year by 2 percent. The IRS simply multiplies $38,000 (your 2005 income) by 1.02 to determine that your 2006 income was $38,760. That figure is then multiplied by 1.02 (or such other CPI amount applicable to that year) to arrive at the alleged 2007 income of $39,535. This procedure is repeated until each year is accounted for.

7. Weighted Averages. A weighted average is a mathematical computation performed when only partial records are available. It works this way: Suppose you have a bank account for eighteen months during 2012 and 2013. In early July 2013, the account is closed and you have no further transactions with any bank. Given this, the IRS has records of income from bank deposits for all of 2012, half of 2013 but none at all for 2014.

To determine income for the last six months of 2013 and the entirety of 2014, the IRS averages the deposits shown for the first eighteen months. That average is then projected over the balance of the eighteen-month period, taking into account likely increases in income determined from the CPI tables. These averages form the foundation of the IRS's claim of income for the eighteen-month period in which no bank records exist.

The Economic Reality Audit

As the years roll by, Congress is faithful to cut the number of deductions legally allowed. As fewer deductions are available, there are fewer to audit. At the same time, the IRS is concerned about the growing underground economy. It has therefore employed a more creative weapon in the fight against alleged unreported income. This weapon takes the form of the so-called economic reality audit. The economic reality audit is based upon one or more of the seven techniques outlined above. However, it goes much, much further, as we shall soon see.

CHAPTER SIX

HOW TO COUNTER
THE ATTACT

ALL FACE-TO-FACE AUDITS BEGIN AT THE SAME point—with a notice from the IRS. The notice says that your return was selected for "examination" and establishes a time and place for the meeting. Generally Form 4564, *Information Document Request* (IDR), accompanies the notice. Sometimes the IRS uses Form 9297, *Summary of Contact*. The substance of each form is the same, as described below. For purposes of simplicity, I refer to the IDR throughout the remainder of this discourse.

The IDR presents a list of items the auditor wishes to inspect. The requested documents relate to the claims in the return subject to review. In many cases, the IDR makes a specific request for production of documents relative to a particular claim, such as evidence to support a mortgage interest deduction. In other cases, the IDR is more general. It may seek "all records relative to your claim of deductible items in the return."

Now that you are on notice of the audit and what the issues are, let us examine the phases of preparation you must undertake to put yourself in the best position to win.

Step One. Audit defense preparations begin with a careful analysis of the notice and the IDR. Ascertain the issues in question. Is the IRS questioning certain deductions or all of them? Are they asking for documents that indicate they are challenging your income? In either event, do not be intimidated if the IDR asks for a laundry list of records. You will quickly notice that much of the material does not exist. The IRS generally paints with a broad brush when seeking records, at least initially. You can narrow the list in a hurry after recognizing that some items do not apply to you and your return.

Step Two. Now begin to determine two essential facts with respect to each item in question. First, what in fact was claimed on the return with regard to that item? And second, are you in possession of sufficient proof to verify that the entry is correct?

Verifying what in fact was claimed is a simple matter. Just look to your Form 1040 or the supporting schedule bearing the entry in question. Note the amount. An example is the mortgage interest deduction. If you claimed $5,000 in mortgage interest on Schedule A, $5,000 is the amount you must prove. If you used a return preparer, meet with your preparer and go over the return to be sure you understand each of the entries in question. Do not proceed to an audit without reviewing the tax return in this manner. If you do, you will have no idea whatsoever as to your burden of proof. You will be completely at the mercy of the auditor.

Step Three. The next step is to match your documentary proof to each item to be sure the two figures coincide. This answers the fact question whether you indeed incurred the expense claimed. Your documents establish that you did. Exactly what type of documentation is considered "sufficient proof" is addressed later in this chapter.

Your preliminary preparation must satisfy this question: Do the documents in your possession or under your control support the amount of income and deductions claimed? If the answer is "no," then you must use one of the methods explained later in this chapter to supplement your proof. If the answer is "yes," then proceed to step four.

Step Four. Now you must determine whether the proof is sufficient from a legal standpoint. This usually involves slightly more effort than just adding up the receipts and checks. It will involve a little work on the Internet.

With the Internet, basic legal research is easier now than ever before. You do not even have to darken the door of a law library to get the information needed to understand the law that controls the issues in your case.

The laws of the United States currently in effect are organized in a publication known as the United States Code, the body of federal law known as "statutes." The statutes are organized within the United States Code by topic. Each topic is assigned a number, known as a "title."

All federal tax laws are found in Title 26 of the United States Code, commonly referred to as "the Internal Revenue Code." Within Title 26, each separate statute is numbered individually, beginning with "1." The statute is then referred to as a "section." Hence, the citation "26 U.S.C. 6511" is a reference to Title 26 of the United States Code (the Internal Revenue Code), at section 6511. Throughout this treatise, I refer simply to the code section without the reference to Title 26, e.g., "code section 6511."

You can find electronic versions of the United States code at several Internet sites. The U.S. House of Representatives sponsors a site at:

http://uscode.house.gov/search/criteria.shtml

There is also a version sponsored by Cornell University Law School, which is accessible through the IRS's website and is available directly at:

http://www.law.cornell.edu/uscode/text

In each case, you can either go directly to a code section within a specific title or you can search by key words and phrases.

You can also do a simple Google search to find the tax code and specific topics within the tax code to ascertain the basic information you need. The Internet is loaded with tax law research and articles designed to provide information to understand basic legal points. However, if you use secondary sources of information, such as articles on the law rather than the law itself, be sure the document is produced by a reputable source. There is a lot of tax non-sense on the Internet. To help protect people from tax non-sense, I have written two research reports that expose common tax schemes. They are *The Untax Promise* and *Why Trusts Don't Work.* Both of these reports are available free of charge by going to www.taxhelponline.com. From the home page menu bar, click on "Resources and Publications," then "Research Reports."

Do not be intimidated by the size and complexity of the tax code. You do not have to become an expert on tax law. You only need understand the very limited number of issues at stake in your case.

The purpose of referring to the code is simple yet important. Expect revenue agents to assume one of two stances with regard to a given deduction. The first and most common is that your proof does not meet or exceed the numbers shown on the return. "Without further substantiation," you will be told, "I can't allow this item. You're unable to prove that you in fact spent the amount claimed." Hence, down the drain goes your deduction, in whole or in part. Remember the GAO study on documentation? Sixty-six percent of all disputed cases have this problem.

But when your proof does match the deduction, the revenue agent claims that while you did indeed spend the money alleged, the law does not allow the deduction. "The law is clear," begins the refrain. "A deduction is just not permitted for money spent in this fashion. I am sorry, but I can't allow it."

In anticipation of this two-pronged attack, proper preparation for the audit must address both the factual aspect (how much was spent, for what, and when) and the legal aspect (what the law say about money spent in this fashion) of a given deduction.

As we have already seen, even IRS agents know little about the law given that so many sweeping changes occur on an ongoing basis. Agents can, however, bluff and intimidate citizens on these points. That is why I recommend everyone have my library of IRS defense materials. The books address your rights and IRS procedures in nearly every kind of tax dispute.

In addition to the Internal Revenue Code where we find the statutes, the body of tax law is made up of other sources of authority, including:

Treasury Regulations. The IRS creates regulations. A tax regulation becomes effective when Congress *fails* to act upon it by expressly voting against its enactment. Through this system of "law by default," un-elected bureaucrats heap thousands of legal requirements on the public each year. In this work, I refer to a tax regulation as a Revenue Regulation, with the abbreviation "Rev. Reg."

Court Decisions. Court decisions interpret the statutes and regulations on a case-by-case basis. Most court decisions regarding the IRS and the tax code come from the United States Tax Court.

Revenue Rulings. Revenue Rulings reflect the IRS's written opinion as to how the law should be applied in a given set of hypothetical facts and circumstances.

IRS Publications. The IRS produces dozens of publications that discuss various aspects of the federal tax law and tax return preparation. These publications are specifically designed for public consumption. However, they present only the IRS's opinion of the law. They do not necessarily state the law correctly in every case. In any event, these publications provide guidance as to how the IRS expects one to complete his tax return and supporting schedules.

Each of these sources of legal authority can help provide support to any single claim you make. Internet research on a tax issue using key words applicable to your situation can turn up hits that may include any or all of the above authorities.

How to Prove Income

In anticipation of the IRS's attack on your claimed income, be prepared to counter with one of the proven methods used to verify that your disclosure is correct. I have distilled four primary techniques, which, when used alone or in concert with one another, ensure that the income portion of your return remains intact. Each of these techniques, together with a real life example, follows.

1. Ledgers. The most effective way to verify income is with records made personally and contemporaneously at the time of earning the income. Records reflecting income are commonly referred to as ledgers, logs or journals. These records are, in the absence of patently contradictory evidence, most persuasive in an income dispute.

A case comes to mind where logs were the difference between paying tens of thousands of dollars in illegitimate taxes and the just conclusion that such was not owed. Dennis went through a tax audit in which he presented to the auditor his bank records and evidence to support his business deductions. Unaware that the auditor was fishing for unreported income, Dennis candidly answered a barrage of questions about the manner in which he operated his business.

As a piano tuner, Dennis made house calls to his many customers. Some of the customers paid by check. Many paid in cash. Naturally, all of the checks were deposited to Dennis's bank account but the cash was not. When the IRS audited Dennis's tax return, they reviewed his bank records. The auditor believed he stumbled upon a major discrepancy in Dennis's finances.

The discrepancy was that Dennis wrote off many thousands of dollars in business expenses on his Schedule C, but deposits to his bank account did not come close to matching those amounts, not to mention the deductions claimed on Schedule A. Even though Dennis declared sufficient income to account for these expenditures, it was obvious he did a large part of his business in cash. This caused the auditor to jump to the erroneous and unfounded conclusion that Dennis significantly underreported his income.

The auditor did all of this gum shoeing without Dennis's knowledge. Had the agent simply asked, Dennis could have provided ample verification of his income. Instead, soon after the audit was complete, the agent mailed Dennis an examination report with a cover letter. Upon reviewing the examination report, Dennis was shocked to find that the agent included thousands of dollars in unreported income. Flabbergasted by the report, we immediately drafted the necessary paperwork to carry out an appeal. See chapter 13 for the appeals process.

During the Appeals conference, we presented Dennis's ledgers. They constituted the primary source of information for the income declaration in his return. The ledgers were not summaries of other documents. As primary source (not secondary) documents, they directly reflected the matters presented. Not being an accountant, the ledgers were rudimentary by professional standards but quite functional for his needs. They were also more than adequate to establish that his income was reported correctly. Remember, the law does not require that you keep records in a "professional" manner. The law requires only that you keep records sufficient to "clearly reflect income." Code section 446(b) and Rev. Reg. sections 1.6001-1(a) and (b). See chapter 5.

Dennis's ledgers looked something like this:

MONTH/YEAR

Date	Name/Address	Job	Paid

Beneath the heading in each column Dennis recorded the data called for. Next to the amounts shown in the "Paid" column, Dennis indicated whether the amount was paid at the time of rendering service or whether he had to bill the customer. At the end of the month, he mailed statements as necessary. The eventual payment was then recorded in the month it was received. At the end of the year, it was a simple matter of adding the amounts received. The total amount was reflected as the gross income on the tax return. Spreadsheet software and other computerized bookkeeping tools make this process very simple.

Verifying income at the Appeals level was not difficult. We provided copies of Dennis's ledgers together with an explanation as to how they were maintained. Dennis's testimony that his ledgers were made contemporaneously with earning the income was critical. That is to say, the documents were not concocted after the audit in the hope of avoiding additional taxes.

In the absence of any specific evidence to the contrary, and given the fact that Dennis's explanation was *plausible*, reasonable and Dennis was an *honest* person and clearly *projected* that, the appeals officer accepted his proof and dropped all of the alleged phantom income.

Many businesses use professional accountants, bookkeepers or computer software to establish ledgers or journals accurately and neatly reflecting the company's daily business. Those without the benefit of experts should take a lesson from Dennis. Be careful not to fall into the trap of creating ledgers that are too complex and difficult to follow. Unless supervised by an accountant, ledgers should be simple and to the point. Most importantly, create the ledgers contemporaneously, that is, at the same time the events being recorded occur. It is important to be able to testify believably that your ledgers were made at the time the income was earned, not on the way to the IRS's office, and that they are primary source documents, not summaries of other documents.

2. Bank Records. Just as the IRS uses bank records to *increase* income, you can use them to refute erroneous IRS estimates of your income. Useful tools include monthly bank statements and duplicate deposit slips. Between the two, a person can fix his income quite accurately. In fact, I maintain that the best and most accurate ledger or journal a

person can have is his business bank account.

When you receive money in the course of your affairs and deposit it to an account, a permanent record is made of the amount and date of the deposit. When the IRS questions income, reliance on bank records as a full and complete record of your receipts is virtually unassailable. This of course assumes the IRS cannot point to large cash expenditures or net worth increases that might betray bank account information.

To illustrate this, I point to a case where the IRS made an estimate of a man's income based on BLS tables as explained in chapter 5. Don did not file tax returns for the two years in question. Don was a plumber, but not a very successful one. Personal circumstances caused his business to dwindle and he was working odd jobs to generate income.

BLS statistics, unfortunately, do not take into consideration whether one is successful in business or not. They are, by admission, mere averages. In order to have an average, there must of course be a high and a low. Don's income was at the low end of the scale, but BLS tables put his income over five times higher than reality. With penalties and interest, the IRS wanted Don to pay more in taxes for the two years than he earned in income.

Using bank records as the starting point, we set out to determine the *accurate* amount of gross income Don earned. Don's wife, Linda owned the bank account in question. Linda was as an employee for a company and earned W-2 wages. She also filed her own tax returns and paid her own taxes. Don deposited his money into her account. As she had no obligation to report his income, she reported only her own wage income on her tax return.

We knew how much Linda earned from her job each month and we knew that she was paid twice each month. We carefully reviewed the bank statements (primary source documents) and with a red pen, drew a line through those deposits we identified as Linda's paycheck. In some cases however, a deposit larger than a single paycheck was shown. In that case, we went back to the deposit slip. A deposit slip identifies each of the individual items that make up a deposit. By referring to the deposit slips, we were able to identify and mark out each of Linda's paychecks.

The remaining deposits represented Don's earnings. Having isolated Don's income on each of the bank statements, it was just a matter of adding the deposits that were his. The total for twelve months was Don's income for the year. Our tally was presented to the Appeals Officer, together with testimony to the effect that all of Don's receipts were deposited to Linda's account. We also proved that Linda's wages were responsible for the other funds deposited to the account. Finally, we showed that Linda already filed her own return and paid all her taxes separately. With no other evidence that Don earned the income claimed by the IRS, the Appeals Officer was forced to accept the facts as presented.

Not all solutions are that simple. Sometimes, a bank account analysis is much more tedious. Further effort is necessary when the IRS skews figures taken from two or more separate accounts. It typically unfolds this way.

A small business owner has two (or more) bank accounts. One functions as a business account, to which he deposits his receipts and from which he pays business bills. The other is a personal account. The personal account is funded by periodic payments from the business account. From the personal account he pays personal living expenses.

During the course of an examination, the IRS reviews the records of both accounts. The deposits to the business account are totaled. Then the deposits to the personal account are totaled. The two figures are then *added together* and the sum is called "corrected income." It happens too often to be called a mistake. Let us look at what such a trick does to one's gross income.

Suppose total deposits to the business account were $200,000. Suppose further the owner of the business takes a "draw" or distribution of $3,000 per month, which he pays to himself with a check drawn on the company account. In the typical sole-proprietor business, all business income and expenses are reported on Schedule C. The difference between company receipts and business expenses is considered personal income to the owner. With very few exceptions, that difference is manifested by the "draw" or periodic distribution.

Under our example, the yearly income of our hypothetical proprietor is $36,000 ($3,000 per month). The $36,000 came from the $200,000 in gross deposits to the business account. However, when the IRS combines the total deposits of *each* account, it concludes that the gross was $236,000, not $200,000. Worse than that, since there appears to be no additional expenses to offset the apparent unreported income, the net income to the proprietor is figured at $72,000, exactly *twice* what he earned.

So, what is the cure? In one case, we explained to the agent that the funds he called unreported income were in fact re-deposits from the business account. We further explained that the money was already accounted for on the Schedule C. Sitting back in his swivel chair he cracked a devilish smile and glibly said, "prove it." So here is what we did.

Beginning with the checks written on the *business* account, we identified each check written to the citizen or his wife. Next, we carefully reviewed the bank statements from the *personal* account. We compared the specific deposits to the personal account with the checks written on the business account. In this manner, we traced the money from its source in the one account to its destination in the other. A yellow highlighter marked the particular line of the statement showing this re-deposit. The clear conclusion was that no money came into the personal account from any source other than the business account.

Next, we tallied the deposits to the business account by reference to the monthly statements. That number was then compared to the one shown on the Schedule C as gross receipts. As anticipated, the two matched.

Back for a second meeting with the examiner, I explained these steps. Pointing first to the checks drawn on the business account, then to the monthly statements for the personal account, I insisted that the evidence plainly showed that the sole source of funds in the personal account was re-deposits from the business account. I then showed that the deposits to the business account matched the Schedule C income, thus proving there was no unreported income as the agent alleged. In the face of this presentation, the agent was forced to agree that all income was correctly reported.

This process is even easier with electronic transfers. In that case, the source bank account shows a transfer to the destination account. The destination account shows a credit originating from the source account. In both cases, the account numbers are generally reflected right in the statement. Now it is just a matter of highlighting the transfers *from* the source account and the corresponding credits *to* the destination account. A spreadsheet with the dates of the transactions makes it easy for the IRS to see exactly what happened.

Bank records do not lie and they are unassailable primary source documents—for better or for worse. For those reasons, they are often extremely helpful in verifying income.

3. Information Returns. Information returns reflect data compiled by a third party and transmitted to the IRS. The information return, usually a Form W-2 or 1099, communicates to the IRS how much a person was paid by an employer, a bank, or other third party. In the absence of contradictory evidence, an information return can be the last word on the question of income.

On the other hand, millions of erroneous information returns are filed annually. As I stated in chapter 2, the Treasury Inspector General for Tax Administration reported that in 2007 alone, 31.7 million information returns were filed with invalid payee data, such as addresses or SSNs. Based on this, it is likely that hundreds of *millions* of erroneous information returns are on file with the IRS at any one time. For the procedures on dealing with erroneous information returns, see chapter 10, under the heading, **How to Dispute an Erroneous Information Return**.

Usually, erroneous returns overstate the income paid. In many cases, they give an incorrect name or Social Security Number. Often, they simply misreport that a person was paid when in fact he was not. As a result, the IRS adjusts one's tax return to match the income shown on the information return. For that reason, it is always a good idea to compare paycheck stubs with W-2s or 1099s to ensure the latter's correctness.

Assuming, however, that the information return is indeed correct, it is a helpful tool when the IRS attempts to increase income for some other reason. Many people who receive wages or commissions do not necessarily keep a journal reflecting their income. For this reason, until they receive their W-2 or 1099, they have no idea what they earned. I discuss a cure for this situation in chapter 19. This makes them prime targets for the IRS to arbitrarily increase their income. This precise thing occurred in the case of a commissioned jewelry salesman.

Paul was audited for a tax year in which is he claimed income from sales in the amount of $18,300. The auditor did not believe Paul could survive on that "little amount of money." Agreeing with the auditor, Paul said, "I couldn't. That's why I had to find a new job." But in her mind, the auditor was convinced that Paul's stated income was "just too low."

"That is all I made," he assured her.

"Well, I would like to see your bank statements for the year" she replied.

"I didn't have a bank account," Paul popped. "There is nothing to show you."

In her audit report, the agent added income, arbitrarily assuming Paul needed an additional $3,900 to live on (ignoring his paltry living habits and expenses) and thus, added that sum to his declared income.

Later, we presented the Form 1099 issued by the person for whom Paul worked. The form verified Paul's claimed income. In addition to the form, Paul submitted a statement from the payer to the effect that the amount shown was all he paid to Paul during the year. Furthermore, Paul provided *his own testimony* (I discuss testimony at length later in this chapter) to the effect that he did not earn money from any other source. Since there was no bank account, these uncontradicted statements were, as they had to be, accepted as the true reflection of Paul's income.

4. Testimony. Oral testimony is the most misunderstood aspect of the audit process. Is the taxpayer's own testimony about his personal or business expenses acceptable proof of income and deductions? And if so, under what conditions is it acceptable? Who other than the taxpayer may provide testimony? These questions are often unanswered by tax professionals and ignored by the IRS. In fact, in my more than three decades of experience dealing with the IRS, I have met precious few agents who fully understand the role testimony plays in a tax audit.

Contrary to what most IRS auditors tell you, testimony is a useful adjunct to the other methods of verifying income and proving deductions. In some cases, it is the only method. The IRS has become quite adept at putting citizens on the defensive, indeed, painting people into corners from which there is no apparent escape.

Let me offer an example. Consider Paul's case, where the IRS arbitrarily increased his income on the theory that "he could not live very well on what he earned." But without bank records, Paul was not in a position to prove with extrinsic evidence that he did not earn the additional $3,900. Furthermore, the auditor chose to ignore the Form 1099 reporting Paul's sales commissions—the only information return issued for Paul that year. So what was Paul left with in the way of proof? His only option was to provide testimony to shed light on the subject. Still, is the IRS bound to accept "his word" on such an important issue? I submit that it is and over the years, several court decisions have agreed.

First understand the posture into which a taxpayer such as Paul is thrust. Under the circumstances, he was forced to prove a negative. Since the IRS's changes to a tax return are "presumed correct," the burden rests with the citizen to prove that such determination is incorrect. It seems that you must therefore prove *you did* not earn the additional income. You must, in essence, prove you cannot fly, something we all know is difficult, if not impossible.

The IRS does not make this task any easier. The agency usually maintains that whatever testimony you offer to support your "negative" position is "inadequate" or (and this is their favorite phrase) "self-serving" and therefore is disregarded. Without corroborating documentation, suggests the hustle, testimony is unacceptable.

However, the courts expressly reject this concept. These are just a few of the relevant court decisions: *Portillo v. Commissioner*, 932 F.2d 1128 (5th Cir. 1991); *Carson v. Commissioner*, 560 F.2d 692 (5th Cir. 1977); *Demkowicz v. Commissioner*, 551 F.2d 929 (3rd Cir. 1977), *Adams v. Commissioner*, 71 T.C. 477 (1978).

When the IRS makes an affirmative claim with regard to income, that claim must be supported by some "foundation of substantive evidence" before the burden shifts to the citizen to disprove the receipt of phantom income. *Weimerskirch v. Commissioner*, 596 F.2d 358 (9th Cir. 1979). (This is *not true* of deductions.) Stated another way, without the IRS itself presenting some tangible proof of the additional income, your testimony that you did not have such income is completely sufficient to defeat the claim.

The Fifth Circuit Court of Appeals in *Carson* put it this way: "So long as the taxpayer found himself unable to prove a negative," the IRS could not rely upon the "presumption of correctness" in connection with its claim. The *IRS*, not the citizen, is forced to present evidence to prove the receipt of unreported income. Without such evidence, the court must "readily reject" the IRS's claim. I expound on this concept further in chapter 10.

Thus we see that the IRS, not the citizen, has the burden to present extrinsic evidence on the question of income. Without such evidence, one may fully and legally rely upon testimony to combat such a claim.

Still, there is great confusion on this point and the IRS uses that confusion to its advantage. The very premise of the economic reality audit is based on the idea of putting the burden to prove a negative on the citizen or face a tax assessment. The IRS almost always demands records to prove whatever may be your stated position. But what happens when there are no records? As you recall, Paul did not keep a bank account. Was he therefore stuck with the determination, albeit arbitrary, that he in fact had additional unreported income? Certainly not.

In one Tax Court case, the citizens gave a compelling explanation of why they had no records of income. The IRS maintained that two ministers had substantial unreported income for several years. To justify its estimate, the IRS pointed to the BLS tables. Both men lived exclusively upon gifts from their family and members of their congregation. Under the tax code, gifts are expressly classified as *non-taxable*. As such, neither man filed a tax return or kept records of how much he received.

The government argued the two failed to prove that they did not have sufficient income to require a tax return. The IRS claimed, that the two

> did not have any books and records that reflected that they did not receive taxable income during the years at issue.

We countered this obviously ridiculous argument with the following diatribe:

> First, why would one keep records to prove there was no need to keep records? Section 6001 of the Code provides in part:

>> "Every person liable for any tax imposed by this title, or for the collection thereof, *shall keep such records,* render such statements, make such returns, and comply with such rules and regulations as the Secretary may from time to time prescribe. * * *"

> If one is not "liable for any tax imposed" by the Code, one is not required, by virtue of that very Code, to keep records. We have seen that code sections 102

and 107 specifically exclude from "income" the only two types of payments received by the taxpayers during the years in question. Why should they keep records of these payments when the law imposed no tax upon such payments, and thus, no duty exists to record them?

The idea that one would record a negative is superfluous. When was the last time this Court saw two parties write a contract solely for the purposes of proving there is no contract between them? What would such a document say?

If there were no contract, then there simply would be no written instrument between the parties. Similarly, if there was no income earned, there naturally and logically would be no records of income. A record, by its very nature, evidences a happening, an event, or an historical occurrence. One cannot record that which does not occur. We do not record the fact that no children were born to a family. We record those that are. We do not record automobiles that are *not* purchased; we record those that are. And we do not record the home that is *not* purchased; we record the one that is purchased. So too, we do not record income that is *not* received; we record only the income that is received. The taxpayers had nothing to record. Hence, no recording was carried out.

It is utter nonsense to suggest that one should create and maintain records to prove a negative. Yet the IRS makes you believe that without such proof, you are stuck with whatever wild conclusion an agent may wish to concoct. As we now know, that is not the law.

What then must one's testimony consist of in order to overcome the IRS's arbitrary decisions? The court decisions cited earlier teach the following:

a. Testimony must be very particular as to the issue. In this regard, "unequivocal denials" of having received the additional income are quite compelling. Testimony is less effective if it is unclear or somehow without conviction.

b. Testimony must be believable and reasonable, not "improbable, unreasonable or questionable." *Lovell & Hart, Inc. v. Commissioner*, 456 F.2d 145 (6th Cir. 1972). To this end, whether one's testimony is credible and believable depends to a large extent upon personality, attitude and demeanor. A person who "appears" to be lying may communicate that his testimony is unbelievable. On the other hand, one who testifies with full knowledge of the facts and is not vague or evasive, and who is capable of explaining the details of the transactions will generally hold up as credible and believable.

c. Testimony should be "uncontroverted." If not uncontroverted, one should be able to cast such doubt on the contrary evidence that the court finds the *contradiction*, and not your *testimony*, to lack credibility. In this respect, if one insists he did not have the alleged additional income, he must be sure the IRS cannot present bank records or substantial cash purchases to controvert the testimony. Similarly, a witness who testifies that one skimmed large amounts of cash from a business will discredit testimony. That is not to say that such contrary evidence kills your position. If a reasonable and plausible explanation, or the outright impeachment of the witness disarms the damaging evidence, the court could very well elect to disregard the contrary evidence. This result is more likely if your testimony is otherwise believable and convincing.

Perhaps the most important lesson from the case law is this: "we believe that the taxpayer was not required to 'corroborate' his testimony in order to meet his burden..." *Demkowicz*, Ibid. Stated another way, you need not keep records to prove a negative.

If the courts have ever come clean on anything, it is the notion that it is impossible to "document" a negative. Even more difficult is the task of anticipating the negatives one may be called upon to prove at some point, then undertaking a recordkeeping sojourn to satisfy those unknowns. The very idea is not only preposterous, but thinking about how to do so gives me a headache.

After years of the IRS taking advantage of citizens in this regard, Congress enacted rules to help prevent this in the future. As part of the Taxpayers' Bill of Rights Act 2, Congress placed the burden of proof squarely at the IRS's door in certain income cases. I talk more about that in Part III, dealing with economic reality audits.

How to Prove Deductions

In the case of deductions, the burden of proof is always on the citizen. As I stated earlier, the courts are fond of pointing out that "deductions are a matter of legislative grace." The person claiming the benefit of a deduction bears the burden to "point to some specific statute to justify his deduction and establish that he comes within its terms." *Roberts v. Commissioner*, 62 T.C. 834 (1974). One is not inherently entitled to claim deductions. Without sufficient proof, the deduction is simply not allowed.

That is why it is important to understand the law controlling the issues in your case. Many people are bluffed out of deductions because revenue agents tell them their proof is legally insufficient or that certain language in the law renders the deduction improper. Ignorant citizens take these statements at face value. Since precious few people have even seen the Internal Revenue Code, and fewer still actually read a provision or two, they are in no position to challenge the agent.

Certain basic elements apply in proving any deduction. Without exception, you must be prepared to prove at least the following four elements with regard to any payment claimed as a deduction:

1. That the money was paid in the year claimed,

2. That the amount claimed on the return was in fact paid,

3. That the character of the payment is recognized by the law as a deductible expense, and

4. That the amount claimed does not exceed any statutory limits.

Let us now examine six ways to prove deductions.

1. Canceled checks. Some people deal exclusively with banks, checkbooks and debit cards. I know people who, rather than carry any cash at all, write checks or use debit cards for every transaction, however minuscule. As this is a routine practice, all their evidence is in the form of canceled checks and bank statements.

This is not all bad. Canceled checks and bank statements provide handy tools to prove deductions. On the face of one document an auditor finds the date the bill was paid, the amount paid, to whom paid, and if the check writer is careful, a notation showing the purpose of the payment. This is all the information necessary to establish the factual elements of a deduction.

The difficulty with canceled checks and debit cards is that people tend to be lazy. For example, one may write a check to William Jones, rather than to Dr. William Jones. The check to William Jones contains no proof on its face that William Jones is a physician and that the payment is a medical expense. Because of the omission, additional evidence is needed.

The lower left corner of the check blank contains a space for recording information relative to the payment. Use it. This space helps to establish the nature of the payment and the fact that it meets the requirements of a deductible expense. If you use a debit card, make the notation on your copy of the charge slip. This is especially important for businesses. Many times proprietors write checks appearing from their face to personal expenses. Checks to "Bill's Supermarket," or "Stan's Repair" may be for purely business purposes and fully deductible. However, without supplemental data, the expenses may be classified as personal and disallowed.

2. Cash receipts or invoices. Cash receipts or invoices function in much the same way as canceled checks, but are susceptible to more loose ends. The reason is that store and shop proprietors who make out receipts may be more harried than those writing checks. In the interests of time, the operator scribbles the amount and sometimes a description of the item purchased. As often as not, the date is missing and the description of the item purchased is too sketchy to allow a third party to figure it out. Even receipts generated electronically can be missing critical data needed for tax purposes. For example, such receipts often show only a product number but no description of the item. In that case, the IRS assumes it was a personal purchase, not a business expense.

When making cash purchases, be careful to have the receipt completed in a manner sufficient to plainly communicate what is purchased, the date, and the amount paid. It is not improper to make your own notes on the receipt. Notes made contemporaneously with the purchase are quite helpful if audited several years later.

Note in your own terms, rather than in the retailer's product number, the item purchased. Also note how the item is put to use. This information is helpful to establish the deductible nature of your purchase. The more detail you provide, the better off you are and the less likely your deduction will be disallowed. It is helpful to combine a canceled check with a cash receipt or invoice because between the two documents, you find all necessary information.

Consider this word of caution about invoices. An invoice is merely a bill that seeks payment for goods or services. Unlike a statement, the invoice is not by itself proof that anything was paid. For example, telephone bills are invoices. The bill contains no independent proof that you in fact paid the amount due. Be careful to provide such proof with an invoice when presented to the IRS.

3. Year-end statements. A year-end statement communicates information compiled by a third party. The most common example of a year-end statement comes from your mortgage company. The document states what portion of the total paid was applied to interest, principal and real estate taxes. The statement is indispensable because even though a person can prove that payments were made to a mortgage company, he generally cannot prove how the payment was applied to interest and principal. Of course, only the interest and real estate tax portion of such a payment is deductible.

It is a very good idea to obtain and maintain year-end statements to the fullest extent possible because they take the guesswork out of proving deductions. All the information necessary to prove a deduction is contained in one document prepared by a third party, not the citizen under audit. Moreover, the IRS is more inclined to believe the statements of third parties as presented in their paperwork than it is to accept the word of the taxpayer. Somehow the IRS believes that hearsay evidence is more valuable then first-hand testimony. I do not mean to suggest that one's own records are inadequate. They of course are not. I mean only to suggest ways to simplify the task.

For example, the secretary or treasurer of a church or other charitable organization, not you, prepares a year-end statement from that organization. It is presented on the letterhead or similar document of the organization. It also states the year the sums were paid and the total amount paid. As explained in more detail below, it should also state that no goods or services were received in exchange for the contributions. With such a statement, it becomes unnecessary to sift through canceled checks or bank statements to find proof of payment to charitable organizations.

And in fact, at least in the case of charitable contributions, the IRS will not allow your deduction without a third-party statement from the organization to which you gave the money. Code section 170(f)(8) specifically states that no contribution is allowed as a deduction without "a contemporaneous written acknowledgment of the contribution" issued by the organization to which you gave the money. The written acknowledgement must state:

a. The amount of cash or a description of the non-cash property you contributed,

b. Whether the organization provided any goods or services in exchange for the contribution, and if so,

c. A description and good faith estimate of the value of the goods or services, and finally,

d. If the goods or services received consist solely of intangible religious benefits, a statement to that effect.

The statement meets the "contemporaneous" requirement if you obtain it on or before the earlier of:

a. The date you file your return for the year in which the contribution was made, or

b. The due date (including extensions) for filing the return. For example, in the case of 2014 contributions, your acknowledgement is considered contemporaneous if the statement is received no later than April 15, 2015, or if you obtained a filing extension, October 15, 2015.

These special rules apply to any one-time contribution of $250 or more, not the total of contributions over the course of a year. Hence, if you write a check for $100 per month to your church, these rules do not apply. However, if you give $250 at any one time, you are required to have the contemporaneous acknowledgement from your church to claim the deduction.

4. Logs. A log is a ledger or diary made as the event being recorded occurs. Examples of common logs are diaries of automobile mileage and related costs, and travel and entertainment (T&E) expenses. The log is either a separate book or is incorporated into an appointment calendar or similar device.

The law is rigid on the type of information required to substantiate travel and entertainment expenses. For this reason, logs are very important. For example, code section 274(d) requires that in order to prove entitlement to such a deduction, one must show:

a. The amount of the expense,

b. The time and place of the travel or entertainment,

c. The business purpose of the expense, and

d. The business relationship to the person entertained. See: Rev. Rev. section 1.274-5(c)(2) and *Rutz v. Commissioner*, 66 T.C. 876 (1976).

It is easy to see that such detailed information is most readily kept in a log made contemporaneously with the travel, etc. Anytime you engage in regular activity, use a log to record your actions. In fact, Rev. Reg. section 1.275-5A(c)(2)(ii) states that a record of T&E expenses "must be prepared or maintained in such manner that each recording of an element of an expenditure is made at or near the time of the expenditure." This clearly describes a contemporaneous record, which is best made in a log or diary. Under the regulation, the record must be made at a time when, "in relation to the making of an expenditure, the taxpayer has full present knowledge of each element of the expenditure, such as the amount, time, place and business purpose of the expenditure and business relationship to the taxpayer of any person entertained."

I like logs because they make the job easier and conform to the regulation. But in the absence of logs, you can still verify deductions using any one or more of the other methods, especially reconstructions, as I discuss in the next section of this chapter.

Logs are also necessary to support any deduction for mixed-use property. This includes property with both business- and personal-use components. For example, if you use your vehicle 50 percent for business and 50 percent for personal purposes, you need a log to support the business use-component. Other mixed-use property might include:

- A computer or similar equipment unless used exclusively at a regular business establishment, and

- Cell phones or similar equipment.

5. Reconstructions. Reconstructions are used when there are either limited or no supporting documents upon which a claimed deduction is based. It is perhaps the least known method of proving deductions. The reason is that the IRS has people convinced that without a piece of paper supporting the claimed expense, the expense simply is not allowable. This is just not true. For decades, the Tax Court has followed the so-called *Cohan* rule to allow citizens to reconstruct records that were lost, destroyed or otherwise not kept. *Cohan v. Commissioner,* 39 F.2d 540 (2nd Cir. 1930). When done correctly, reconstructions are every bit as valid as the other methods of proof.

In fact, many court decisions suggest that you have a duty to reconstruct records if they are somehow lost or destroyed. Your burden of proof is not extinguished merely because you lost your records. *Robbins v. Commissioner,* 42 T.C. Memo. 809 (1981). Thus, the fact that you lost certain records is not a defense to your inability to prove your deductions.

In order to sustain deductions based on reconstructions, the *Cohan* rule states that you must first establish a foundation of evidence upon which to base the reconstructions. That is to say, you must provide a factual basis to support the idea that you incurred the expenses. Let me illustrate. Suppose you lost records necessary to prove your business expenses for advertising, rent and utilities. The foundation of evidence needed to reconstruct these expenses must include your testimony or other proof of the following:

a. That you operated a business during the periods in question,

b. A description of the nature of the business and exactly how income was earned,

c. A definitive statement that you incurred expenses for advertising, rent and utilities,

d. An explanation of how the amounts presented in the reconstructions were arrived at,

e. The reason the records were lost or not kept in the first place, and

f. Copies of whatever documents you do have to support any of the above in order to lend credibility to your statements.

As to item (c), it is important to state clearly that you incurred the specific expenses in question. Your testimony cannot be vague or equivocal. To lend credibility to the statement, explain how you advertised and the companies used to execute your advertising; where you rented your business premises and who you paid; and the fact that you paid for electricity, gas, water, trash removal, etc., during the period of occupancy. These are foundational facts that allow the reader to conclude that payment of such expenses in some amount did in fact take place.

As to item (d), you must provide some accounting to support your reconstructions. For example, as to rent, you can state that your rent obligation per the lease was $1,000 per month. A copy of the lease agreement (per item (f)) establishes the lease amount. Proof of payment in the form of checks or year-end statements from a prior year can also establish the amount. Finally, your testimony that you paid rent, advertising and utilities for each month during the year in question supports the deduction without proof of the actual payments.

Present this information to the IRS in the form of an affidavit, which I describe in detail later in this chapter. In my book, *The IRS Problem Solver*, I provide specific examples of affidavits and how they are used to reconstruct records.

In one case, the taxpayer had full and accurate records of his business farming operation for the years 2004 and 2005. The IRS agreed that his records were adequate and granted all his deductions for those years. However, he had no records for several years behind 2004. The taxpayer testified that his business operations were the same from year to year and that he incurred essentially the same expenses during the earlier years as he did in 2004 and 2005, the years for which he had solid records. This established the foundation of evidence needed to invoke the *Cohan* rule. The Tax Court ruled that he was allowed deductions for expenses in the prior years based upon the nature and amount of the expenses he proved for 2004 and 2005. See: *West v. Commissioner*, T.C. Memo. 2011-272 (2011).

The IRS claims that T&E expenses under code section 274 are not subject to reconstructions. However, Rev. Reg. section 1.274-5A(c)(5) disproves that statement. The regulation provides, in part, as follows:

> Where the taxpayer establishes that the failure to produce adequate records is due to the loss of such records through circumstances beyond the taxpayer's control, such as destruction by fire, flood, earthquake, or other casualty, the taxpayer *shall have a right* to substantiate a deduction by reasonable reconstruction of his expenditures." (Emphasis added.)

Citing this very regulation, the Tax Court in *Cioffi v. Commissioner*, T.C. Memo. 1980-223, stated:

> *Of course*, where the taxpayer establishes that failure to produce adequate records is due to the loss of such records through circumstances beyond the taxpayer's control, such as destruction by fire, flood, earthquake or other casualty, the taxpayer may substantiate his claimed deductions by *a reasonable reconstruction* of his expenditures. (Emphasis added.)

The following history demonstrates how reconstructions are useful. Kathy was a traveling sales rep for a clothing firm. She traveled all across five Midwestern states and did so for three years. Often using her American Express card, she went from town to town peddling her wares. As an independent contractor, she was responsible for her own costs, including travel and related expenses. These expenses climbed into the tens of thousands of dollars for each year she was on the road.

Due to a series of residential moves during a traumatic period of her life, she lost her records. When called for an audit of the tax returns claiming the greatest amount of travel and related business expenses, she did not have one scrap of paper to document a trip around the block, much less across the region several times. Without sympathy for her hard luck story, all of the business expenses were disallowed.

IRS issued a Notice of Deficiency and Kathy appealed to the Tax Court (a process I discuss in chapter 13). We then began the process of reconstructing three years of her life. As a starting point, we had her address book in which she recorded the names and addresses of the various retailers who purchased her wares and upon whom she called, whether or not they purchased. We also knew Kathy used her American Express card to pay expenses while on the road.

She requested copies from American Express of the monthly statements for the three years at issue. The charges were itemized with the name, address and date of the item charged. The statements showed most hotel and meal charges. Moreover, IRS procedures expressly allow one to prove deductions with the records kept by such institutions when originals are lost. See: Revenue Procedure 92-71, 1992-2 C.B. 437.

The American Express material proved very fruitful. The first statement showed Kathy spent a night in Fargo, North Dakota. Looking to her list of actual and prospective customers, she ascertained, then listed on a separate sheet, each of the retailers she called on in Fargo and the surrounding area. When we were able to pin down the specific amounts spent on food and fuel, they were noted. When we were unable to do so, the amounts were estimated on the basis of reason and common sense.

We followed this process for each of the thirty-six months at issue. When we completed the task, Kathy was able to document nearly all of her expenses. Where there was a gap in time or place due to the incompleteness of the American Express records (the card was not used 100 percent of the time), we supplemented the estimates with testimony. Her testimony and the address book established the foundation of evidence needed to prove that Kathy indeed did the traveling she claimed. The reconstructions were allowed—to the penny.

By their nature, reconstructions are estimates and to the best extent possible, attempt to recreate a picture of reality as it was in years past. They are not perfect. Because they are not "self-contained" as are canceled checks or cash receipts, they must be supported with testimony. For example, in many cases, Kathy's charge slips showed a hotel expense evidencing that she spent the night in a distant town, but did not show any cost for food. Common sense dictates that one must eat on a daily basis. For that reason, we were careful to provide testimony to the effect that food was purchased on the days no food charges appeared.

When used in conjunction with oral testimony, which is "credible, consistent and uncontroverted," reconstructions are as valid a method of proving deductions as any. *Mantell v. Commissioner*, T.C. Memo. 1993-420 (1993).

6. Oral testimony. Testimony in the context of proving deductions is nothing more than your oral representations and assurances that the amounts claimed were in fact paid. When such proof is offered to a revenue agent, the most common response is

something like, "You may be telling the truth, but I can't take your word for it. I must have some kind of proof."

This statement assumes that your word is not "proof." The courts take a completely different view of this, however. Courts regularly allow deductions when the only proof offered is testimony, that is, "your word." How is that so? When the testimony is plausible, believable and credible, the IRS cannot refuse to consider it. Testimony that meets these criteria is just as valid as any piece of paper. *Mantell v. Commissioner*, supra; and H*ough v. Commissioner,* T.C. Memo. 2006-58.

Even the tax code provides for the use of testimony to support deductions.

For example, code section 274(d), the travel and entertainment section we discussed above, contains the following language:

> No deduction or credit will be allowed. . .unless the taxpayer substantiates by adequate records or by sufficient evidence corroborating *the taxpayer's own statement*. . . (Emphasis added.)

The express language of the law allows one to prove these touchy deductions with oral testimony supplemented with other evidence. Furthermore, an IRS news release issued in 1986 states that, with respect to the business use of a motor vehicle, a citizen could substantiate such use "with any type of evidence, including the taxpayer's own oral statements corroborated with no more than circumstantial evidence." Announcement IR-86-37 (March 28, 1986).

Circumstantial evidence is evidence that tends to make a particular fact more (or less) probable. It is not direct evidence such as that of an eyewitness, or in a tax case, a canceled check. Circumstantial evidence may consist of countless different types of proof which, when considered as a whole, make your claim that you paid certain expenses more probable.

To be effective, oral testimony must be specific. Qualified claims and vague recollections will not carry the day. Be sure that all your explanations are seasoned with as many hard facts as humanly possible. Specificity leads to credibility and in turn, believability.

A Final Word on Testimony

Testimony plays a key role in the audit process, both in establishing your income and proving deductions. The question now is how do you present the testimony without going to court? The process is surprisingly simple. You present testimony in writing through a tool known as an affidavit. An affidavit is nothing more than a detailed letter of explanation you have notarized. This makes it a sworn statement that carries essentially the same weight as testimony presented under oath in a courtroom.

Affidavits are needed not only to augment reconstructions, but any time a claimed deduction involves an "intangible" issue. An intangible issue is one for which, under no circumstances, will you have a piece of paper to support your claim. Let me give three examples.

When claiming a deduction for an office in your home, the law requires you to prove a number of things, including that the space in the home is not used for any purpose other than business. This is the so-called "exclusive use" test. Code section 280A. No piece of paper I can imagine will prove the exclusive use test. Only your own testimony, and perhaps that of others such as a spouse, can establish the fact that your home office is not used for any personal purpose whatsoever.

The second example involves mileage expenses. To be deductible, auto mileage must have a legitimate business purpose. You will likely never receive a slip of paper showing that your auto mileage was racked up for a given purpose. Only your testimony can establish the business purpose of your auto mileage.

My last example is a major concern for small businesses. As I stated earlier, one of the IRS's primary attacks on small businesses is to claim they are not businesses at all, but rather hobbies. To prove your business is legitimate and you are entitled to all business deductions, you must prove a "profit motive." Code section 183. The IRS looks to several factors to determine a profit motive. Chief among them is the nature of your business, and your goals, objectives and profit potential. These elements are presented primarily in the form of testimony. Details on the hobby rules are discussed in chapter 12.

Affidavits must be complete, detailed and specific. When referencing particular documents, attach copies whenever possible. Affidavits are quite useful in settling a number of IRS disputes, audits being just one example. For that reason, I included a lengthy chapter on affidavits in my book, *The IRS Problem Solver*. Because that chapter is so thorough, I do not restate the material here. When making an affidavit to help in your audit, refer to chapter 3 of the Problem Solver for more guidance.

Looking to the Future

As we learned in chapter 5, adequate records are the key to settling most audit disputes. While this certainly comes as no surprise, the reality is most people have no idea how to keep such records in the first place. This topic is the focus of much discussion in my book *How to Double Your Tax Refund.* There I dedicate two chapters to showing you how to set up a recordkeeping system necessary to prove your claims.

CHAPTER SEVEN

THE INFORMATION DOCUMENT REQUEST, QUICKBOOKS AND SUMMONS ENFORCEMENT

AS YOU KNOW BY KNOW, IN ANY ROUTINE CIVIL examination, the IRS has almost no burden of proof. That is to say, the agency never has to prove that you made a mistake. You have to prove your return is correct. Because the IRS generally has no burden of proof, the process of examining a tax return historically was very simple for the IRS.

As explained in chapter 5, the process begins with a letter in which an agent requests specific documents and information to verify the correctness of your return. The letter usually provides a list of the issues in the case and seeks documentation as to each issue. For example, if the audit questions your business expenses, the agent would identify the specific expenses in question and ask to see the material to support them. As the examination progresses and new issues arise, the agent might issue an Information Document Request (IDR) asking for the additional information. Once all the requested material is provided, the agent determines whether the data are sufficient to verify the claim. If so, the claim is allowed. If not, the claim is disallowed.

But what happens if no material is provided sufficient to satisfy the agent's curiosity? In that case, the IRS has two options. The first is to push you to release the data using the administrative summons, a discovery tool that I discuss in chapter 3, under the heading, **The IRS's Summons Authority**. The second option is to simply disallow the deduction because you failed to provide the information needed to support the deduction. And because the IRS has no burden of proof when it comes to disallowing deductions, this approach proves to be a quick and easy way to dispose of the issue—a sort of "Mr. Nice Guy" approach to the problem.

At that, if you wish to challenge the agent's determination, the only way to do so successfully is to provide sufficient documentation to support your claims. Thus, as I have said all along, the burden lies solely with you to carry the water with respect to all your deductions.

No More "Mr. Nice Guy"

A recent IRS directive indicates that the agency may be abandoning the "Mr. Nice Guy" approach to gathering records. In January 2014, the IRS issued a memo that addresses information gathering, the issuance of IDRs and the use of summonses to force the issue if the requested information is not provided. At the time of issuance, the memo was pointed at only large businesses. However, it is clear that the agency will push the practices "more deeply" into the system, exposing more taxpayers to their pitfalls. Because of this, I fully expect the IRS to utilize "strong arm" tactics more often in pressing for documents in all audits, particularly those related to business income and particularly with respect to computerized recordkeeping systems.

What are the Strong Arm Tactics?

What are the tactics we can expect the IRS to use if you fail to provide the requested data? While I address this in step-by-step fashion later, the short answer is the agency will resort to the use of administrative summonses faster and more often than it has in the past.

As I explain in chapter 3, an administrative summons is a document issued by the IRS that requires the production of specified information. It is a discovery tool akin to those available to litigants in a civil proceeding, but without the necessity of the IRS having to go to court. Of course, this proves to be rather handy for the IRS and more than just an inconvenience for taxpayers.

You may be asking why the IRS is changing focus from simply disallowing deductions to forcing the issue by serving a summons for documents and testimony? The answer is quite simple. As established throughout this work, a growing percentage of audits, especially those of businesses, focus on the *income* side of the ledger, not the deductions. I expect summons to be directed at income issues.

While it is true that deductions are a matter of legislative grace and taxpayers bear the burden to prove they are entitled to their claimed deductions, that is not so regarding income. As we learned earlier, this is one of the rare exceptions to the burden of proof rules. The IRS cannot unilaterally add alleged unreported income to a tax return simply because it believes that a person may have earned more income than was reported. The law mandates that the IRS must establish a foundation of evidence to support any claim that a person earned income he did not report. Likewise, the IRS cannot put a person in the position of having to prove a negative simply by asserting that he earned income he did not report, then forcing him to prove otherwise.

And while the IRS believes as a matter of policy that all taxpayers cheat by hiding at least some income, the question for the IRS is, how do we prove that? The answer lies in getting as much information from the taxpayer as humanly possible about his lifestyle, business habits, spending patterns, assets, earning history, etc, etc. In fact, there is no such thing as too much information when it comes to the ability to ascertain the extent to which businesses and individuals may hide income. This attitude is the driving force behind the IRS's never ending push for more information reporting laws, which I discussed in chapter 2.

How the New Policy Operates

IRS Memo LB&I-04-1113-009 (November 4, 2013) establishes the enforcement policy that became effective January 2, 2014. The policy sets forth the IRS's IDR Enforcement Process in three steps. The key here is that the "process is mandatory and has no exceptions." That is to say, if the information sought in an IDR is not provided, the auditor is mandated under this policy to push for the information using these three steps:

1. A Delinquently Notice. This is a letter to the taxpayer stating that he is delinquent in providing the requested information. The notice must state exactly what information is missing and it must provide a deadline of no more than fifteen calendar days from the date of the notice in which to comply. The agent is also required to discuss the notice with the taxpayer and explain the process of enforcement if the information is not provided. A copy of the notice must be mailed to the IRS's Office of Area Counsel, the attorneys who represent the IRS in most civil litigation.

2. A Pre-Summons Letter. If the information is not released by the deadline stated in the delinquency notice, the agent must report to his manager and the Counsel attorney that the IDR has not been complied with. At that point, the manager must make contact with the taxpayer, again explain the process and point out that a summons may be issued for the material. This must be done as quickly as possible, but no more than fourteen days after the response date set in the delinquency notice. The pre-summons letter must demand compliance no later than ten calendar days from the date of the pre-summons letter.

3. The Summons. If the taxpayer "does not provide a complete response to the IDR by the response date in the pre-summons letter," the IRS goes to the next and final step. That is, both management and the Counsel attorney are again informed of the failure and a summons for the missing information is issued. The summons carries enforcement ramifications that are very serious, which I discuss below.

The IRS also published guidance on the issuance of IDRs. In fact, if the IRS follows the policies regarding the issuance of IDRs in the first place, it may be that there will not be a substantial increase in summons litigation for failure to comply. The key, of course, is that you must understand these procedures and hold the IRS to following them.

IRS Memo LB&I-04-1113-009 lists thirteen requirements examiners must follow when issuing an IDR. (As I stated earlier, as of this writing, this policy applies only to large business audit, but I fully expect it to migrate deeper into the IRS sooner than later. Therefore, it is best to understand it now.) The list reads as follows:

1. Discuss the issue related to the IDR with the taxpayer.

2. Discuss how the information requested relates to the issue under consideration and why it is necessary.

3. After this consultation, determine what information will ultimately be requested IDR.

4. Ensure the IDR clearly states the issue that is being considered and that the IDR only requests information relevant to the stated issue.

5. Prepare one IDR for each issue.

6. Utilize numbers or letters on the IDR for clarity.

7. Ensure that the IDR is written using clear and concise language.

8. Ensure that the IDR is customized to the taxpayer or industry.

9. Provide a draft of the IDR and discuss its contents with the taxpayer.

10. After this discussion, determine with the taxpayer a reasonable timeframe for a response to the IDR.

11. If agreement on a response date cannot be reached, the examiner will set a reasonable response date.

12. When determining the response date, ensure that the examiner commits to a date by which the IDR will be reviewed and a response provided to the taxpayer on whether the information received satisfies the IDR. This date should be noted on the IDR.

13. If the information requested is not received by the response date, the examiner will follow the IDR Enforcement Process.

As you can see, these procedures do not allow the IRS to issue IDRs in an arbitrary or indiscriminate way. All information sought must be relevant to a specific issue in the return and examiner must establish a clear connection between the requested data and the issue in question. The IDR must be provided to the taxpayer in draft form and must be discussed with the taxpayer before being issued formally. That discussion must include a reasonable response date for the information sought.

Obtaining Enforcement of a Summons

Failure to respond to an IDR and the pre-summons enforcement steps mentioned above will lead to the issuance of a summons, and while this is a serious matter, the summons is not self-enforcing. As I explain in chapter 3, the IRS has no independent authority to enforce the summons, such as the ability to issue a fine or penalty for failure to comply. Therefore, the agency looks to the federal courts to enforce its summonses.

However, as pointed out in chapter 3, the process of obtaining enforcement of a summons is not particularly difficult. To win, the IRS need only established the four so-called *Powell* elements. In just about any civil audit, the IRS would be able to do that with an affidavit from the examiner attesting to those four facts. The likely result would be an order from the court requiring the citizen to cough up the records.

Once such an order is issued, you would face a contempt of court charge that could land you in jail if you fail to comply. For these reasons, it is very important to treat IDRs very seriously. You must deal with them directly and deliberately. You cannot ignore these formal requests for information.

IDRs and Electronic Records

As more businesses and individuals turn to computerized recordkeeping systems, the IRS has taken to scrutinizing those records more closely. As part of routine records requests, the IRS now commonly demands the production of original computer files (not just the paper printouts) from programs such as QuickBooks, Quicken, MS Money, Peachtree, etc., and in some cases, tax preparation software, such as TurboTax.

Why does the IRS want the computer files? Are not the printouts sufficient to provide the needed data? Whether the printouts are sufficient or not, the IRS also looks at the so-called "metadata." The metadata are the behind-the-scenes data generated by the software (not the operator) that records how, when and by whom a particular item or set of information was collected, created, accessed, modified and formatted. These data are automatically created as the software is accessed and utilized in the day-to-day course of operations. QuickBooks, for example, stores metadata in what it calls an Audit Report file, which is somehow accessible by those who know what they are doing with QuickBooks.

The IRS summarizes the need to review such data as follows:

> In many instances, the Service's examinations would be advanced by accessing metadata that identifies the original date a transaction was entered in the electronic records, the dates of any changes to the entries, and the username of the person who made the entries. The value inherent in an examiner's ability to obtain the date and source of recorded entries is self-evident; the information tends to support or undermine the credibility of the entries in the business records. IRS Chief Counsel Advice Memo. 2011-46017, November 11, 2011, pg. 3.

It should come as no surprise that the IRS's position is that you must release a copy of your original computer files generated by the accounting software. As stated in the Chief Counsel Advice Memo quoted above, if an examiner can point to changes, additions or deletions in the computer file, that fact might somehow undermine (or support) the correctness of the tax return. It should also come as no surprise that the IRS believes it can summons the data if you refuse to produce it.

Please recall from our discussion in chapter 3 that the IRS's summons authority is very broad. Code section 7602(a) gives the IRS the authority to summons "any person" in connection with an examination or investigation. Moreover, the summons authority extends to examining "any books, papers, records, or other data which *may be relevant* or material to such inquiry" (emphasis added).

Given this breadth and scope, you would think there essentially *no* limits to what the IRS can get from you or a third party, including metadata from the likes of QuickBooks. In fact, as to metadata, the IRS justifies the "may be relevant" argument, saying,

> . . .it is apparent that metadata associated with a taxpayer's electronic business records "may be relevant" within the meaning of code section 7602(a) because the nature of the information contained in the metadata, especially the dates on which the entries were made or modified and the identities of the persons entering the data, may support or undermine the credibility of the records offered to substantiate the accuracy of the return. IRS Chief Counsel Memo, pg. 5.

How Does Metadata Show the Correctness of a Tax Return?

So the question is not whether the IRS has the broad authority to get the metadata. The question is how may the data be relevant to the correctness of the tax return. Let me answer that question in the context of: 1) your duty to keep records, and 2) how a computerized recordkeeping program fits into your recordkeeping scheme. Let me address each issue in turn.

1. Your duty to keep records. We already addressed this matter at length in chapter 5. The tax code creates a duty to keep records that are permanent, accurate and which allow the IRS to determine your correct tax liability. It is just that simple. The law also makes it clear that "no particular form is required" for making and keeping records. Rev. Reg. 31.6001-1(a). As long as an auditor can examine your records and correctly determine your income and allowable deductions, your recordkeeping system is adequate. A computerized accounting system or bookkeeping system may be a part of that process or not, at your sole discretion.

2. How does QuickBooks fit into this scheme? At its most basic level, QuickBooks (QB) and similar programs merely add, subtract and categorize data derived from other records. As such, QB reports are mere summaries of the original data, but are not themselves primary source documents of income and expenses. Rather, as I explained in chapter 6, primary source documents are bank records, cash register receipts, credit card payment data, etc. In the final analysis, only the primary source documents control the issue.

For example, if QB says you had $50,000 of income but bank statements show $100,000 of deposits, to which data do you believe will the IRS defer? Any examiner will go by the bank statements showing gross deposits unless you can show why they include deposits that do not constitute income (i.e., loans, gifts, etc.). Even if a QB entry stated that the extra $50,000 came from a bank loan, the IRS will not accept that as true without the loan documents to support the QB entry.

The same is true with deductions. A QB report might show $10,000 of advertising costs but without canceled checks, invoices, etc., the IRS will not allow the deduction. Source documents—not summaries—are necessary to prove income and expenses. Thus, QB reports are largely irrelevant to the determination of taxable income as they are merely summaries.

Even if metadata in a particular QB file shows several inconsistencies—correcting entries, mistakes, deletions and misclassifications—what does that prove regarding the correctness of a tax return? Again, the primary source documents are the key. In the case of an income ledger, for example, suppose an auditor finds that several items of income were entered then deleted from the QB files. Does that mean, suggest or even hint that the income on the tax return is understated? If the source documents (bank statements, etc.) back up the reported income, why does it matter that the QB files were changed or corrected at some point—or that they are a mess from top to bottom?

And what about such a mess? I had a client who ran a small construction business. She used QB as her accounting program. At her audit, it was determined that she underreported her income by about $30,000 over three years. She swore that she captured all her income in QB as it went into the bank. Well, she did not because, as it turned out, she did not understand as much about QB as she thought she did. A full bank deposits analysis showed that she missed quite a bit of income. Thus, her Schedule Cs were wrong. Neither the auditor nor the Appeals Officer were the least bit impressed with the QB reports and it would have made no difference whether the metadata showed either no correcting entries or a massive number of them, or even who made them. In all events, the bank deposits controlled—period.

This is not uncommon. Most small business owners using the likes of QB make numerous errors in their "accounting" processes and most have no idea they are doing so. I can take one look at a QB Profit and Loss Statement prepared by an uninformed small business owner and spot several errors right off the bat. Why show such a document to an auditor who is looking for errors in the first place?

Even when business owners do catch their mistakes, many simply delete the entry rather than making a correcting journal entry so a third party can follow a trail to see what happened and why. But most small business people are not accountants. Debits, credits and journal entries mean little or nothing to them. That is why primary source documents alone are the key to the accuracy of a tax return, not QB files.

QB summaries can become helpful *after* primary source documents establish that the summaries are accurate. For example, suppose an auditor asks for all documents to support every deduction on Schedule C. You might limit the scope of such an aggressive audit by suggesting that the agent pick three deductions at random, for which you will provide all the canceled checks, invoices, etc., to prove those items. You will provide the QB summaries as to each other item. Once the agent is satisfied that, as to the three selected areas, the QB summaries are accurate, he can then accept the QB summaries for each of the other areas. This greatly limits the time, scope and expense of an audit. But keep in mind that you cannot force an agent to accept summaries as proof since only primary source documents establish what expense was paid, when and for how much.

To Produce or Not to Produce

So the bottom line question is, do you produce QB electronic files that you know or believe may contain errors, or not? If you know the QB files are sound, what can it hurt to produce them? On the other hand, if they are riddled with errors, as most are, now what? If you refuse to produce the information, will the IRS attempt to force the issue by serving a summons for the data? And if they do serve a summons, what is your duty to comply? I address each question in turn. Then the ultimate question becomes, how do you avoid a summons in the first place?

1. The likelihood of a summons. In the face of a flat refusal to produce QB documents, I believe there is a strong likelihood the IRS will summons the

data, especially considering the IRS's IDR policy I outlined earlier in this chapter. Therefore, you cannot *flatly* refuse to provide information. But that does not mean you necessarily have to provide the specific information the agent asks for.

Rather, make it clear to the agent that you are in fact providing the primary source documents that do "clearly reflect income." Likewise, make it clear that the QB summaries do *not* "clearly reflect income" and give some specific reasons why. This might include: a) they are not primary source documents, b) an untrained person made the entries, c) various correcting entries were required for whatever reason, etc. The bottom line is that the QB summaries do not clearly reflect income.

Keep in mind what I said in chapter 5 about code sections 6001, 446 and the regulations. Your duty is to keep and provide records that are accurate and that clearly reflect income. We know that QB reports are not records that reflect income. They are merely summaries. Summaries do not meet your burden of proof. Only primary source documents meet the burden of proof.

Thus, if you produce primary source documents and make it clear that the documents are complete and accurate records that correctly show the receipt of income, I believe you can avoid the summons confrontation in the first place. That is to say, do not "flatly refuse" to provide records. Rather, make it perfectly clear that the primary source documents (which are provided) are the key to the audit. They correctly reflect income and the summaries do not.

If the agent follows the IDR enforcement procedures set forth above, you will have ample opportunity to explain your position before any summons is issued. For example, after you refuse to provide QB data in response to an IDR, a manager is supposed to contact you in writing with a warning that if the data are not provided, a summons could be issued. At that point, you need to respond with a letter such as I outline later in this chapter. By proactively asserting your position as outlined below, you will likely avoid a summons.

2. Would a summons likely be enforced if issued? Once a summons is issued, the game changes. As I explain in chapter 3, courts are very quick to enforce summonses. The chief reason is that the IRS's burden in establishing its case is very light. Remember, the IRS only has to establish the four simple *Powell* elements to get its summons enforced. And the burden to prove these elements is "slight."

Thus, if you get to the point where a summons enforcement proceeding is instituted, it is virtually assured that the summons will in fact be enforced. At that point, the failure to comply may lead to a contempt citation, something you want no part of.

So that begs the question, how do you keep the IRS from seeking enforcement of the summons if they do issue one? One answer is that you can just cave in and deliver the QB files to the IRS and be done with it. The other option is to hold your ground and see if they take the next step. To hold you ground, you must appear in response to the summons at the time and place set by the agent. At the summons hearing, you must raise your objection to providing the data. In this case, you would reiterate that the electronic files are not reliable for whatever reason and that you already disclosed all the primary source documents. Thus, the IRS has everything necessary to determine the correctness of the return. You then leave the meeting.

The next step is you will likely hear from a Counsel attorney before the IRS moves to enforce a summons. Counsel attorneys are responsible for reviewing the case and deciding whether to refer it to the Justice Department for enforcement. At this point of review, Counsel's office generally issues a letter explaining that if the material is not provided, they will seek court enforcement. You must quickly respond to the letter by explaining the "accurate records" argument under code sections 6001 and 446 and the fact that QB documents are not primary source documents. The outline of my letter goes like this:

I would employ the *Powell* elements to my advantage. I would remind counsel that in order for the IRS to get a summons enforced, the IRS must prove that the information sought is "not already in the IRS's possession." I would point out that you already provided all the primary source documents, which clearly reflect income as required by law. I would point out that you have no other information in your possession that constitutes primary source documents the IRS does not already have. I would implore counsel to drop the issue since you have fully complied with your duties under code sections 6001 and 446.

I might even employ a "may be relevant" argument in my letter. But recognize that the IRS believes *anything* "may be relevant" and as the Supreme Court said in the *Arthur Young* case cited in chapter 3, the IRS cannot know what is relevant until they see it. Specifically as to metadata, the IRS believes the "value" of the data is "self-evident." But is it?

If a person with either limited or no accounting knowledge made the QB entries, I might argue that the information can have *no* value. Sure, there would be a host of errors, adjustments, deletions, etc., but so what? The primary source documents control in any event. Even assuming the QB entries are pristine—prepared by the world's greatest accountant—will an examiner accept a return as filed based *solely* on the QB reports? That is simply not going to happen. Given that, there is no relevance to the QB metadata.

After sending such a letter to counsel, then wait and see.

Given these facts, I might expect counsel to drop the issue and that would be the end of the QB fight. But of course, there is no way to guarantee that. If counsel does not back off but insists that you provide the information, you have to know that continued refusal will likely lead to a summons enforcement proceeding and with that, the likelihood that a court will enforce the summons.

CHAPTER EIGHT

UNDERSTANDING YOUR ESSENTIAL TAX AUDIT RIGHTS

THE IRS IS UNDER AN AFFIRMATIVE DUTY TO APPRISE taxpayers of their rights in both audit and collection situations. In fact, on no fewer than four occasions, Congress commanded the IRS to produce materials that clearly and simply communicate to taxpayers what their rights and remedies are when dealing with the agency. The first came in 1988, with the passage of the initial Taxpayer Bill of Rights. Congress required the IRS to notify taxpayers in "simple and nontechnical terms" about their rights during audits, appeals and the collection process.

This is the law that gave birth to IRS Publication 1, *Your Rights as a Taxpayer*. The problem is that the publication is just two pages long. It is woefully incomplete. Another publication, Publication 1-EP, which deals with certain business audits, states that, "IRS employees will explain and protect your rights as a taxpayer throughout your contact with us."

Sadly, we know that the IRS's efforts to explain your rights are inadequate at best and negligent at worst. As the National Taxpayer Advocate stated in her 2013 Annual Report to Congress, "IRS employees do not always clearly communicate these rights to taxpayers at appropriate times." NTA, 2013 Annual Report, pg 51. This fact, combined with the news that the IRS systematically targeted certain conservative political action organizations for heightened and unreasonable scrutiny between the years 2010 and 2012, led to the release of a statement by IRS Commissioner John A. Koskinen regarding taxpayers' rights. The statement declared that the IRS adopted a "Taxpayer Bill of Rights that will become the cornerstone document to provide the nation's taxpayers with a better understanding of their rights." See: IRS News Release IR-2014-72, June 10, 2014.

And while I am encouraged that the IRS claims to be taking the matter of taxpayers' rights seriously, the so-called Bill of Rights presented in the June 2014 statement is merely a conceptual statement of rights. It does not reference specific provisions of law, regulations or published IRS procedures upon which a taxpayer may rely to defend himself. The fact is the tax code is loaded with specific taxpayer rights that people just do not know about. The 2014 Bill of Rights does not add to the rights already existing, nor does it make those rights any more user-friendly, or for that matter, enforceable. It remains true that if you do not know your rights, you simply do not have any.

The ten provisions that make up the 2014 Bill of Rights are as follows:

1. The right to be informed,

2. The right to quality service,

3. The right to pay no more than the correct amount of the tax,

4. The right to challenge the IRS's position and be heard,

5. The right to appeal an IRS decision in an independent forum,

6. The right to finality,

7. The right to privacy,

8. The right to confidentially,

9. The right to retain representation, and

10. The right to a fair and just tax system.

Commissioner Koskinen stated in the announcement that the "concept of taxpayer rights is not a new one for IRS employees: they embrace it in their work everyday." Unfortunately, this statement is pure *farce*—perhaps owing to the fact that Commissioner Koskinen was on the job with the IRS for less than one year as of the time of issuing the statement. He might very well believe what he said but as I have documented throughout my work of over thirty years, and as the National Taxpayer Advocate grimly confirmed in her 2013 Annual Report to Congress, the IRS cares little about taxpayers' rights when those rights somehow stand in the way of the agency getting the money.

Therefore, it falls to me—as it has for more than three decades—to explain your rights as a taxpayer and to show you how to exercise them properly and effectively. So in no particular order, what follows is a discussion of the most important rights you have in the tax audit environment.

The Time and Place of the Audit

One of the most common complaints I hear about audits is the IRS is insensitive and inconsiderate when it comes to setting the time for a face-to-face meeting. Audit notices dictate that the examination must be conducted on "Thursday, at 9:00 AM," or an arrogant phone call exclaims that if you are not in the office by "the 20th, enforcement action will be taken." Citizens are deliberately left with the impression that they have no say in determining the date or time of their audit. This is just not true.

Code section 7605(a) states in part:

> The time and place of examination pursuant to the provisions (of the code) shall be such time and place as may be fixed by the Secretary and as are *reasonable under the circumstances*." (Emphasis added.)

Historically, there has been a tremendous amount of abuse by the IRS on the question of what is "reasonable under the circumstances." The IRS's regulation directs employees to "exercise sound judgment in applying these criteria to the circumstances at hand" to "balance [the] convenience of the taxpayer" with the needs of the IRS when scheduling the audit. Revenue Regulation section 301.7605-1(a)(1).

This is not a bright line so there is much abuse in this area, especially considering that many auditors lack "sound judgment." As such, it seems that the regulation asks the impossible. However, the gray language can actually work to your advantage. I regularly make it my business to insist that pre-scheduled audits be reset to accommodate either calendar concerns or to facilitate further preparation.

To claim your right under section 7605(a) and have a voice in determining what is "reasonable," you must be assertive. Failure to be assertive means the IRS alone dictates where and when you meet.

Consider Paul's case. The IRS notified him of the pending audit of his tax return. The auditor set up a meeting, sent a document request and waited for the appointed date. Two factors, of which the agent was unaware, prevented the audit from coming off as she might have hoped.

First, Paul was an independent salesman on the road almost four full weeks per month. He worked in a season-sensitive business and had to travel from early March through October's end. Any time off during that period seriously impacted his earnings. Secondly, Paul moved subsequent to filing the return in question. Thus, most of his records were lost. Those that were available were in disarray.

Time was needed to either locate the lost records or reconstruct them if they could not be located. We also had to organize and make sense of the records that were on hand. This had to be achieved during the industry's few off-peak months if Paul were to earn a respectable living. The agent was notified, not asked, that circumstances dictated the scheduled meeting must be postponed. We explained the facts to demonstrate that the request was "reasonable under the circumstances." The date originally set was ignored and Paul went about his business.

Finally, after the records were located and the peak season came and went, Paul attended the audit. During the audit, the agent made the remark that she was handed, but did not want to delve into Paul's return for the next tax year. "I just want to get this one finished and off my desk," she said. "You're just too hard to get a hold of."

Had Paul sheepishly appeared on the date first set, two undesirable consequences were certain. First, his records were not in order so many, if not all of his deductions would have been disallowed. Secondly, since the auditor did not seem to understand that appeal rights exist (a right discussed later in this chapter), she may well have convinced him to accept the disallowances. The outcome would have been the payment of taxes, interest and penalties Paul did not owe.

Do not be forced to attend an audit for which you are ill prepared. Furthermore, the IRS has no authority to force you to attend an audit at a time that would prove costly or otherwise inconvenient to you.

Assistance of Professional Counsel

The right of representation before the IRS is absolute. Publication 1, *Your Rights as a Taxpayer*, states, "Taxpayers have the right to retain an authorized representative of their choice to represent them in their dealings with the IRS." This language derives from section 7521(c), which holds, in part:

> Any attorney, certified public accountant, enrolled agent, enrolled actuary, or any other person permitted to represent the taxpayer before the Internal Revenue Service who is not disbarred or suspended from practice before the Internal Revenue Service and who has a written power of attorney executed by the taxpayer may be authorized by such taxpayer to represent the taxpayer in any interview. . .

IRS Form 2848, *Power of Attorney*, is used to provide written authorization to a professional to represent you. Without Form 2848 properly prepared and executed, the IRS will not talk to your representative. The power of attorney (POA) should be submitted to the tax auditor prior to any meetings.

Once a POA is executed and delivered to the agent, the agent is not authorized to contact you directly. All contacts, whether verbal or written, must be channeled through the representative. Furthermore, the IRS agent "may not require a taxpayer to accompany the representative" to any meeting or conference in the absence of a summons. Code section 7521(c).

Even if you begin an audit without counsel, you have the right to stop the proceedings in mid-stream to get help. Section 7521(b)(2) states clearly that even while an interview is pending, if you express a desire to consult counsel, the auditor "*shall suspend* such interview regardless of whether the taxpayer may have answered one or more questions." (Emphasis added.)

It is common for the IRS to ignore these legal requirements. One way this happens is due to a provision within section 7521(c) that allows an agent to contact the citizen directly when the agent and his immediate supervisor believe your representative "is responsible for unreasonable delay or hindrance of an Internal Revenue Service examination or investigation of the taxpayer." A letter claiming that your representative is responsible for unreasonable delay is sometimes mailed to a citizen when his representative does not allow the client to turn out his pockets. It is an intimidation tactic designed to create distrust between the client and the tax pro. It is also intended to bluff the representative into caving in on whatever matters he is holding out on.

In one case, Tom represented a corporate taxpayer and refused to allow the agent to enter the company's premises. Since there was absolutely nothing in the corporation's tax return that could be verified by a site inspection of the premises, there was no need for a visit. It would serve only to disrupt the work environment and Tom would have no part of it.

The agent huffed and puffed, then mailed a letter to both the client and Tom, saying it was his opinion that Tom was guilty of unreasonably delaying the examination. The agent mailed the demand for a site inspection directly to the corporation. The corporate officer responded with a simple letter saying, "take it up with my lawyer." Tom issued another letter, citing chapter and verse from the IRS's regulations about site inspections, saying if the agent could justify his request in accordance with the regulations, he was welcome to view the premises. The agent could not and that was the end of the matter.

The Correspondence Audit

Are you good under pressure? Do you talk too much? Or do you have a propensity to freeze up or even worse, to babble when presented with questions and demands by an authority figure? Many people fall apart when confronted by authority, and most assuredly, the IRS. When I suggest one has the ability to deal with the IRS without the need of an expensive professional, the typical response is, "There is no way I can confront those sharks and win. They will trap me and that will be the end of it."

Without a doubt, much of the IRS's audit techniques revolve around asking questions and seeking information designed to "trap" you. The agent knows in advance the purpose of a particular line of questioning, but does not reveal it. Instead, he asks the questions without providing any answers of his own. This is especially pronounced in the economic reality audit in which the agent probes for hidden income.

Not only is this practice unfair but it has the effect of rattling an ignorant citizen. If you are easily rattled or intimidated, or you are afraid that you might "talk too much," staying out of danger is simple. Just stay away from the face-to-face audit.

I am not suggesting you should refuse to be audited. On the contrary, as I illustrated earlier, you have the obligation to prove that your return is correct. I am suggesting there is an alternative to your physical presence at an audit. It allows you to comply with your legal requirements without subjecting yourself to a painful and intimidating confrontation.

Larry was the kind of person I just described. He was nervous at the very thought of dealing with the IRS and the last thing he wanted was to face an auditor, even if he did not have to take time off work. Consequently, when he received an audit notice, he was adamant that he did not want to personally appear. Under these circumstances, Larry demanded that his examination be handled via correspondence.

The so-called "correspondence examination" is very common and the IRS routinely uses it to verify returns. It grows from Revenue Regulation section 601.105(b)(2)(ii), which states in part:

> * * * Examinations are conducted by correspondence only when warranted by the nature of the questionable items and by the convenience and characteristics of the taxpayer. In a correspondence examination, the taxpayer is asked to explain or send supporting evidence by mail. * * * (Emphasis added.)

In its description to the public of the correspondence audit, the IRS says in Publication 1, *Your Rights as a Taxpayer*, the following:

> We handle many examinations and inquiries by mail. We will send you a letter with either a request for more information or a reason why we believe a change to your return may be needed. You can respond by mail or you can request a personal interview with an examiner. If you mail us the requested information or provide an explanation, we may or may not agree with you, and we will explain the reasons for any changes. Please do not hesitate to write to us about anything you do not understand.

To assert his right to a correspondence audit, Larry mailed a simple letter to the agent. It pointed out that he did not wish to appear personally. He further explained that he would answer all questions in writing and would provide copies along with written explanations of all documents and receipts necessary to verify the correctness of his return.

As the audit progressed, Larry was asked to provide copies of bank statements, canceled checks and other data relevant to the examination. Each time, he responded in writing by submitting the applicable material with needed explanations. When all was said and done, Larry never set foot in an IRS office. He never laid eyes on a tax examiner and never lost one hour of work. Most importantly, Larry never placed himself in an environment where his own fear and ignorance might come back to haunt him.

Sometimes agents refuse to conduct the audit by correspondence, claiming that there "must" be a face-to-face conference because this is a "field" audit and not a correspondence audit. In that case, do not argue with the agent about Publication 1 or the regulations. Simply mail the requested information to the agent and provide a written explanation of the items, just as Larry did. If the agent continues to insist on a face-to-face meeting, explain in writing that all information and documents needed to make a decision were provided. There is nothing more to discuss. If the agent claims there are more questions, ask that they be submitted in writing and you will respond in writing.

The Right to Record the Audit

In every court hearing, the authorities make a record of the proceeding. This is to provide proof later of what was said. This is not a bad idea for tax audits. The problem is the IRS provides no reporter to make a record. At the same time, however, it cannot refuse to allow you to make your own audio recording.

Code section 7521(a)(1) provides that IRS personnel conducting interviews must allow you to make an "audio recording of such interview at the taxpayer's own expense and with the taxpayer's own equipment." The proviso is that the citizen must make an "advance request" to make the recording.

The term "request" as used in the statute is misplaced. You need not ask permission to make the recording. You need only give notice in writing at least ten days in advance of the meeting. You must also bring your own recording equipment. IRS Notice 89-51.

Similarly, the IRS has the right to make a record of the hearing. The agent must tell you before hand of his intent to record and you have the right to obtain a copy of the transcript. Code section 7521(a)(2).

The success of an audit from the IRS's perspective is often dependent on bluff and intimidation by the agent, and the fear and ignorance of the citizen. When an audit conference is recorded, you can be sure the overt incidents of such tactics diminish substantially.

The Repetitive Audit

"I've been audited four years in row, now. Each time, they pick on the same deduction. And each time, I end up owing no taxes. This is getting old. What can I do to stop it?"

I hear this question quite often. The answer involves both good news and bad news. The bad news is the IRS has the right to examine any return for any year, provided the assessment statute of limitations (discussed later) has not expired. The fact that the IRS may have examined a prior return and found no taxes owed does not preclude the examination of a subsequent year, even on the same issue. For example, just because you proved your charitable contributions for 2010 does not mean you can prove them for 2011. Each tax year stands alone.

The good news is the IRS has an examination policy designed to guard against unnecessary repetitive audits. The policy is expressed in Internal Revenue Manual section 4.10.2.8.5 (January 2012). The policy provides three key elements. They are:

1. An audit was performed for either of the two preceding tax years,

2. The issues raised in the current audit are the same as those in the prior audit, and

3. The prior audit resulted in either "no change or small tax change."

When each of these elements is present, the case can be closed without further examination activity. However, the repetitive audit rules generally do not apply to Schedule C (small business) or Schedule F (farmer) tax returns, nor to they apply to business entities, such as corporations or partnerships.

To argue the repetitive audit defense, respond in writing to the IRS's initial contact letter. Explain that you were audited for one or both of the previous two years. Assert the repetitive audit guidelines of the IRM and ask that the audit be closed. To prove your claim, send the auditor a copy of the initial contact letter for the prior audit, the audit report issued by the previous examiner and the final letter explaining there was no change (or small change) to your tax bill.

Even if you cannot find all the above documents, assert the defense anyway and provide what documents you do have. In that situation, the IRM commands the agent to "requisition" the files. He must then review them to determine whether the issues in the current case are the same as those raised in the prior audits. The agent is to postpone the audit until a determination can be made on the repetitive audit claim.

The defense can also be asserted during your first meeting with the agent. This might be necessary if the initial contact letter did not specifically describe the issues in question in the current audit. However, it is best to have these issues established in writing beforehand, a process I discuss later in this book. At that point, you can assert a repetitive audit defense in writing, before meeting the agent.

Though the IRS is not required by law to close a repetitive audit, the IRM definitely instructs the agent that when the above three conditions apply, "the current examination can be closed." Ibid.

The Right to Present Evidence

Tax auditors can be fickle about the burden of proof question. On the one hand, they pound you on the fact that you have the burden of proof on all matters. On the other hand, they try to limit your ability to present evidence. They do this two ways.

First, they try to cram the presentation process into an unreasonably short envelope of time, e.g., "You must have the material to me by Monday or I will not allow it." The second way is by the effort to prevent witnesses from attending the audit conference who can testify to relevant issues, e.g., "No one is allowed at the audit except an attorney, accountant or enrolled agent."

Neither the tax code nor the regulations hand the auditor the authority to arbitrarily set unreasonable or unrealistic time constraints on your ability to present evidence. The single time restraint that governs this situation is the assessment statute of limitations, which I discuss later in this chapter.

When the IRS is up against the assessment statute, it has the right to demand records within sufficient time to allow it to evaluate the records. However, the assessment statute is generally three years from the date the return is filed. In the garden-variety audit, the IRS selects the return well in advance of the statute expiring. Therefore, it does not risk missing the statute by affording you reasonable time to collect records, gather facts and otherwise present your case.

Presentation of facts includes the presentation of testimony on material matters that cannot be proven by documentation. I outlined just a few examples of these items at the end of chapter 6, under the heading, **A Final Word on Testimony**. I refer to items that cannot be proven with documents as the "intangible" elements of a deduction. Ideally, the presentation of testimony should be done in writing, through an affidavit. However, there are times when presenting the facts live may have more impact.

You have the right to present live witnesses and the IRS cannot refuse to allow the presence of such a person merely because he is not an attorney, etc. The argument used to keep such people away is that they are not "authorized to obtain confidential tax information about you." This argument is based only on partial truth. It is true that without proper authorization, no person can obtain your confidential tax information. It is also true that it is usually not enough for you to "tell the agent" that it is okay to talk about your tax matters in the presence of another person. The authorization must be in writing.

However, it is not true that only an attorney, accountant or enrolled agent can obtain such authorization. Any person can be authorized to receive your confidential tax information if you deem it necessary, and the IRS created a form for doing just that. It is Form 8821, *Tax Information Authorization*. Use it expressly for the purpose of authorizing disclosure of your tax information to a person not actually representing you. Such a person could be a witness needed to present material facts to the agent. With a signed Disclosure Authorization in hand, the agent cannot preclude that witness's presence at the audit.

Assert Tax Advantages Not Claimed in the Return

One of the most common defense mechanisms people use to mitigate the potential negative financial consequences of an audit is to fail to claim all the deductions they are entitled to. In the event of an audit, they intend to present proof of unclaimed deductions as a means of offsetting any disallowances.

While I question the wisdom of this approach for a number of reasons, the IRS has developed a response of its own. The response is to ignore the additional deductions. In one case, a citizen was told that in order to consider additional deductions, he would have to file an amended return. However, while a return is currently under audit, the IRS will *not* process an amended return for that same tax year. Once the case is in the hands of a revenue agent, that agent controls the matter entirely. Thus, you simply must present your evidence of additional, unclaimed deductions at the audit while the case is under consideration. It is not likely that you will have a chance later.

Moreover, the claim that additional deductions can be claimed only on an amended return is just flat wrong. In fact, the regulations expressly provide that overlooked deductions may rightfully be claimed at an audit. Rev. Reg. section 601.105(b)(2)(ii) reads in part as follows:

> During the interview examination, the taxpayer has the right to point out to the examining officer any amounts included in the return which are not taxable, or any deductions which the taxpayer failed to claim on the return.

This regulation gives you two specific rights. The first is the right to change the "income" by demonstrating that certain income was in fact, not taxable for whatever reason. For example, you might have claimed capital gain income from the sale of your main home, only to find out that most or all of the income was excluded because of the exemption that applies to capital gains from the sale of a principle residence. This has the effect of reducing taxable income.

Secondly and very clearly, you have the right to assert any additional "deductions" not claimed on the return. We all understand the effect of this. You have the burden of proof as to both items.

A Conference with a Manager

You always have the right to request a meeting with the agent's manager in order to discuss issues in the case. Generally, a meeting with the manager is used to discuss the proposed final report if you disagree with it but that is certainly not the only reason to request a conference.

Anytime you face an impasse on an issue, ask to speak the agent's manager. This might happen if there is a scheduling conflict. Suppose you cannot appear at the time set by the agent or you are unable to fully prepare by the time set for the audit. If the agent is unreasonable, speak to the manager. As another example, suppose the agent refuses to allow a witness to appear or will not accept your submission of an affidavit. Discuss the matter with the manager.

When the examination is complete, expect the agent to issue an examination report. The report is often referred to as a thirty-day letter, because it provides thirty days in which to act. Three optional courses of action are presented in the letter. First, you can submit more information. Second, you can request a conference with the manager. And third, you can request a conference with the IRS's Office of Appeals.

I recommend that you first exhaust the remedy of meeting with a manager, but do not be deluded. Be mindful of the purpose of the Examination function. I summarized it in three words earlier in this discourse: get the money. For that reason, it is usually necessary to bring the matter to the Appeals Office, as discussed next.

The Right of Appeal

The right to appeal the decision of tax examiners is absolute. Revenue Regulation 601.105(b)(4) provides, in part:

At the conclusion of an office or field examination, the taxpayer is given an opportunity to agree with the findings of the examiner. If the taxpayer does not agree, the examiner will inform the taxpayer of the appeal rights.

This right applies equally to face-to-face examinations or correspondence audits. Regardless of the context, the decisions of tax auditors are never final. This is very important to understand given that the decisions of auditors are wrong so often.

To describe the appeals process in more detail, the IRS offers Publication 556, *Examination of Returns, Appeal Rights, and Claims for Refund.* Under the heading, "If You Do Not Agree," Publication 556 explains:

If you do not agree with the proposed changes, the examiner will explain your appeal rights. If your examination takes place in an IRS office, you can request an immediate meeting with the examiner's supervisor to explain your position. If an agreement is reached, your case will be closed.

If you cannot reach an agreement with the supervisor at this meeting, or if the examination took place outside of an IRS office, the examiner will write up your case explaining your position and the IRS's position. The examiner will forward your case for processing.

First, let me give you a word of caution about this statement. Do not rely on the examiner to "write up your case." It is true that he must forward your case to Appeals if you wish, but you must take the lead in filing the request. I show you exactly how to do this in chapter 13.

Next, do not let the idea of an "appeal" scare you. This is not a court appeal. The cost of an appeal is equal to a postage stamp and the brief time it takes to write the required protest letter. As we saw in chapter 4, the audit process is fraught with errors and the appeals function is intended to correct them.

Freedom From the Tax Audit—
The Statute of Limitations

"The IRS can chase me 'til I'm dead." This is the belief most people have about the agency's power. But it is not true. As I already stated, the IRS is governed by a statute of limitations in all its actions, including the power to audit a return.

According to code section 6501, the IRS must make a tax assessment within three years of the date the return is filed. Thereafter, the agency's ability to assess evaporates. The IRS is therefore generally precluded from examining a tax return after three years from the date of filing. For example, suppose your 2008 return was filed on time on April 15, 2009. The IRS had until April 15, 2012, to examine it and make any additional assessment of taxes. After April 15, 2012, the 2008 return is considered a "closed year." It can be examined only under especially extenuating circumstances, which I address later.

But first, let us examine important rules that apply when determining the starting point of the three-year period of limitations.

1. The return must be complete. The return must disclose gross income, deductions and taxable income in such a manner as to enable the IRS to determine its correctness. A return that does not disclose information from which a tax can be computed is not a return. That does not mean the return must be perfect, if that is even possible. The return need only evidence an honest and genuine attempt to comply with the law. Inadvertent omissions or inaccuracies do not suspend the statute of limitations.

2. Returns filed early. Code section 6501(b)(1) provides that returns filed before the April 15 filing deadline do not trigger the three-year period on the date filed. Rather, the limitations period begins to run on the due date of the return. Even though you may have filed your 2010 return on January 31, 2011, the statute of limitations began to tick on April 15, 2011.

3. Returns filed late. Conversely, for late-filed returns, the statute of limitations starts on date the IRS receives the return. Thus, if the IRS received your 2010 return on July 15, 2011 (without a valid filing extension), the statute of limitations expires on July 15, 2014.

Let us now turn our attention to the various exceptions to the general three-year period of limitations. In some circumstances, the period is merely extended. In other situations, the period of limitations is suspended.

1. Certain amended returns. Section 6501(c)(7) extends the statute of limitations when certain amended returns are filed. An amended return filed during the sixty-day period immediately before the expiration of the statute extends the statute for sixty days from the date the amended return is received.

For example, suppose the assessment statute covering your 2007 tax return was set to expire on April 15, 2011 (three years from the due date of the return). Suppose further that on March 15, 2011, (during the sixty-day period immediately before the expiration of the statute) you file an amended return. The statute of limitations is extended to May 14, 2011, sixty days from the date of filing the amended return.

2. Substantial omission of income. There are two elements to this exception. The first is found in section 6501(e)(1)(A)(i), which provides that when one omits "in excess of 25 percent of the amount of gross income stated in the return" the assessment period is extended to six years. For purposes of determining whether more than 25 percent of gross income was omitted, the calculation is made without respect to any deductions or credits that may be taken against such income.

There is an important restriction on this rule. As you now know, the citizen generally bears the burden of proof on all items claimed in the return. When the IRS asserts the more-than-25-percent omission rule, however, the agency bears a two-pronged burden of proof. It must prove both that you had more income than reported and that the amount omitted should have been included in gross income.

The second element is found in section 6501(e)(1)(A)(ii), which addresses income from a source outside the United States. Under that provision, if you omit more than $5,000 of income generated from an asset held offshore, say capital gain income from a foreign stock account, the statute of limitations on assessment is extended to six years from the date the return is filed. I address offshore issues in chapter 19, under the heading, **How to Handle Undisclosed Offshore Income and Assets**.

3. Failure to report foreign assets. Code section 6501(c)(8)(A) provides that if a citizen fails to provide any of the information required in Form 8938, *Statement of Specific Foreign Financial Assets,* the assessment statute of limitations for the return in question does not start running until the information is in fact provided. At that point, the statute does not expire until three years after the information is provided. Thus, if your foreign assets are not reported, the IRS can audit your return and make an assessment of tax *at any time*. See chapter 19 regarding the process for curing disclosure failures.

Section 6501(c)(8)(B) has a reasonable cause provision that potentially limits the damage that can arise as a result of there being no assessment statute of limitations if Form 8938 is not filed. That section reads as follows:

> If the failure to furnish the information referred to in subparagraph (A) is due to reasonable cause and not willful neglect, subparagraph (A) shall apply only to the item or items related to such failure.

For example, suppose you had interest income of more than $5,000 attributable to foreign bank accounts that was not reported on your tax return. Suppose further that you can establish "reasonable cause" for not reporting the income. In that case, the suspended statute of limitations applies only to the unreported interest income, not to the entire tax return. However, if you cannot establish reasonable cause as to the unreported interest income, the IRS is at liberty to audit the entire tax return, assessing taxes, interest and penalties, regardless of whether the adjustment was attributable to a foreign financial asset.

This provision is among the most egregious of all the potential penalties applicable to the failure to report foreign financial assets. Because the statute of limitations does not begin running until the required information is provided, you are never out of the woods on a return for a year in which you held foreign financial assets. And if the IRS makes a tax assessment, say for a tax year that is five years earlier, it also assesses the interest on the tax beginning from the date the tax *should have been paid*, not from the date the tax is assessed. This fact alone can double a tax liability (or more) and penalties are added on top of that. If you have foreign income or assets that have not been reported to the IRS, I strongly recommend you seek counsel to ascertain your options for dealing with that situation. The penalties for failure to report such assets can be egregious.

4. Loss and credit carry-backs. Under certain circumstances, operating losses incurred in connection with a business, capital losses incurred in connection with investments and unused credits may be carried back to previous years. This operates to reduce taxes for the previous years, usually resulting in a refund. Sections 6501(i) and (j) provide that when a loss or credit is carried back to a prior year, the statute of limitations on that year stays open as long as the year in which the loss or credit was generated is open.

To illustrate, suppose you incur a capital loss in 2012 and you carry back a portion of that loss to tax year 2011, resulting in a refund for 2011. The normal statute of limitations for 2011 expires April 15, 2015 (assuming there was no filing extension). The loss was incurred in 2012 and the normal statute of limitations for 2012 expires April 15, 2016 (assuming there was no filing extension). Therefore, tax year 2011 (the year to which the loss was carried) remains open until April 15, 2016, one year longer than usual.

5. False or fraudulent return. Code sections 6501(c)(1) and (2) suspend the assessment statute of limitations in either of two circumstances. The first is when a return is filed that is false or fraudulent "with the intent to evade the tax." The second is where the citizen attempts "in any manner to defeat or evade tax." These are the so-called fraud exceptions to the statute of limitations. When invoked, the IRS may assess taxes for the year it proves fraud, regardless of age.

However, to sustain the fraud exception, the IRS has the burden to prove with clear and convincing evidence one of two facts: either that the citizen, 1) filed a false or fraudulent return with the intent to evade taxes, or 2) he committed an affirmative act calculated to deceive or mislead the IRS, in an effort to evade or defeat payment of the tax. Unless the IRS can prove fraud, it cannot assess taxes beyond the normal three-year statute unless some other exception applies.

I must point out here that the "no statute" rule for fraud applies only in civil cases. Criminal prosecutions for fraud are governed by a separate rule.

6. No return filed. If you fail to file a tax return for any year, the IRS may assess those taxes regardless of how much time has passed. As with the fraud rule, this rule applies only in civil cases. Separate rules govern criminal prosecutions for failure to file.

7. Substitute for returns. When the IRS believes a false return was filed or a citizen failed to file a return, the agency is authorized by code section 6020(b) to make a return for him based upon "available information." Such a return is referred to as a substitute for return (SFR). The normal statute of limitations on assessment does not apply to SFRs. Because SFRs are made only in cases where the citizen filed a false return or failed to file entirely, the statute of limitations on assessment is suspended.

8. Judicial actions. Under some circumstances, judicial actions undertaken by a citizen can toll the assessment statute of limitations. Here are two of the most common examples.

a. Tax Court. If you cannot reach an agreement with the IRS after either an audit or appeal, the agency mails a Notice of Deficiency (NOD) asserting additional tax due. You then have the right to file a petition with the U.S. Tax Court to have the NOD reviewed. You must file the petition within ninety days of the date on the NOD. The IRS may not assess the tax while the ninety-day petition-filing period is pending, nor can the IRS assess the tax once a timely petition is filed. The tax may be assessed after the petition-filing period expires if no petition is filed. Assuming a petition is filed, the IRS can assess only the amount the Tax Court later says is owed. Code section 6215.

At the time of mailing the NOD, the assessment statute of limitations is tolled—that is, it stops running. The statute remains tolled until the earlier of: 1) the expiration of the ninety-day petition-filing period, or 2) a ruling from the Tax Court. The statute begins running sixty days after the occurrence of either event. Code section 6503(a)(1).

b. Summons enforcement. The IRS has authority under code sections 7601 and 7602 to issue summonses to third parties, such as banks, etc. Code section 7609 affords the citizen the right to ask a federal court to "quash," or prevent, the summons from being enforced.

When a citizen moves to quash a summons through the judicial process, all applicable statutes of limitation are suspended while the proceeding is pending. Code section 7609(e) (1). Additionally, if the summoned party does not release the records sought within six months of service of the summons, all applicable statutes of limitations are suspended. The suspension begins with the date six months after service of the summons. It ends on the date of compliance. Code section 7609(e)(2).

9. Voluntary extensions. The assessment statute of limitations may be suspended if both you and the IRS agree in writing to a suspension. The agreement is formalized on Form 872, *Consent to Extend Time to Assess Tax*, otherwise known as an assessment statute waiver. Once executed, the waiver extends the assessment statute until the date shown on the form.

It is common for the IRS to ask a person to sign Form 872 while an audit is pending in order for the agency to have more time to assess the tax. The statements agents make when asking for this waiver are almost always wrong and intended to mislead. Let me give you some background.

Suppose you are under audit for tax year 2011. The return was filed on time in April 2012 so the IRS has until April 15, 2015 (three years from the due date) to complete the audit and make an assessment. At some point during the fall of 2014, the agent asks you sign an assessment statute waiver. The agent states that the IRS needs at least ninety days to process a closed audit case and since the statute is coming up in April 2015 and the audit is still not complete, they need more time. A signed Form 872 gives them the time needed.

This statement is accurate so far as it goes. The IRS does require a window of time for a completed audit to be reviewed and all the closing paperwork to be processed. The ninety-day timeframe for doing so is common. However, it is the next part of the agent's presentation that is false and misleading.

In order to pressure you to sign Form 872, the agent tells you that unless you sign it, the IRS must: 1) make its decision based upon the information already in the file, 2) that you will have no further opportunity to present information and arguments, and 3) you will lose your appeal rights. Each element of this statement is flat wrong. Let me explain why.

As to the claim that you lose your appeal rights, the fact is the IRS cannot assess any additional tax without first mailing a Notice of Deficiency. I discussed this earlier, explaining that an NOD is required before any tax can be assessed and that the NOD gives you the opportunity for a Tax Court appeal. The Tax Court, not some auditor, then makes the determination as to what you owe, if anything.

Upon filing a petition with the Tax Court, the IRS then involves the Office of Appeals in an attempt to resolve the case without the need of a trial. In 100 percent of the audit cases before the Tax Court, the file is sent back to Appeals with instructions to work with the taxpayer to negotiate a settlement. Moreover, while your case is in Tax Court, you have every right to provide whatever additional information, documents, evidence and arguments are necessary to support your case. There is no limitation on your right to do so. The reality is that 97 percent of all Tax Court audit appeals are settled without a trial. So it is flat not true that you will lose your rights to appeal and to provide more information if you do not sign the assessment statue waiver. See chapter 13.

What is true (but not explained) is that the audit appeal path changes if you do not sign the waiver. The usual appeal path is this: IRS issues the final audit determination. You then have thirty days to appeal by filing a protest letter, which causes the case to be sent to the Office of Appeals. If you reach agreement there, the case is closed. If not, the Appeals Office mails a Notice of Deficiency, which then gives you ninety days to file a Tax Court Petition. By filing the petition, the case is resolved through the Tax Court process. Signing Form 872 at the audit level means this appeals path will be followed.

But if you do *not* sign the Form 872 at the audit level, the IRS will simply mail the Notice of Deficiency to keep the statute of limitations from expiring. Thus, there is no thirty-day letter and there is no intermediate trip to the Appeals Office. However, by timely filing a petition with the Tax Court, your case is sent back to Appeals for full consideration and settlement negotiations, and as stated above, the likely full settlement of the case. While working with the Appeals Office, you have every right to provide all the information, documents, evidence and arguments necessary to support your case. There is simply no restriction on this. Thus, you get an appeal but follow a different route to get there.

So the question becomes, "Do I sign Form 872 or not?" The answer is, "It depends." I have put together a list of factors to consider in determining whether to sign the waiver or not. Let me discuss them here.

Consider *signing* the waiver if:

- Your auditor is reasonable, understanding, appears to be—or in fact is—willing to work with you to arrive at the correct tax liability in your case, rather than simply trying to get more money;

- You are dealing with simple issues and you have solid evidence to support your case. In that situation, you can expect to resolve the case without going to Tax Court or even the Office of Appeals. If you can avoid both of these steps, you shorten considerably the time it takes to ultimately resolve the problem; or

- You are under audit for multiple years but the IRS wants a wavier on just the earliest year. In that case, you might want to maintain continuity of the case so that one tax year is not following a different path from the other tax years.

- Even if you decide to sign a waiver, understand the difference between Form 872 and Form 872-A. Form 872 is a fixed date waiver. It expires on the date expressed in the form itself. Form 872-A is an open-ended waiver. It remains in effect until you revoke it by submitting Form 872-T, *Notice of Termination of Special Consent to Extend Time to Assess Tax*. Form 872-A has an advantage in that you can terminate it at any time, whereas Form 872 is good until the date stated in the form.

- Signing a waiver does not have to be a "take-it-or-leave-it" proposition. You might consider negotiating the terms of the waiver. For example, suppose there is one year left on the assessment statute and the IRS asks for a waiver. At that point, I would suggest to the agent that we work hard for the next six months to get the audit completed so there is no need for either a waiver or an appeal. Point out that you are willing to provide whatever documents, etc., are necessary to get the matter resolved. If, after six months, the matter is still not resolved, you will then consider signing a waiver. As another example, suppose the IRS asks for a one-year waiver at a time when there are just four months left on the statute. You might suggest just a six-month extension because you do not want the matter to linger for another year. You want to get it resolved. You can also suggest using Form 872-A rather than Form 872. Recall that with Form 872-A, you have the right to terminate the waiver at any time.

Consider *not* signing the waiver if:

- The assessment statute expiration date is very close. If there are fewer than six months left on the statute, it is possible the IRS simply cannot get the paperwork done in time to beat the expiration date. And if even they do beat it, you still have your appeal rights as explained above;

- You are dealing with an auditor that is unreasonable, does not know the law, repeatedly demands documents already provided, or otherwise makes it clear that she is just working to get more money. By not signing a waiver, the case will be taken from the auditor when you file your Tax Court petition;

- You wish to pressure the IRS to settle the case. Most people cringe at the idea of filing a case with the Tax Court, believing that the IRS will go harder on them for filing an appeal then otherwise might be the case. The opposite is true. In the typical audit scenario, the more you fight, the better deal you will likely make for yourself. Once the case is in Tax Court, the pressure is on the IRS to settle. Because there are tens of thousands of cases filed with the Tax Court each year, the IRS simply cannot litigate each one fully through the trial process. They have to settle these cases and they work hard to do it;

- You wish to speed up the process. Often, the IRS asks for at least an additional year on an assessment statute waiver. By not signing, the case will end up in Tax Court. It is then assigned to an Appeals Officer who must make the case a priority precisely because it is a Tax Court case. This can often speed the process of settlement because you bypass the one-year extension the IRS asks for, the additional time spent with the auditor, and you skip the intermediate appeals step.

One Audit Per Tax Year

The IRS does not have open season for unlimited audits of your tax return, even apart from the statute of limitations issue. While the statute of limitations restricts the IRS in terms of when it may examine your return, code section 7605(b) limits the number of times the IRS can audit a given return. That section reads:

> No taxpayer shall be subjected to unnecessary examination or investigations, and only one inspection of a taxpayer's books of account shall be made for each taxable year unless the taxpayer requests otherwise or unless the Secretary, after investigation, notifies the taxpayer in writing that an additional inspection is necessary.

Thus, the IRS gets one bite of the apple per tax year. Once an audit is "closed," the IRS will not reopen it unless one of three circumstances is present.

First, let us define what consists a closed case. The IRS says an audit is considered closed when the IRS notifies you "in writing" of any adjustments to your account or that your return is accepted without change. See: Revenue Procedure 2005-32, sec. 4.01(1). If a Closing Agreement (Form 866 or 906) is used to resolve the case, the case is considered closed when the Closing Agreement is signed by an IRS official with the proper authority to bind the IRS to the agreement. Code section 7121. A Closing

Agreement generally removes all doubt as to whether an audit case is closed and when it was closed. That is why I recommend that any audit not appealed to the Tax Court be finalized with a Closing Agreement. Your signature on any other form carries the possibility that the IRS may not consider the case "closed" for purposes of code section 7605(b).

The three conditions under which the IRS may open a case closed after examination to make additional adjustments against you are:

1. When there is evidence of fraud, malfeasance, collusion, concealment or misrepresentation of a material fact in connection with the audit,

2. The case involved a clearly-defined, substantial error based on an established IRS position existing at the time of the examination, or

3. Other circumstances exist indicating that a failure to reopen the case would be a serious administrative omission. Rev. Reg. section 601.105(j).

These are very rare circumstances, which leads me to the conclusion that if you have a closed case for a given tax year, the IRS will not be able to reopen that case and audit you again.

Recommended Reading

While I often accuse the IRS of not telling the truth in its information publications, there are some worth reading. When it comes to the tax audit process, I recommend two in particular, both of which were mentioned already. You can easily get them from the IRS's web site or have a copy mailed to you by calling the IRS. The first is Publication 1, *Your Rights as a Taxpayer*. The second is Publication 556, *Examination of Returns, Appeal Rights, and Claims for Refund*. Read both publications carefully as you embark on the audit journey.

PART THREE

THE IRS ON THE ATTACK

[The] lack of awareness of taxpayer rights is further compounded when IRS employees themselves do not sufficiently understand taxpayer rights. Only some employees receive initial training about taxpayer rights, and this information is not regularly reinforced during later periodic training, such as Continuing Professional Education (CPE). Information about taxpayer rights is scattered throughout the Internal Revenue Manual and pertains to narrow circumstances for specific phases of taxpayers' dealings with the IRS.

NATIONAL TAXPAYER ADVOCATE
2013 ANNUAL REPORT TO CONGREE

Chapter Nine

THE DANGERS OF AN ECONOMIC REALITY AUDIT

Stirring the Pot

KEITH SAT AT THE TABLE WITH HIS WIFE. HE FIDGETED nervously as the agent poured over bank statements. With each notation the auditor made, Keith's heart pounded a little harder. His obvious concern was not lost on the agent. "Sure wish I could see what he's writing," he thought. Looking at his wife, he knew she was thinking the same thing.

When they were notified that their tax return was to be audited, Keith and Nancy were naturally concerned, but confident too. As the owner of a small construction business, Keith used a downtown accounting firm to prepare his returns and was convinced there could be no real problems. After all, he's honest—reports all his income. Doesn't do anything under the table. He has nothing to hide.

But none of that changed the fact that his stomach knotted up like a phone cord when he saw the letter in the mailbox. And reading it floored him! He expected questions about his business expenses, interest payments—things like that. Instead, they wanted to know about every dime he spent and how he spent it.

"Look at this," Keith said to Nancy. "I can't believe it. They want us to list how much money we spent on food and clothes during the year."

"What is that?," Nancy asked.

"It's a laundry list of things we're suppose to come up with," Keith said, handing it over.

Nancy read the sheet accompanying the audit notice. It was IRS Form 4822, *Statement of Annual Estimated Personal and Family Living Expenses*. It asked them to classify by cash, check or credit how much they paid for such things as groceries, clothing, laundry, barber, beauty shop and cosmetics, mortgage payments and utilities, recreation, club dues, contributions, gifts and allowances, even reading materials and smoking supplies. The list went on and on, covering every possible aspect of their life. To Keith's amazement, none of it had anything to do with his tax return.

"This will take weeks to organize," Nancy moaned.

To make matters worse, the letter demanded the material within two weeks, and set a meeting in three weeks—at their home!

Keith and Nancy did their best to gather the material. The accountant was little help. Since most of the items were non-deductible personal expenses, he didn't asked for or use any of the data in the tax return.

After burning the midnight oil for an impressive string of evenings, Keith and Nancy assembled a package they believed was responsive to the demands. "The only people who will make out on this deal is the paper company," he said sarcastically while dropping the package in the mail.

Now that the agent was in his kitchen looking over everything imaginable, Keith couldn't help thinking he did something wrong somehow. But what? He could only guess—and wait.

The agent was especially concerned about their lifestyle, the boat in particular. He asked an awful lot of questions about it, questions Keith would never have thought possible in a tax audit. The funny thing is, Keith never claimed the boat as a deduction. The accountant said it was a gray area. And even though he entertained plenty of customers and probably was entitled to some deductions, why take a chance?

Wasn't an audit supposed to be about your tax return? Instead, the agent wanted to know when Keith bought the boat, how much he paid for it, whether he made any substantial repairs or improvements to it, how much it costs to operate, how much he spent on accessories, and, get this, how often—and whom—he entertains on the boat.

"What's that got to do with our tax bill," Keith asked, just a little indignant.

"It's important for us to construct a full picture of your economic activity to determine the accuracy of your tax return," the agent replied in a stoic but well rehearsed way.

"I can certainly understand the financial part," Nancy said, puzzled. "But why does it matter who our friends are and how often we have them on our boat?"

Without answering, the agent just fired another question. "Now you keep your boat at the Hidden Bay Marina, right?"

"Yes," Keith answered, wondering how he knew that.

"It costs about $4,000 a summer to rent a slip in that marina, doesn't it?"

"Well it depends on the size of the boat, but that's about right for what we have."

Shuffling through the heaving pile of bank statements and work papers, the agent picked up the personal living expense statement Keith and Nancy worked on so carefully. "I'm curious," he said. "You didn't show that expense on your Form 4822. Why not?"

"We don't actually pay the bill," Keith explained. "My company did some remodeling work at the marina. The owner paid for the materials and I provided the labor. I worked on it during the winter months, while both of us had spare time. He helped too. He agreed to give me three years worth of free slip rental."

"I see. So you got three years of slip rental, worth about $4,000 per year."

"Yea. That's about right," said Keith, wondering about the significance. He was afraid to ask.

As the agent was making notes, Keith felt pressure to offer more details on the marina arrangement. He didn't want the agent to think he was getting away with something there. "We still have to pay for pump outs, pulling the boat out for service, things like that."

The agent looked up from his work and slowly nodded his understanding. After making more of the notes that were driving Keith and Nancy mad, he came back with another question. "You mentioned pump outs and pulling the boat for service. What's that all about?"

Cautious, Keith said, "Well, the holding tank for the toilet has to be pumped out when it gets full and they charge for that. And sometimes the boat needs to be taken out of the water for service, like fixing the prop, and they charge for that too."

"How often do you have to do that?"

"It depends. If we use the boat a lot, then it has to be pumped more often. And with repairs, you never know. Last year we never had a problem, but this year I've gone through two props already, plus a bilge pump. They had to pull the boat to get to the props."

"I notice those costs don't show up on your personal living expense statement either. You'll have to itemize those and get them to me."

"Sure," murmured Keith, dreading more midnight labor.

"I also notice from your property tax statement that the assessed value of your home went up quite a bit. Did you make substantial improvements to your home?"

"Yes. We finished the basement and converted a large closet upstairs into an extra bathroom," Keith explained.

Nancy joined in. "My mother is getting up in years and she stays with us most of the time now. We needed the space, so we put in two bedrooms downstairs and moved the boys down there. The extra bathroom is for mother. She needs special equipment like grab bars around the toilet, things like that."

"Do you provide food and other living expenses for your mother when she's here?"

"Why, of course," replied Nancy. "She's my mother, but she helps too. She chips in for groceries, watches over the kids while I'm gone in the afternoon and does light housework. She can't really do that much, but it's important to her to help. And we don't have to pay babysitters. That saves a lot right there."

"How much time did she spend here last year," the agent asked.

"In all, about six or seven months."

"And how much do you suppose she contributes each month."

Looking at one another and wondering out loud, the two figured mother must kick in about $500 to the family fisc. And the baby-sitting? That probably saves $200 a month or so.

The agent made more notes, then turning to Keith he inquired, "How much did you spend on the remodeling?"

"Well, counting the stall we added to the garage, I suppose about twelve, maybe fifteen thousand. I haven't added it all up. I did the work myself. The boys helped some. Some friends helped with the trade work. My neighbor is a plumber. He did the bathroom. Nancy's brother did the electrical work. It really saved us a lot. And I helped them in return, you know. Nancy's brother built a garage and I installed the siding and roofed it for him. Sort of a pay back."

"But your checking account doesn't show any where near that amount for home improvement expenditures. Where did you get the money," the agent asked with more than a bit of accusation in his tone.

"We used some savings," Keith pleaded, exasperated.

"But I don't see any evidence of that in the documents you sent me," the agent rebuffed. "By the way," he continued, "Would Nancy's brother be willing to confirm that he did work for you?"

"Of course he will," barked Nancy. "Bill's completely honest and we have nothing to hide." Before they knew it, Keith and Nancy were providing the names of all those who helped in exchange for a return favor. The agent made even more of the notes that were really starting to get on Keith's nerves.

All at once, the agent put his pencil down, organized his papers, then looked up, first at Keith, then Nancy. "It appears from my preliminary analysis that you had income you didn't report on your return. You had barter income from the marina of at least $4,000 in one year alone, and that appears to carry into other years. So I'll be picking up the returns for those other years. That doesn't include the barter income from the plumber or Nancy's brother. Also, you spent thousands on your home with no apparent means of paying for it. You're paying expenses for the operation of a boat that don't show up anywhere. And, you're providing support for your mother. Not only that, but your mother pays rent to you worth about $4,900 a year in the form of groceries, housework and babysitting. On the basis of this information, you must have had at least twenty to thirty thousand dollars more in income than you reported on your return. There is no other way to support all those activities."

Keith and Nancy sat stunned, staring back in utter disbelief. They would never dream of hiding income from the IRS. And how can taking care of your mother count as income anyway? Even if Keith didn't want to, his accountant was adamant about reporting all income. "You don't want any fraud problems," he would say. Boy, is that the truth!

"That's not right," Keith protested. "That just can't be. I've always reported every dime."

"You didn't report the barter income," the agent popped. Gesturing to the tax return in front of him, the agent asked pointedly, "Did you claim $4,000 worth of free slip rental as income on your return?"

Keith, surprised and confused, said, "Um, well, no. We never actually got $4,000.

I mean, he never gave us any money. Just the use of the slip."

The agent quipped, "What you got was barter income and it's taxable. You should have reported it and paid taxes on it just as if it were cash. The same is true of the electrical and plumbing services you received while remodeling the house."

Keith's heart sank. Instantly he began to realize why he felt so awkward throughout the entire audit process. He had no idea where this guy was coming from and now was sure this wouldn't be the last time he got blindsided. Then his mind began to race. "If I got barter income from Bill, then he must have gotten barter income from me." He suddenly grew sick at the idea that he just unknowingly and certainly unwillingly turned his own brother-in-law into the IRS.

He barely heard the agent say, "I'll expect the additional information I asked for within two weeks so I can complete my report."

Keith snapped back to the moment as the agent handed him a sheet of paper. "This is an Information Document Request," he explained. "I've listed the items I want you to provide by the date indicated on the top of the form, right there. If you have any questions, you can feel free to call me. Otherwise, get that material to me by the deadline." The agent then unceremoniously packed his briefcase and got up from the table.

Before he reached the door, his attention was grabbed by the wall on which Nancy lovingly hung dozens of family photos. "That's a nice shot," he said, in a tone more personable than he used to that point as he gestured to one of the photos. "Where was it taken?"

Nancy, suddenly collecting herself if just a bit, said, "Florida. We took the kids there last year. Visited Disney World and Tampa. My sister lives in Tampa. That was at the beach. We had a wonderful time."

Turning to face the couple, the agent very calmly announced, "You didn't include the vacation costs on your living expense statement. Please add them to the list."

He turned and walked out the door.

The Economic Reality Audit Explained

Economic reality is an aggressive audit strategy pointed squarely at the income reported on a tax return. With the decline in the deductions available to most people, the IRS is less able to generate enforcement revenue by focusing audit activities on deductions. It can be more productive attacking income. This is true even for those who claim relatively low income. Since the premise is that all people hide income, people with low reported income may be even more likely to be earning substantial income off the books.

The IRS always had the authority to question income. That is not new. In chapter 5, we spend a good deal of time discussing the "traditional" ways it does so. It is plain to see, however, that the economic reality approach goes far beyond "traditional" techniques.

Historically, the audit process called upon a citizen to prove only that his various tax return entries were correct. If the IRS questioned, say, a $2,000 charitable contribution, the citizen was asked to prove the claim. This is known as a "verification" audit.

In the context of economic reality, the IRS goes beyond the matter of merely verifying that $2,000 was given to charity. In the context of economic reality, the IRS asks the question, "How can the citizen *afford* to give $2,000 to charity in the first place?" In this way, simple verification audits have been transformed into "investigative" audits.

In the over six hundred pages of IRS documentation on economic reality audits issued at the outset of the program, such audits are defined as one "whereby the financial status of an individual taxpayer, as measured by his/her standard of living and operating in the community, is evaluated in relation to information reported on the return." "Examining for Economic Reality," Facilitator's Guide to Workshops 1 through 6, Training Aid 3302-127, pg i.

Is it an exaggeration to refer to this process as a full-scale investigation? Certainly not, for in many ways, it resembles a criminal investigation. The IRS itself refers to economic reality as an "investigative" audit and describes the "objectives of economic reality" as follows:

> Evaluate the whole taxpayer (including consideration of related tax entities) from an economic reality point of view instead of only focusing the audit on some narrow aspect of tax consequence.

> Perform investigative audits instead of verification audits. Ibid. (emphasis added).

To build the economic profile of the citizen, the IRS focuses upon five questions. They are:

- What is the standard of living?

    What does the citizen and "dependent family" consume? How much does it cost to "maintain this consumption pattern?" Is reported net income sufficient to "support the standard of living?" Facilitator's Guide, Training Aid 3302-101, pg T1-6a.

- What is the citizen's accumulated wealth?

    How much has the citizen expended in the "acquisition of capital assets?" When and how was this wealth accumulated? Is reported income "sufficient to fund the accumulations?" Ibid, pg T1-6b.

- What is the citizen's economic history?

    What is the "long term pattern" of profits and return on investment in the citizen's business? Is it "expanding or contracting?" Does the reported business activity "match with the changes" to the citizen's "standard of living and wealth accumulation?" Ibid, pg T1-6c.

- What is the business environment?

    What is the "typical profitability and return on investment" for the nature of the business, given its location? What are the "typical patterns of non-compliance" in that business? What are the "competitive pressures and economic health" of the business? Ibid, pg T1-6d.

- Has the citizen made assertions to receipt of funds considered non-taxable?

  Do such claims "make economic sense?" How credit worthy is the citizen in view of his "assertion that funding was secured from loans?" If the citizen claims funds were received from sources other than conventional lenders, "what was the lenders' source of the funds?" Ibid, pg T1-6e.

You may why, in our fictional account of Keith and Nancy's interview, the agent spent so much time on matters not relating directly to the return. The boat and its operation are critical elements of their lifestyle, spending patterns and asset acquisitions.

Remodeling the house has several implications. First, where did the money come from to do the remodeling? Even if Keith claimed he obtained a bank loan, the agent would have delved into his credit-worthiness and banking history to see whether such a claim makes "economic sense." Furthermore, the agent would have asked to see the loan application Keith submitted to determine whether Keith reported more income to the bank than he did to the IRS. But Keith claimed the money came from savings. This of course raises the question whether Keith had sufficient net income over the years to amass enough savings to fund his project. That would have opened a full spectrum of questions regarding prior years' income and spending activities. In fact, if even the statute of limitations on assessment for prior years were closed, the agent might demand to see income records for those years to verify that savings were accumulated as claimed.

The agent also spent time on the support of Nancy's mother and their Florida vacation. These items directly relate to the cost of maintaining the family and the resources needed to support their spending patterns.

The big item is that Keith was involved in bartering services in connection with his business. Barter income is taxable, yet most people are unaware of this. At the same time, many people, especially tradesmen, do exactly that. Economic reality audits always spell trouble for people if they handle it the way Keith did.

The Components of an Economic Reality Audit

The IRS instructs agents to "create an economic profile of the taxpayer." In turn, the IRS uses this profile (read, "dossier") to attempt to answer the five broad questions outlined above. To build the dossier, the agent is to evaluate a person's lifestyle elements. IRS Training Aid 3302-102, entitled, "JOB AID 1, Components of Economic Reality," identifies forty-seven different aspects of a person's life as some of the elements of the dossier. Here are just a few:

- Neighborhood

- Home
- Age and number of dependents
- Investment income
- Number of years in business
- Recreational vehicles
- Automobiles
- Changes of address
- College tuition
- Trips
- Club memberships
- Hobbies
- Weddings of children
- Legal actions
- Level of sophistication
- Cultural background
- Education and work experience
- Type of business
- Insurance coverage/what covered
- Marital history
- Gambling
- Personal property
- Loan information, and the like.

Given this, it should come as no surprise that the fictional account I presented in chapter 1 pictured an agent following Keith to his boat. Since the IRS is deeply concerned with recreational vehicles, club memberships and hobbies, we can well imagine the agent spying to uncover facts surrounding the boat. It might, after all, reveal some hidden source of unreported income used to fund the boat—obviously a high-ticket expenditure. At the outset of the fictional audit, the agent followed Keith to the boat then questioned marina employees or picked up literature about slip costs at the facility. As the audit developed, the agent discovered Keith earned barter income by doing remodeling work for the marina in exchange for slip rental.

Another piece of the economic reality puzzle is the personal living expenses paid during the years under audit. The "Personal Living Expense (PLE) Checklist" developed by the IRS, JOB AID 3, Training Aid 3302-104, instructs agents to have citizens itemize all personal living expenses paid during the audit years (not the year of the audit). You might recall that Keith and Nancy worked long into the night to gather and document their living expenses. The agent gave them IRS Form 4822 on which to present the results. Much to their chagrin, they left off items the agent believed essential and he sent them back to the drawing board. The following are just a few of the items you might be called upon to document:

- Food, consumed both at home and away from home

- Alcoholic beverages

- All housing expenses

- All utility expenses

- Expenses for household operations

- Laundry and dry cleaning

- Housekeeping supplies

- Household furnishings and equipment

- Apparel and services

- Entertainment

- Jewelry

- Personal care

- Reading materials

- Education

- Tobacco and smoking supplies, and so on.

How serious is the IRS about documenting these expenses? To quote the Training Aid, the PLE is "extremely important." Training Aid 3302-127, pg 2-11. Personal living expenses are the key to the entire audit. Since they do not appear on a tax return, the IRS must get the data from you in order to have any idea whether you live beyond your apparent means. The following statement illustrates just why you might be asked to document every nickel you spend and where you spend it:

> Most taxpayers will not intentionally deposit skimmed funds, but will use the cash to increase their standard of living. This will include day-to-day cash expenditures for payment of living expenses, down payments and/or purchases of assets and other investments.

The more information an examiner can develop, the larger the understatement (of tax). The development of the personal living expenses can be extremely critical in this process. "JOB AID 9, Indirect Methods," Training Aid 3302-110, pg 1.

Do you still believe it is implausible for the IRS to follow a person to his boat? Do you believe an "investigative audit" will not seek to answer the question how the citizen was able to buy the boat in the first place? And how much did it cost? Was the purchase financed? How much does it cost to slip the boat? How much fuel is used? How much is spent on maintenance? How much food and beverages are consumed on board? Whether the beverages are alcoholic or not?

And how much was spent on items ancillary to the boat, such as life preservers, ropes, linens, pillows, kitchen utensils, covers, hoses, power cords, batteries, tools, accessories like radios, audio equipment, TVs, lights, cleaning supplies, ladders, spare fuel tank, pumps, charts, bumpers, beverage coolers, binoculars, chairs, rafts, swim toys, personal care items such as shampoo and soap, grill, fire extinguisher, anchor, etc.?

The bigger questions, of course, are whether these items were purchased by credit or with a check or by cash? If by cash, what was the source of the cash? Was the cash properly reported on the return? PROVE IT!

Just because you do not have a boat does not mean you will not come under this kind of microscope. Review the elements of economic reality. The forty-seven items (I list only a few) cover every aspect of life. The economic reality investigation is all encompassing.

Still, the IRS does not rely solely upon your statements. "JOB AID 4, Internal/ External Sources of Data," Training Aid 3302-105, offers a host of data sources the agent may pursue such as I outlined in chapter 1. "Internal sources" refer to items found within the IRS's own records, including:

- The tax return
- Prior audits
- Information returns such as Forms W-2 and 1099
- *Currency Transaction Reports*, IRS Form 4789
- *Report of Cash Payments Over $10,000*, IRS Form 8300,
- IRS Collection division information
- Criminal Investigation information, etc.

It comes as no surprise that the IRS would rely upon its own data when building its file. What is shocking is the extent to which it pursues outside sources of information. Such information includes:

Other government agencies, including the U.S. Postal Service, Department of Motor Vehicles, Social Security Administration, OSHA, Department of Agriculture, Department of Social Services, local law enforcement agencies, and so on

Court records showing divorce, marriage, liens, probate, property records, mortgages, bankruptcy, etc.

- Trade associations
- Credit applications and credit reports
- City Directory and Internet information
- Banks, credit unions and savings and loans
- Suppliers

- Insurance providers

- Subscriber information such as is available from Dun and Bradstreet, Robert Morris, LEXIS and of course, the Custom Comprehensive Report I talked about in chapter 3

- Newspaper articles, etc.

Dun and Bradstreet is an information resources company. It gathers financial and other data about businesses then compiles databases. It sells the information to anyone willing to pay for it. Companies purchasing the data use it to determine the health and standing of those they may wish to do business with. Such reports often form the basis for ascertaining potential customers, credit limits, payment requirements, etc. The IRS uses the information as building blocks in the process of constructing the financial dossier.

And the IRS does not stop there. As we have already discussed, the agency regularly contacts third parties who might have information about you. The contacts include:

- Landlords

- Employers

- Employees

- Other business and personal associates

- A former spouse, and

- Friends and neighbors.

If these sources do not prove adequate, the agent may even develop "informants." Training Aid 3302-105, pgs 2-3 (emphasis added). In the routine "investigative" audit, the IRS cultivates among American citizens the practice of spying upon one another.

You are probably saying, "Hey, I'm honest. I don't skim. I keep good records. I have nothing to hide." Keith said the same thing and look what happened to him. The reality is, good records and honesty have little or nothing to do with surviving an investigative tax audit for two reasons.

First, as we learned in chapter 5, the tax code does not define good records. Citizens struggle to comply with recordkeeping requirements they do not understand. This is one reason the majority of disputes with the IRS involve inadequate recordkeeping. Secondly, even if a person does have legally adequate records, the IRS uses bluff and intimidation to get him to part with his money anyway. Good records are always critical to winning a fight with the IRS, but standing alone, they will not do the job.

Second and even worse, the IRS is predisposed to disregard your records. Economic reality manuals discuss at length the process of adding unreported income to a return. The introductory language to one states its purpose is to "get examiners and managers to feel comfortable" using various methods of adding income. "JOB AID 9, Indirect Methods," Training Aid 3302-110, pg 1 (emphasis added).

The premise is simple. When your records "do not clearly reflect income," the IRS has the legal authority to reconstruct it. According to economic reality guidelines, there are four circumstances under which the IRS believes it has the authority to "reconstruct" your income. They are, "when the taxpayers books and records:"

- are non existent,

- are not available,

- are incomplete, and [now get this]

- "*appear to be correct.*" Training Aid 3302-110, pg 7 (emphasis added).

Not only are good records alone insufficient to defeat the intentions of an economic reality audit, they in fact may be the very reason the IRS adds income to your return. It seems that the act of keeping good records (records that actually "appear to be correct") is a sign that you set out to throw an unwary auditor off the trail.

Much of what economic reality entails is pointed at small businesses. Business owners have the tendency to dismiss potential IRS threats with a somewhat cavalier attitude. "Hey, I'll just have my lawyer or accountant deal with this. Sure, it might cost a few bucks, but that has to be better than dealing with them at my place of business, or trying to answer a million questions about how I earn income and where I spend it." Do not be so sure.

The training aids put agents through a "brainstorming session" on how businesses might hide income. The opening question is to agents is: "What would you do to omit income if you owned a bar or restaurant?" "Facilitator Guide," Training Aid 3302-101, pgs 4-3 and 4-4. The manual goes on to list seventeen different ways it might be done. To cope with these potential tactics, agents are instructed to:

- Check with state alcohol authorities to see if you have been investigated for dealing with illegal liquor

- Contact your suppliers to see whether you pay bills in cash

- Contact vending machine owners, including video games and pool tables, to determine how much and in what fashion you are paid

- Observe your party room facilities and activities to determine whether you earn cash income from parties

- Look for payments to subcontractors or unusually large payroll expenses to determine whether you engage in off-premises catering

- Observe your day-to-day operation to determine whether you earn income from betting pools

- Observe your day-to-day operation to determine whether you have cash income from sales of inventory items such as hats, tee shirts, etc.

- Observe what you do with empty containers such as cans and bottles to determine whether you have cash income from recycling or bottle refunds

- Observe your day-to-day operations to see whether you accept credit cards in your business, then check bank records to verify credit card deposits

- Observe your day-to-day operations to determine whether you earn cash income by renting space

- Observe your day-to-day activities to determine whether you earn cash income by cashing checks for customers. Ibid, pgs 4-5 and 4-6.

The training aid goes through a similar exercise for an auto body shop and a vending machine business. In each study, the agent is called upon to "imagine" how such a business might omit income then develop audit techniques to address the answers. Regarding the body shop, the agent is asked to "look for pictures of special jobs" to see whether the owner is earning income from repair or paint jobs for "special customers." Ibid, pg 4-10.

Now then, is it so impossible to believe our fictional agent noticed a photo on the wall in Nancy's home then asked her about it? His training taught him to be aware of how the simple things around him can lead to evidence of unreported income.

This description of business audit techniques should leave you with the clear impression that your books and records, however "good" they may be, are not enough to do the job. Instead, it is clear the agent intends to park himself, perhaps under cover, in your place of business. How else can he "observe" your day-to-day operations to see for himself what is going on? And in fact, for years the IRS did just that in a number of "tip income" investigation projects it operated in casinos in Las Vegas and Atlantic City to determine how much unreported tip income was earned by servers and bar tenders throughout those hotels. I discuss these projects in chapter 10.

The agent also makes it clear to every supplier and relevant state and local government agencies that you are a target of an "investigative" audit. What other message is sent when he asks how you pay bills, when, in what amounts, and for what kind of items, etc.? And how might local government agencies react when contacted by IRS examiners to see whether you have been under investigation for any business related illegal activity? My guess is you may have some explaining to do. That is why you need to be aware of the techniques I discuss in chapter 3 to keep the IRS from contacting third parties.

If you think I am over-reacting, that the IRS does not really intend to park itself at your business to spy on your operation, consider this. After describing the various ways to determine the unreported income of the hypothetical bar owner, the IRS asks the following question of its agents (but before I state the question and answer, I want to make it perfectly clear that the use of emphasis in the statement below is *not* mine. I restate this sentence exactly as it appears in the training aid):

- "Q. Do the results of the brainstorming give you a clue as to where the audit needs to be conducted?

- "A. AT THE TAXPAYER'S PLACE OF BUSINESS!!!" Training Aid 3302-101, pg 4-8.

The last thing our fictional agent did before leaving Keith and Nancy's home was to engage them in a bit of small talk about a photo hanging on the wall. We already know why he was attuned to stumbling upon such a thing, but what made him use that comfortable, seemingly innocuous conversational style to discover the Florida vacation?

The training aid spends a good deal of time teaching agents various "interview techniques." Job Aid 8, "Interview Techniques," Training Aid 3302-109, lists sixty-one different tricks and gimmicks to trip people up during the interview process. These are just a few:

- Put taxpayer at ease
- Read taxpayer's non-verbal language (body language)
- Appear interested
- Be creative and observant
- Be skeptical
- Use perseverance
- Be observant
- Feign ignorance when appropriate (act dumb)
- Use appropriate small talk
- Be an investigator
- Verbally pin down the taxpayer when appropriate
- Maintain composure
- Work to establish rapport
- Maintain an inquisitive mind
- Contain your excitement. Ibid, at pgs JA8-1 through JA8-4.

The facilitator guide adds to this list, explaining that "successful economic reality examiners" are "street smart," assertive and aggressive. They are "risk takers," ask the tough questions, and have sufficient self-confidence to "maintain their position when challenged." Facilitator Guide, Training Aid 3302-101, pg 1-12.

The economic reality audit can best be described as a sneak attack. Agents may present themselves as sheep, but in reality, they are ravenous wolves intent on devouring those unable to cope with these aggressive and deceptive audit tactics. The chapters to follow specifically address how to keep from falling into the traps that ensnared Keith and Nancy.

CHAPTER TEN

UNDERSTANDING THE BURDEN OF PROOF

THE IRS'S ATTACK ON THE INCOME SIDE OF THE
ledger has gone on for years. For example, in 1996, Thomas W. Wilson, then the Acting
Assistant IRS Commissioner for the IRS's Examination function, issued a memorandum
to all compliance officers regarding economic reality audits (referred to in the memo as
"financial status" audits). The memo came in response to a series of complaints lodged
by frustrated tax professionals over the economic reality audit tactics used by the IRS.
The memo extols the virtues of economic reality audits and better than anything I can
say, exposes the danger of proceeding through such an ordeal without understanding
what is taught in this chapter. At page three of the memo Mr. Wilson declared:

> When used appropriately, financial status analysis audit techniques are
> successful. For example, in 27 cases (involving 65 tax years), examiners
> found understatements of taxable income averaging over $180,000. * * *

A key reason for such a staggering increase in taxable income is not that citizens cheat
on their tax returns. Rather, it is because they do not understand their burden of proof.
And to make matters worse, the IRS does not tell the truth about it. You no doubt noticed
that throughout this discourse I repeat the axiom that the burden of proof in tax cases lies
with the citizen. Expect the IRS to beat you over the head with this rule.

But there are important exceptions I have alluded to already. I shall develop a critical
one in this chapter to the end that you will not be blindsided in your audit. We begin by
briefly reviewing the basics.

The Burden of Proof Basics

As we already know, the law requires you to keep records necessary to clearly reflect
income and the payment of deductible expenses. If your records do not reflect income, the
IRS has the authority to "reconstruct" your income to obtain a more accurate accounting.

The burden of proof is squarely on you to show that your deductions are proper. This is
true both in terms of the amount and legality of the claim. If the IRS disallows a deduction,
it need not support its action because the law places a "presumption of correctness" on
the IRS's determination. The legal presumption is akin to the "presumption of innocence"
that cloaks a defendant throughout the course of a criminal prosecution. A criminal
defendant never has to prove he is innocent. The government has to prove he is guilty. On

the other hand, with regard to deductions, to defeat the disallowance of your deductions, *you* must overcome the presumption of correctness with credible evidence sufficient to prove your claim.

The Burden of Proving Income

The rules *are not* the same regarding income. True, the IRS may attack income but it cannot force you into a position of having to prove a negative. We all know that is usually impossible. The agency cannot say, for example, "We believe you had $20,000 worth of income you did not report," then merely rest on the presumption of correctness to see whether you can disprove the claim.

It can, however, "test" your claim of income. In other words, it can probe your records to see whether they were somehow cooked or are otherwise inaccurate. For example, if you report $50,000 of income, the IRS can require you to present a foundation of evidence to support the disclosure. Such proof might be a Form W-2 showing wages coupled with bank statements showing like deposits to your checking account.

Suppose, however, bank records reveal $60,000 of deposits, while the Form W-2 shows $50,000 of wages. In such a circumstance, the law places the burden of proof on you to explain the $10,000 difference. It may have come from a bank loan. It may have come from an inheritance or gift. It may reflect re-deposits from your savings account to your checking account. It may be a non-taxable return of capital from the sale of stocks or bonds. However, if you cannot offer a suitable explanation with some proof, the deposit will be considered income.

By offering proof to support your income claim, you build a foundation of evidence that you can stand on. Having erected a foundation, the IRS—*not you*— bears the burden to prove you earned income not reported on the return. Hence, your foundation of evidence effectively shifts the burden of proof to the IRS, but only where income is concerned. At that point, to support its claim of unreported income, the IRS must present firm, credible evidence that you earned income and did not report it.

Let me illustrate. As we know, the IRS regularly uses Bureau of Labor Statistics to "estimate" personal living expenses. Economic reality literature instructs agents to build a BLS profile of your living expenses even before contacting you. BLS numbers thus become the yardstick by which to measure the supposed accuracy of your disclosures.

Imagine that BLS tables for your area and family size indicate you must spend $30,000 on living expenses. Most personal living expenses do not show up on a tax return simply because they are non-deductible. Suppose further that your tax return shows $25,000 in disposable income. For purposes of this discussion, disposable income is the money available to spend on all your living expenses *after* paying all federal, state and local taxes. The IRS also subtracts the expenses claimed on your tax return, such as mortgage interest, charitable giving, etc. The IRS refers to this exercise as a "cash transactions" or "cash T" analysis. On one side of the ledger the agent lists all known income. The other side is made up of all known expenses, most of which come off the tax return. However, the IRS does not know what your personal living expenses are, therefore it guesses using

BLS tables as the benchmark.

In my example, it appears from the BLS numbers that you spent $5,000 more than you reported. BLS numbers indicate that it requires $30,000 to live your lifestyle. However, you had just $25,000 in disposable income on the basis of your tax return disclosures. In such a case, the agent might claim "you must have earned more than you reported" because the BLS tables show you could not live on what was left after paying all expenses reflected on the return.

Think back to the case of Paul that I discussed in chapter 6. There, the auditor made exactly such a claim. At the end of the audit, she asserted $3,900 in unreported income solely on the basis of her suspicion that he "just couldn't live on what he reported." BLS numbers for the city Paul lived in drove her suspicion.

Parenthetically, we should note that BLS numbers are merely averages, composites of living costs in a given area. By their nature, they cannot possibly reflect reality in your specific case. Averages are, after all, nothing more than a balance between known highs and lows. They are not intended to be an exact measure of what happens in an individual situation.

Can BLS numbers—or for that matter, any IRS reconstruction—place the burden on you to prove you did not earn the extra income suggested by the data? Not if your own income records provide a foundation of evidence upon which to rest your initial claim. Where you have valid and credible evidence to support your income disclosure, *the IRS must prove its case with a foundation of extrinsic evidence.* Without a strong base of evidence to buttress its assertion, the agency cannot rely upon the presumption of correctness. One example of how it might present such evidence is through credible testimony from customers or clients claiming they paid you in cash and that cash was, a) never deposited to your bank account, and b) not reported on your tax return.

Amazingly, economic reality guidelines recognize this limitation in the IRS's power. The instructions are not clear, however, and the IRS colors the issue to its own liking. As a result, agents in the field hold unwitting citizens to an unrealistic and legally unsupported burden of proof. In the manual entitled, "Indirect Methods," Job Aid 9, Training Aid 3302-110, the IRS discusses procedures for reconstructing a citizen's income when his own books do not "clearly reflect income." It points out that the IRS has the right to "test the reliability of the books." Ibid, pg JA9-1. It goes on to note, however, that:

> Before we can challenge the accuracy of the taxpayer's books and records and show by another method of income reconstruction that the records of the taxpayer do not properly reflect income, *we must exercise special care* in testing the validity or accuracy of the taxpayer's records. Ibid, pg JA9-2; emphasis added.

That same manual goes on to point out that the IRS "has a special responsibility of thoroughness" in reconstructing income. Citing the warning issued by the Supreme Court in *Holland v. United States*, 348 U.S. 121 (1954), the IRS observes that it carries the burden to, 1) "prove a likely source of unreported income," 2) negate "all possible non-taxable sources," and 3) check and negate all leads furnished by the citizen "with respect to likely sources of non-taxable receipts." Ibid, pg JA9-4.

The conclusion is plain: the IRS is not free to summarily reject your records and testimony in favor of its own income reconstruction simple because an agent believes that you "could not have lived on that amount of income." The IRS must be able to present some hard evidence to establish that your records are unreliable. In sum, BLS numbers or any other form of reconstruction the IRS may employ are without moment when clear evidence to back them up is lacking.

How the Courts Rule

There are two reasons the IRS ignores these facts. The first is people do not understand the rules. Because of that, they are bluffed or intimidated into believing they carry the burden to prove a negative fact and cannot meet the challenge. Secondly, the burden of proof rules vis-à-vis income *are not delineated in the Internal Revenue Code!* As hard as that is to imagine, it is nevertheless true. For that reason, we cannot expect poorly trained revenue agents motivated simply to "get the money" to turn up rules of law crafted to favor the citizen. Expect agents to merely regurgitate the "presumption of correctness" doctrine as though it is the alpha and the omega.

For a true grasp of these rules, we must examine court authority on the matter.

Case Study No. One — *Portillo v. Commissioner*, 932 F.2d 1128 (5th Cir. 1991).

Ramon Portillo was a self-employed painter from El Paso. He contracted with builders to paint residential and commercial projects. General contractors paid him on a weekly basis so he could pay his crews doing the work. Each payment was carefully recorded in his ledger at the time he received a check. As such, his records were contemporaneous in nature.

Ramon did not have a bank account. Consequently, after recording a check in his ledger, he cashed it. He used the cash to pay employees and purchase supplies. Ramon maintained all his payroll records in a separate ledger.

At the end of each year, Ramon used Forms 1099 issued by the various contractors to confirm the gross receipts shown in his ledger. He then handed the ledgers to a paid preparer to complete his income and employment tax returns. In 1984, however, the preparer did not have a 1099 from a particular contractor because it was not filed on time. Thus, the preparer determined gross receipts paid by that contractor strictly by reference to Ramon's own ledger.

In mid 1985, that contractor filed a Form 1099 with the IRS. In 1987, Ramon was audited for tax year 1984. When the agent reviewed the form and crosschecked it with Ramon's tax return, he discovered an important discrepancy. Checks paid to and cashed by Ramon totaled $13,925. However, the contractor's Form 1099 said he paid Ramon $35,305, a difference of $21,380.

Ramon denied receiving any more money from the contractor than his own records reflected. The agent questioned the contractor, asking him to provide records of his payments. The contractor was able to produce checks showing payments of $13,925, exactly as Ramon claimed. The contractor claimed the difference was due to cash payments, but had no evidence to verify his claim.

Despite this, the agent asserted that Ramon received $21,380 in unreported income. The agent prepared his report accordingly and presented it to an IRS reviewer. The reviewer was concerned about the discrepancy in the contractor's statements. The reviewer explained that there were "several ways" to "follow up," to check if Ramon indeed received cash. The auditor refused to follow up at all, saying, "It was Portillo's burden to prove that he did not get the payments." The auditor concluded that the Form 1099 was "presumed correct" and shrugged off the reviewer's concerns. The final audit report held Ramon responsible for tax, penalties and interest on the alleged unreported income.

Ramon appealed. On appeal, he testified he did not receive $35,000 from the contractor in question. He presented his ledgers showing what he actually received. This established the factual premise that the Form 1099 was false. In addition, the contractor produced his records showing payments of just $13,925. No proof existed for anything else.

Using the burden of proof rules presented above, Ramon challenged the IRS's decision. Recall that the burden of proof lies with the IRS to establish a foundation of evidence upon which the determination of unreported income can securely rest. Without such a foundation, the courts have universally held such a determination is "naked" and does not enjoy the presumption of correctness. "Several courts, including this one," reads the decision in Ramon's favor, "have noted that a court need not give effect to the presumption of correctness in a case involving unreported income if the Commissioner cannot present some predicate evidence supporting its determination."

The court laid a clear, affirmative duty at the feet of the IRS. The agency must support its claim with hard evidence. The court demanded that the IRS "engage in one final foray for truth in order to provide some indicia that the taxpayer received unreported income." In the court's mind, the "final foray for truth" translates to the responsibility to investigate the facts and determine whether indeed the citizen received the income he is accused of earning.

Here, the IRS found no records to prove anything beyond what Ramon reported. That should have told the agency that the contractor either made an error or deliberately falsified the 1099 (something that happens too often, and which I address later in this chapter). Apparently, these alternative conclusions never entered the auditor's mind. Then again, the alternative conclusions would have made the agency no money. Consequently, the IRS charged ahead, lacking any credible evidence. It made no effort to engage in "the final foray for truth" required to support its claim. In the final analysis, Ramon was relieved of the impossible duty of having to prove a negative.

The *Portillo* case is a seminal decision on taxpayers' rights and protection from the kind of over-zealous and uninformed auditor that Ramon faced. The decision led to Congress actually changing the law on the IRS's burden of proof when a citizen challenges the accuracy of an information return. In that situation, the IRS now has a clear statutory responsibly to engage in the "final foray for truth" that the *Portillo* court described. I discuss that process later in this chapter.

Case Study No. Two — *Krause v. Commissioner*, T.C. Memo 1992-270 (1992).

One example of how the IRS uses statistics to make otherwise naked assertions of unreported income occurred in Atlantic City during 1984 and 1985. Agents of the IRS's Criminal Investigation function conducted surveillance of all local gaming casinos. The Atlantic City Tip Project was specifically designed to uncover tip income earned by casino employees. The project focused on servers, bartenders and gaming dealers.

After completing the surveillance, the IRS audited a targeted group of employees. On the average, the IRS claimed the employees earned tip income of about 13 percent of their reported wage income. If at least that amount was not reported on the employee's tax return, the IRS added it to the employee's income.

In the Atlantic City project, teams of two IRS agents observed cocktail servers for periods of thirty minutes at a time. The agents went to locations chosen at random by computer and observed the tips given to a server. The agents were instructed to make certain conservative assumptions. For example, if they could not clearly see the denomination of a bill, they were to assume it was a dollar. If they could not clearly see a coin, they were to assume it was a quarter.

During 1984 and 1985, there were sixty-three half-hour periods of surveillance conducted at each of the ten gaming casinos in Atlantic City at the time. In 1987 and 1988, forty-two half-hour spying sessions took place at each of twelve casinos. IRS statisticians in turn developed a formula said to represent average tip income earned by employees in those casinos. The figures varied according to work shift. The evening shift, for example, was said to earn more tips per hour than the day shift.

In case after case, the IRS hit casino employees with tax on unreported tip income based solely on the statistical analysis. The Tax Court approved the IRS's reconstructions because each of the citizens hit lacked any evidence to support their own claims regarding tip income.

Judy was a bartender at the Sands hotel. She was swept up in the dragnet and ended up in Tax Court for 1985. She lost. The Court found that what few records she bothered to keep did not "clearly reflect" tip income. It approved the IRS's reconstruction, which alleged that she earned tips equal to $6.77 per hour on the strength of the surveillance evidence.

Judy learned a valuable lesson from her bitter experience. After the audit, she began keeping contemporaneous, detailed records of her tips using a log. She carried a small notebook to work with her every day. In it, she entered the amount of tips earned that day, either immediately after work or when she arrived home the same evening. At the end of each pay period, she reported her total tips to her employer. The tip income was then included on her weekly pay stub and the appropriate income and social security tax was withheld. On her Form W-2, those tips were in turn reported to the IRS.

When the IRS took another crack at Judy for a later tax yea, she was ready. Judy claimed $6,473 in tip income in a subsequent year. According to IRS statistics, she should have claimed $12,324. The IRS asserted unreported income of $5,852. While this is precisely the problem she faced earlier, this time she had a solid foundation of evidence to support her claim, and in turn, discredit the IRS's assertion.

At trial, Judy presented her contemporaneous log. She testified about her habit of carrying the log with her to work each day and recording her tips. She also explained that she made a report to her employer so the tips were included in Form W-2. This way, she provided for both income and social security tax withholding. The IRS, on the other hand, argued that their statistical analysis showed Judy "must have" earned $12,300. The agency hung its case solely on the analysis. It tried to box her into the cage of having to prove a negative.

However carefully the IRS may have observed the casino employees, and however scientific its analysis may have been, it does not change the fact the IRS did nothing more than guess at Judy's tips. They had no way to know exactly what her tips were.

This time around, the Tax Court agreed with Judy. It specifically found that the IRS's otherwise valid statistics "do not reflect (Judy's) income as accurately as her own daily records." By presenting the foundation of evidence to establish the validity of her income claim, the burden shifted to the IRS to present clear evidence to contradict it. The evidence of its spying operation was not enough to outweigh Judy's documentation.

Case Study No. Three - *Senter v. Commissioner*, T.C. Memo 1995-311 (1995).

The IRS claimed Chuck failed to file tax returns for years 1987-1990. An auditor mailed him a letter saying that because there was no record of his filing, he should either mail copies of the returns or appear at an appointed date to allow the agent to review his records. The agent was going to determine whether Chuck was required to file, and if so, prepare the returns for him.

Chuck responded by saying he could not provide any information without counsel and because he could not afford a lawyer, he would not attend the meeting. After another failed attempt to get records, the IRS mailed a Notice of Deficiency claiming tax liabilities for all the years. It determined his income and tax using the Consumer Price Index (CPI) for each of the years. Just as I illustrate in chapter 5, the IRS took the income from Chuck's last return and applied the CPI to each of the succeeding years to project his income.

Chuck petitioned the Tax Court contesting the proposed deficiency. During the proceeding, he made a bold move—one that I do not recommend. He presented *no evidence* whatsoever concerning the IRS's claim. Rather, he sat back and challenged the IRS to prove he received any income. Naturally, the agency could do no such thing.

Instead, the IRS hauled out the argument that Chuck had the burden of proof. It asserted that its determination enjoyed the "presumption of correctness." The Tax Court, fresh from the teachings of the *Portillo* case, refused to countenance the argument. Acknowledging the general rule that a citizen bears the burden of proof and the IRS's determination is presumed correct, the court noted:

> However, an exception to this general rule is recognized by several courts of appeals for situations where the Commissioner determines that the taxpayer received income that was not reported on the taxpayer's return. The rationale for this exception is based on the recognized difficulty that the taxpayer

bears in proving the non-receipt of income. Citing *Portillo*, supra, *Sealy Power, Ltd. v. Commissioner*, 46 F.3d 382 (5ᵗʰ Cir. 1995), and *Anastasato v. Commissioner*, 749 F.2d 884 (3ʳᵈ Cir. 1986).

In *Portillo*, you will recall, the IRS hung its hat on an erroneous Form 1099. The Fifth Circuit said that was not good enough. In the *Senter* case, the IRS "provided no predicate EVIDENCE" whatsoever to support its conclusion that Chuck earned any income during those years (emphasis in original). The court therefore easily concluded the IRS's determination was "arbitrary and erroneous" and struck it down.

What Chuck did in presenting no records was extremely risky. The approach taken by Judy and Ramon is more advisable. It is better to establish *your* foundation of evidence to shift the burden to the IRS. This is done with affirmative proof that your income declaration is correct. Having done that, it is unquestionable that the IRS has the burden to prove its claims of unreported income. And the sooner you provide this proof, the better chance you have resolving the matter favorably *before* the matter ends up in Tax Court.

Provided you are not an outright tax cheat who indeed failed to report income, the IRS will likely have no success attempting to reconstruct your income. Furthermore, if it ignores these rules (which through arrogance it often does), it runs a growing risk. For example, Ramon was able to extract an award against the IRS for the fees and costs he incurred fighting its determination. *Portillo v. Commissioner*, 988 F.2d 27, (5ᵗʰ Cir. 1993). I discuss the procedures for recovering fees and costs in chapter 18.

Further Case Studies. My analysis of the burden of proof is not novel. The Supreme Court addressed this topic in 1935, in the case of *Helvering v. Taylor*, 293 U.S. 507 (1935). However, as the IRS grows more brazen with its approach to reconstructing income, there are more cases slamming the door on those efforts. Another case is that of *Carson v. Commissioner*, 560 F.2d 693 (5ᵗʰ Cir. 1977), in which the court quite ceremoniously said, "The tax collector's presumption of correctness has a Herculean muscularity of Goliath-like reach, but we strike at the Achilles' heel when we find no muscles, no tendons, no ligaments of fact."

How to Dispute an Erroneous Information Return

Erroneous information returns are the source of a great many problems for citizens. Approximately two billion information returns are filed every year (and growing) and they crosschecked with more than 146 million individual tax returns. We know from our earlier discussion that there are millions of errors made in preparing, filing and processing this mountain of data. When errors arise, the IRS smugly asserts the "presumption of correctness" and errantly presses the citizen to attempt to prove a negative.

However, the Taxpayers' Bill of Rights Act 2 included a provision pointed specifically at addressing erroneous information returns. The provision, a direct response to the *Portillo* case, puts a clear burden on the IRS to make a "reasonable investigation" into the facts when a citizen disputes an information return. I refer to code section 6201(d), which reads as follows:

In any court proceeding, if a taxpayer asserts a reasonable dispute with respect to any item of income reported on an information return filed with the Secretary. . .by a third party and the taxpayer has fully cooperated with the Secretary (including providing, within a reasonable period of time, access to and inspection of all witnesses, information, and documents within the control of the taxpayer as reasonably requested by the Secretary), the Secretary shall have the burden of producing reasonable and probative information concerning such deficiency in addition to such information return.

Under this provision, the IRS may no longer blindly rely on the presumption of correctness in disputes over the accuracy of an information return. Instead, as long as the citizen "cooperates" with the IRS by providing information, documents and access to relevant witnesses, the IRS has a burden to produce "reasonable and probative information" to support its claim. In a word, the agency has to carry the ball to support its claim that you had unreported income. It simply cannot force you to prove a negative.

The key to invoking the protections of section 6201(d) is that you must advance a very specific challenge to any information return you claim is erroneous. A mere "vague contention" as to the form's accuracy will not suffice. See: *Sanders v. Commissioner*, T.C. Memo. 2010-279 (2010). So this begs the question, how does one challenge an information return believed to be incorrect? The answer involves a three-step process, which is just about exactly what Ramon Portillo did in his case. Here are the required steps.

1. Write the company with your specific complaint. The minute you receive an information return you believe is incorrect for any reason, you must voice your complaint in writing to the company that issued it. Be very specific and detailed. While it is not necessary to prove a negative, you must be forthright about any affirmative facts. For example, as in the *Portillo* case, if the amount of income received was X not Y, say so clearly. If you dispute any of the underlying facts regarding the income, say so clearly. Avoid vague or general assertions or mere denials that lack specificity.

Expressly insist that the company either issue a correct form or withdraw it entirely. Give the company a deadline by which to act. Since your tax return generally is due by April 15 of the year following the year in question, the deadline you suggest should give you enough time to accurately prepare your return. Send your letter by certified mail and be sure to keep a signed copy of the letter along with the certified mailing documents, including proof of delivery.

2. If the company fails to respond or does not satisfy your objection, you need to file your tax return and handle the errant information return in the tax return itself. Do this by including Form 8275, *Disclosure Statement,* with your tax return when you file it. The *Disclosure Statement* is a form that allows you to provide information with the tax return that answers any questions raised in the tax return. I discuss this form in more detail in chapter 19.

On the Disclosure Statement, provide the IRS with an explanation of why you believe the information return is incorrect and therefore the amount stated is not included (in whole or in part) as income on your tax return. Give the details of the steps you took to get the company to correct the form and provide copies of your letter to the company along with the certified mailing documents. This will put the IRS on notice as to your dispute and set you up for the protections of section 6201(d), if necessary.

3. Finally, you have to "cooperate" with the IRS. Cooperation means providing all information and documentation relevant to the dispute and giving the IRS the names and contact information of any person who has information that might shed light on the dispute. This has to be done "within a reasonable period of time." Code section 6201(d). In my mind, that means the sooner you provide the information, either proactively or in response to an IRS request, the better off you are.

Assuming you follow these steps and you can demonstrate some "reasonable basis" for disputing the information return, the IRS will have the affirmative duty to produce evidence to support the accuracy of the information return. That means the IRS will have to mine documents and information from the company in question and present a witness to support its claim. What do you suppose the chances are that the IRS will be able to produce such evidence?

Deliberately False Information Returns

A phenomenon that has arisen of the over years as a result of ubiquitous information reporting laws is the act of filing deliberately false information returns as a means of retaliating against another person. I have seen such returns filed by disgruntled workers in contract disputes, by former business partners—even scorned ex-spouses. Often people file false information returns just to trump up deductions for their own business tax returns. I suspect this is what happened in the *Portillo* case. But because there are no restrictions or limitations on who can file an information return and when, and because the IRS generally undertakes no effort whatsoever to determine the correctness of such forms unless there is a dispute, the agency merely processes the form and uses it in the administration of the tax laws.

Due to the dangers associated with false information returns, code section 7434 provides a remedy to persons injured by a deliberately false information return. The law provides:

> If any person willfully files a fraudulent information return with respect to payments purported to be made to any other person, such other person may bring a civil action for damages against the person so filing such return. Code section 7434(a).

If you have cause to believe that a person deliberately filed a false information return on you, you must immediately demand that such person withdraw the form. Do this in writing by certified mail as I discussed above. In your letter to the culprit, point out his potential liability for damages under code section 7434. The person who files a false form is liable for damages of either $5,000 or the actual amount of damages suffered by the victim as a result of the false form, whichever amount is greater, *including* all costs attributable to resolving the problems caused by the false form. Moreover, the victim can recover reasonable attorney's fees incurred in bringing the lawsuit. Code section 7434(b).

A person files a false information return "willfully" under section 7434 if he did so as part of a "voluntary, intentional violation of a legal duty." That is to say, the act was not a mistake or due to inadvertence, or otherwise attributable to some good faith explanation. See: *Vandenheede v. Vecchio*, 541 F. App'x 577, 580 (6th Cir. 2013).

An information return is not "false" merely because it is inaccurate. Millions of inaccurate returns are filed annually due to any number of good faith mistakes. To be false, the return must not only be inaccurate but the person filing the form must have had no "good faith basis for believing" that the form was correct when he filed it. See: *Shiner v. Turnoy*, Docket No. 1:13-cv-05867, July 11, 2014 (U.S. District Court, ND Ill).

By invoking code section 7434 in your letter demanding the withdrawal of the form, you not only strengthen your position for purposes of code section 6201(d), you can set yourself up to recover the damages you suffer as a result of the deliberately false form.

CHAPTER ELEVEN

HOW TO NEUTRALIZE THE ECONOMIC REALITY AUDIT

Recognizing an Economic Reality Audit

KEITH AND NANCY NEVER KNEW WHAT HIT THEM.
They spent sleepless nights gathering records to show purchases of toothpaste and plastic water toys before they had any idea *why* the agent asked for such extraneous information. They never pressed the obvious question, "What can that information possibly have to do with our tax liability?" When they were told that their many hours of work were not sufficient and that they had to go back for even more documents, Keith sheepishly responded by simply saying "sure." The agent's every request was met with nothing more than a cross look.

In the end, every bit of data was somehow used against them. This is entirely consistent with the IRS's teaching to its agents. For example, in "JOB AID 9, Indirect Methods," the manual states, "The more information an examiner can develop, the larger the understatement [of tax]. The development of the personal living expenses can be extremely critical in this process." Training Aid 3302-110, pg 1. It is for this reason alone that the IRS might ask for documents regarding every purchase imaginable, *including* the kitchen sink. The demand to disclose personal living expenses is a key characteristic that betrays the identity of an economic reality audit.

Three items typically portend an economic reality audit. The first we already addressed. It is IRS Form 4822, *Statement of Annual Personal and Family Living Expenses,* discussed in chapter 9. The second is the Information Document Request (IDR), which I discussed in chapter 7. But understand that nearly every audit involves one or more IDRs at some point. The IDR is the most common tool the IRS uses to request data. However, in an economic reality audit, the IDR is *very broad* and effectively all-inclusive as to personal data. By contrast, an IDR in a non-economic reality matter addresses documents relating to one or more deductions claimed in a tax return or very specific items of income, such as a stock sale. Review my discussion in chapter 7 on how the IRS uses IDRs.

Examples of the kind of documents and information the IRS might request in an IDR are discussed in the IRS's analysis of a hypothetical audit. The list includes:

1. All books and records concerning income and expenses, including bank statements, canceled checks and deposit slips,

2. Records of loans obtained, including credit applications and financial statements,

3. Records of loans paid off,

4. Records of purchases of assets, including home, cars, boats, motorcycles, etc.,

5. Records of all non-taxable income received, including gifts, inheritances, loans from friends, family or other third parties,

6. Records concerning money not kept in a bank,

7. Records of business assets purchased,

8. Records of all business expenses, including equipment and inventory, and

9. All accountant's work papers used to prepare the tax return, including deprecation schedules.

Notice that much of the requested information has nothing to do with claims that might be found in a tax return. Item 1, for example, seeks "all books and records" relative to income "and expenses." It is not limited to documents relative to deductible expenses. Rather, it asks for data on "all expenses."

Item 4 seeks information about the purchase of personal assets, such as "automobiles, boats, or motorcycles." This paragraph points out how the IRS intends to sneak up on people. In the hypothetical case portrayed in the IRS's training material, a citizen purchased a boat using cash. The IRS learned of the purchase through Form 8300, *Report of Cash Payments Over $10,000.* This form must be filed by any business that receives payment in excess of $10,000 in cash or cash equivalent. The latter includes cashiers checks, money orders, foreign currency and bank drafts.

The IRS's description of its sample IDR states:

> Notice how the IDR is prepared asking for information about the boat. Because a Form 8300 has been filed indicating an *unusual method of payment for a businessperson*, the question about the boat is included with questions about an automobile and motorcycle. The IDR *does not indicate* the requester knows about a boat purchased with cash or cash equivalent. That information may be of the type that if the taxpayer knew you were aware of the transaction, *they may be unwilling to talk to you.* This type of transaction, that which *may produce an unwanted action* on the part of the taxpayer, could be referred to as *volatile information.* Facilitator Guide, Training Aid 3302-101, pg AK1-8; emphasis added.

The various presumptions implicit in this statement indicate the IRS's predisposition in audit situations. First, the agency presumes legitimate business people do not pay cash for personal assets, as though cash is used only by criminals or in some criminal context. Next, the IRS assumes it must hide the fact that it knows about the purchase; otherwise a person may lie or conceal the truth. That alone seems curious because the citizen had to provide information to the seller to allow him to complete Form 8300 in the first place.

Why would any reasonable person believe the IRS does *not know* about a transaction that was clearly and expressly reported to the IRS? Third, the IRS assumes citizens will lie or refuse to talk about the boat when asked. As a result, the IRS feels the need to orchestrate a sneak attack.

The third badge of an economic reality audit is the type of questions an auditor may ask during the audit. Certain questions indicate the direction the agent is moving. Please think back to the probing personal questions asked of Keith and Nancy. They included, among other things, 1) the use of their boat, 2) the improvements made to their home, and 3) how they spent their family vacation. Exploring these and other highly personal areas of your life usually indicates an attempt by the IRS to illustrate a pattern of spending not justifiable by your reported income.

The auditor may ask, "How much cash did you have on hand on January 1, 2013?" The typical response is, "Well, I don't know. Not very much I guess." Believing it is best to keep the amount low, when pushed for an answer, a person may say something like, "Just a few hundred dollars, I suppose."

The purpose of that question—which the auditor will *never tell you*—is to prevent you from later claiming that you had a "cash hoard" available to fund any cash purchases. A cash hoard is a stash of money that generally does not appear in a bank account. The citizen claims it was earned and saved over the years. By asking you how much cash you had on hand at the beginning of the year, and anticipating a small amount in response, you are later foreclosed from defending an unreported income claim by saying, "We saved cash over a long period of time then used it to buy our boat."

Diffusing the Economic Reality Audit

Now that you know you are in the midst of an economic reality audit, let us address specific techniques for controlling it. To defuse an economic reality audit—and by extension any other audit—and keep from being victimized as Keith and Nancy were, you must understand the legal limits of your responsibility. You have the burden to prove your tax return is correct. I have said this time and again. Here is one area where that truth becomes critical. You *do not* have the responsibility either to keep or produce records if they have no bearing upon the correctness of your return. Much of what is asked for in connection with the income probe has *nothing whatsoever* to do with the return.

In a 1996 memo to all IRS compliance officers, then Acting Assistant Commissioner for Examination Thomas Wilson described the circumstances under which the economic reality audit is *not* appropriate. Page two of the memo reads:

> For the average wage earner, the IRS is able to verify virtually all income and most deductions by matching information returns (Forms W-2 and 1099) with the individual income tax return. Thus, these audit techniques are generally not appropriate in an examination of a wage earner unless there is an indication of income not subject to information reporting.

Turning his attention to the business owner, the memo goes on to state:

> However, examiners are not to assume that an audit of a business or self-employed taxpayer automatically means that there is unreported income and therefore use in-depth income probes on every audit. Examiners must evaluate the facts and circumstances of each case and apply judgment. It is not an efficient use of resources to have examiners perform in-depth income probes and ask questions about personal assets and personal expenditures when there is no reasonable indication of unreported income. *The more in-depth probes should only be employed when there is a reasonable indication of unreported income.* (Emphasis added.)

Prior to that, Mr. L.E. Carlow, at the time the sitting Assistant Commissioner for Examination, issued a memo of his own. It came in direct response to my many radio appearances during which I blasted economic reality audits for all the reasons discussed thus far. The memo is dated August 8, 1995, and went to all Regional Chief Compliance Officers. In it, Mr. Carlow states:

> I want to emphasize that examiners must assess the facts and apply sound judgment in determining the scope [of an audit] on a case-by-case basis. We have been alerted to instances where in-depth initial interviews were routinely used to explore a taxpayer's financial situation when there was not (sic) indication of such a need. This may not be appropriate.

While these statements are not the world's clearest and most binding guidance on the matter, they constitute guidance nonetheless. You can be sure if I had not been on the radio talking about these audits there would be no guidance whatsoever.

The issue of economic reality audits drew a lot of attention during the Senate Finance Committee hearings into IRS abuse. The IRS Restructuring Commission later addressed the topic head-on. My testimony to the Finance Committee discussed how overzealous agents used the weapon against honest citizens, turning routine civil audits into what amounted to a full-scale criminal investigation. What grew from my testimony to the Senate Finance Committee and my work with the Restructuring Commission's investigation into IRS abuse is code section 7602(e), added by the IRS Restructuring and Reform Act of 1998. The code section reads:

> The Secretary shall not use financial status or economic reality examination techniques to determine the existence of unreported income of any taxpayer unless the Secretary has a *reasonable indication* that there is a likelihood of such unreported income. (Emphasis added.)

This statute gives real teeth to the policy statements of Wilson and Carlow. Thus, the tax code itself provides the legal authority needed to limit economic reality audits. This authority has been on the books for over twenty years yet the IRS simply ignores it and most citizens (including too many tax pros) do not know it even exists. Therefore, you must understand the IRS's legal limitation under the law and you must assert that limitation when presented with an audit that is dripping with unfounded economic reality characteristics.

As you can see, agents simply *are not* authorized to use these sweeping techniques in every case. In fact, they are to use them only where there is a "reasonable indication" of unreported income. See chapter 5 for my discussion of how the IRS attacks one's reported income for examples of what such indications may be. Without something concrete to suggest you might be hiding income, there is no reason you should be subjected to the kind of treatment meted out to Keith and Nancy.

In combination with the burden of proof teachings presented in chapter 10, code section 7602(e) provides the formula needed to defuse a full-scale economic reality probe. You must do two things to effectively limit such an attack. I address them here.

Step One: Provide affirmative proof of income. The burden of proof law teaches that if you establish a foundation of evidence upon which to support your claimed income, the IRS cannot put you into the impossible position of having to prove a negative. Code section 7602(e) states that economic reality audits are improper where there is no indication of unreported income. This is especially true in the case of W-2 wage earners whose income is reported by their employers.

Therefore, step one is to provide affirmative proof that your income is correctly reported on the return. I recommend this be done with an affidavit, accompanied by bank records, income logs and other materials that tend to confirm your claim. Let us consider the example of a typical W-2 wage earner.

A wage earner receives Form W-2 showing all the wages paid by his employer. However, the W-2 does not address what others might have paid the individual, or what he might have earned through part time, self-employment activities. Therefore, a wage earner must address those potential questions head on. The affidavit should state that the Form W-2 (or Forms W-2, if you had more than one wage job) represents "all income earned" during the year in question. It should also expressly state that "there was no other source of income" beyond that shown on the W-2.

Suppose the W-2 shows $40,000 in wages and there was no other source of income. Suppose all payroll checks were deposited to a single bank account. In that case, the account statements should reflect deposits about equal to the wages. The affidavit should clearly describe these facts. You should also provide copies of the account statements and illustrate the fact that bank deposits match the wages paid.

Now let us suppose there are substantial differences in bank deposits versus the reported wages. Those differences *must be explained* in the first instance. Do not wait to see if the auditor "discovers" them. Assume he will and explain them on the front end. This eliminates the potential negative inference the agent might otherwise draw and will likely keep the matter from mutating into a full-scale lifestyle audit.

Let me illustrate this. Suppose your bank account shows $50,000 in deposits but the W-2 shows $40,000 in wages. You received $5,000 from Uncle Ed's estate when he died and borrowed $5,000 from your sister to pay off credit card debt. On the face of the bank statements reflecting the deposits of this money, use a marker to highlight the deposits. In your affidavit, specifically refer to the deposits and explain why they do not constitute taxable income. In this example, inheritances are not taxed and loan proceeds are not considered income.

In the event a deposit is taxable, you should point to the line on the tax return where the deposit is claimed as income. Suppose the $10,000 came from a stock sale. Specifically describe in your affidavit what was sold and point out that the profit was reported on Schedule D, *Capital Gains and Losses*. In turn, provide records to support the facts surrounding the purchase and sale of the stock.

This is important because the taxable profit from a stock sale is likely quite different from the amount of the sales proceeds that make up the deposit. If you sell 1,000 shares of the ABC Company for $5 per share, the total proceeds of the sale are $5,000 and the amount deposited to the bank will likewise be $5,000. However, if you bought the stock for $4.75 per share, the taxable profit is just $250.

Self-employed persons use a variation of the same process. Many self-employed persons operate as independent contractors. As such, they receive Forms 1099 from the persons or companies for whom they perform services. Describe in your affidavit for whom you worked and expressly declare that all income is shown on the 1099s provided by those companies. You should use your own ledgers to confirm the 1099 amounts the way Ramon did as illustrated in chapter 10. In turn, reconcile your ledgers and the 1099s with your own bank statements. When these three items substantially match the income reported, you have successfully established a firm foundation of evidence to support your claimed income.

The income of many self-employed people is not reported on 1099s. Those with retail operations and those who perform services for the public (as opposed to business-to-business services) are prime examples. They sell goods and services to the public and in most cases, no reporting requirements attach to those transactions. Because of that, self-employed people are more susceptible to being dragged into the economic reality audit because they are less able to confirm their income exclusively through third-party statements.

If you are such a person, it is fundamentally important to have a good income log or journal. The log must reflect all payments to you and the nature of the payments. In some cases, small business people use only their business checking account as an income log. Deposits show up on the bank statement each month, thus making a clear record of income. This is fine as long as all income was in fact deposited to the account. Therefore, it is critical that your affidavit expressly state that "all income was deposited to the account" and therefore "bank statements reflect 100 percent of the income earned."

Just as we did with the W-2 wage earner, substantial differences between bank deposits or log entries versus income reported on the return must be identified, pointed out and *explained*. Otherwise, discrepancies found by the auditor will likely be looked upon in a more negative light. By pointing them out and explaining the differences, you display honesty and thoroughness.

I strongly recommend that both wage earners and self-employed persons develop and use income logs. This is the best way to establish the foundation of evidence needed to support your income claim. My book *How to Double Your Tax Refund* has a chapter showing exactly how to do it.

Step Two: Establish sound reporting and return preparation techniques. Once you have clearly established the amount and source of your income, you must illustrate that you exercise strong, consistent controls over your recordkeeping to show that your records are reliable. In reviewing the language of the two memos above and code section 7602(e), we find that *the lack* of hard evidence of unreported income, combined *with affirmative evidence* of strong controls over the recordkeeping and reporting processes add up to a tax return *not subject* to economic reality audit techniques.

To establish that you exercise controls leading to accurate records, describe in an affidavit exactly how you record your income. For wage earners, this process is very simple. You might simply record the income figures from your check stubs along with indicating any deductions for taxes and other withholding, such as union dues, etc.

Next, show that all checks are deposited to your bank account. In that case, the bank statements therefore "show 100 percent of the wage income earned." You might include a statement in your affidavit declaring words to the effect of: "Each paycheck earned during the year was deposited to the bank account." This establishes the fact that your income logs and bank statements accurately reflect income. If you work more than one job, have an income log for each job. Paychecks from each job should be recorded in their respective logs before being deposited to your bank account.

Lastly, the affidavit must declare that "the income reported on the return was determined on the basis" of these records. If you prepare your own return, it is a simple matter of explaining how you took the income numbers from your W-2 and income logs and entered them on the tax return (or in return preparation software) in the appropriate place. If you employed a tax pro, specifically declare that you provided the preparer with the W-2 and income logs so the pro could "accurately report all income."

By following this example, you illustrate that your W-2 is tied directly to your paychecks, which in turn are tied to the income log, which is then finally tied to bank account deposits. This creates a chain of evidence plainly showing strong controls over the accounting process and in turn, buttressing the reliability of your records.

The process for self-employed persons is the same. Whether we are talking about Forms 1099 or W-2, the information returns must be tied to your own income logs and bank deposits as shown above.

In cases where there are no 1099s, you must by necessity concentrate on your income logs. The IRS's question in such a case is, "How do we know all income is recorded in the log?" This is where testimony about your recordkeeping practices is essential.

Describe the process by which you record income. Explain, for example, that when paid by a customer or client, the payment is "always recorded in an income log." Point out that such payments are recorded "whether by cash or check." This establishes the fact that no cash is left "off the books." You might even point to bank records showing cash deposits to the account.

Next, explain that deposits are made periodically to the bank and bank deposits are reconciled with your log entries. In this way, you illustrate control over the receipt of income and the performance of practices that ensure the completeness of your income logs and bank statements.

The ultimate task is to show consistency between your income logs, bank statements and tax return declarations. Just as I explained regarding W-2 wage earners, self-employed persons must make this connection. If you prepared your own return, simply declare that your "income logs and bank statements provide the basis of the income claimed." If you used a tax pro, state that he was provided with the income logs and bank statements to enable him to correctly report your income.

Take the initiative with regard to these two steps if the IRS gives the slightest indication of questioning your income. Such an indication is plain if you receive a Form 4822 or the IDR betrays curiosity over your earnings. Do not wait until the agent is asking you to document the number of haircuts you get each year. By following these two steps, you will likely avoid all of that.

The specific process of drafting affidavits is presented in my book, *The IRS Problem Solver*.

Avoid the Personal Living Expense Statement

Dale Carnegie is famous for his advice on building professional relationships, salesmanship, public speaking, etc. His advice about how to win an argument is profound. He says simply, "Do not get into one."

This is precisely how to avoid the pitfalls of the Personal Living Expense (PLE) statement, whether on Form 4822 or in any other manner. Please note that the IRS itself recognizes it does not have the legal authority to force you to complete such a statement. In the Facilitator Guide, the IRS states that "no specific authority exists to require the taxpayer to fill out a PLE." Training Aid 3302-101, at pg 3-11.

Apart from the fact that there is no legal obligation to complete a PLE or to answer a myriad of questions about your toilet paper consumption, such information is simply unreliable. Keep in mind that all of the information sought, with few exceptions, is for items that are not legally tax deductible. As a result, you have no legal obligation to keep records of such items and very few people do keep such records. In fact, why would anyone in his right mind keep track of expenditures for "personal care items" such as toothpaste and haircuts?

As a result, it is impossible to accurately state how much money you spend on these items. Therefore, the process of completing the PLE is reduced to mere guessing. To complicate matters, remember that any current audit is always for a *prior tax year*. For example, if an audit is being conducted *during* 2014, the audit is probably examining *tax year* 2011 or 2012. That means you are guessing *in 2014* at what you might have spent on haircuts and soda pop two or three years earlier. Please tell me how that can be done in a way that gets one even remotely close to reality.

In short, asking you to guess at what you spent on these items is no more reliable than using BLS tables to find a number. However, what is reliable are hard records showing hard numbers. In nearly every case I have seen, any person attempting to scale the PLE precipice ends up with high estimates. The IRS then uses the taxpayer's *own statements* against him to support a claim of unreported income.

So while you should not get caught in the quagmire of the PLE, you must establish your foundation of evidence with hard records that show hard numbers. This is done using an affidavit and the two-step process outlined above.

Should the agent press the issue of the PLE, ask the question, "It is important to establish my income using reliable records, isn't it?" What do you suppose his response will be? Then ask, "Shouldn't the information I provide *accurately* reflect *all* my income?" Guess at his answer. Finally, point out that, "The PLE is unreliable because it cannot be based upon actual records. I do not keep records of what I cannot claim as a tax deduction. However, I have accurate and *reliable* records of income that I already provided and which do show that my return is correct. I opt to stand by those."

How can he argue?

Handling the Belligerent Revenue Agent

The vast majority of tax auditors conduct themselves in a professional and polite manner. That is not to say they are inclined to do you favors or lose sight of their goal; they merely do not act like thugs in the process. Occasionally, however, you do run across one who watches too many movies. Such a person may make unreasonable demands for records. He may ask you to perform accounting tasks unnecessary to determine your correct tax. He may make multiple demands for information either already submitted or wholly irrelevant.

Such a person can be arrogant and unwilling to recognize the limitations of his office. Indeed, such a person often believes, or at least tries to imply, that there are *no limitations* to his power. He may threaten to increase penalties for "failure to cooperate." He may suggest the IRS can "seize everything you have" if you do not cooperate. He may even go so far as to claim you could "go to jail" for the perceived malefaction.

There are two things you must never do when presented with such an attack. First, *do not* argue or otherwise contend with the agent. Second, *do not* succumb to the threats and intimidation. Arguing gets you nowhere. It may only play to his attempt to frustrate you and emphasize your apparent lack of power. At the same time, his resolve is strengthened by your inability to intellectually push him off the point.

But that is not to say you should concede. The single most effective way to deal with unreasonable, belligerent agents is to, a) kindly point out the improper nature of the request, b) reiterate that the material you provided is all that is necessary to prove the accuracy of your return, and c) ask that he rescind his demand. If he does not, explain that as far as you are concerned, the audit is *over*. Ask him to prepare a final report *at once* based on the information submitted and transmit it to you without delay. Explain that you will in turn exercise your absolute right of appeal. Be polite and professional, but firm and direct. I address the appeals process in chapter 13.

Expect the agent to respond in one of three ways. The first is to explain in a huff that all of your deductions will be "disallowed." "If that happens," he may assert, "you will owe substantial additional tax, interest and penalties." However, that claim is simply not accurate. As I explain in chapter 13, you have the absolute right to appeal the auditor's determination. The assessment is never final until *after* your appeal is considered.

The second potential reaction is that he may threaten to issue a summons for the information. However, as I discuss in chapter 7, an IRS summons is not self-enforcing. And when you already provided the substantive information necessary to determine the correctness of your tax return, it is highly unlikely that IRS counsel will push to enforce a summons for either the same material or material that is wholly extraneous. The key here, however, is that you must be sure you already provided the original source documents to show the correctness of your return.

The third and more likely reaction is that an uncontrollable spirit of reasonableness will overcome him. It suddenly becomes unnecessary for him to press those issues and demands which, just moments ago, were critical to the disposition of the case. He may begin to understand your argument and see your point of view. You can now move toward a reasonable resolution of the case.

Keeping the IRS Out of Your Home

I can think of few things more intimidating and outrageous, or more offensive to the notion of personal liberty than the idea of an agent of the Internal Revenue Service sitting in your home taking inventory of your family photos, suits and dresses, and rummaging through your underwear drawer looking for the twenty bucks he thinks you might have stashed there.

Just as with the case with the PLE, the IRS has no legal authority to unilaterally gain access to your private residence. Often the IRS points to the regulation regarding a "site visit" as its "authority" to enter one's personal home. I refer to Revenue Regulation section 301.7605-1(d)(3)(iii). Let us examine it carefully:

> Regardless of where an examination takes place, the Service may visit the taxpayer's place of business or residence to establish facts that can *only be established* by direct visit, such as inventory or asset verification. The Service generally will visit for these purposes on a normal workday of the Service during the Service's normal duty hours. (Emphasis added.)

As you can see, there is no language compelling you to allow an auditor into your home. The regulation says the agent "*may visit*" your residence. What it does not say is that he must have your *express permission* to *enter* the residence unless he has a court order signed by a judge authorizing such entry. Such a court order would come in the form of either a Writ of Entry or a search warrant.

The circumstances are very narrow under which the IRS may obtain either a Writ of Entry or a search warrant authorizing access to a private residence. Generally, search warrants issue only in criminal investigations, and then only when a Special Agent specifically testifies under oath that he has probable cause to believe the premises contain evidence of a specific tax crime. That will simply never happen in a routine tax audit situation.

A Writ of Entry is used to enter private premises for the purposes of carrying out collection. Do not confuse a tax audit with tax collection. The audit is nothing more than the process of determining the correctness of a return. The collection process is engaged only *after* a tax is assessed, and even then, only after a person fails or refuses to pay the tax. To obtain a writ, a revenue officer must testify before a federal court that he has reasonable cause to believe there are items within the premises that can be used to satisfy the liability. *G.M. Leasing Corp. v. United States*, 429 U.S. 338 (Supreme Court 1977). Just as with a search warrant, this is not going to happen in a garden-variety tax audit.

The Supreme Court was quite clear in the *G.M. Leasing* case. Without court authorization obtained in strict compliance with the dictates of due process, the IRS has no right to enter the private property of a citizen. Where a business open to the public is concerned, the IRS may enter the public areas of the business without a warrant. However, it cannot access any private areas without the express consent of the business owner.

For example, suppose you operate a restaurant. The business consists of a dining room where patrons eat, a kitchen where food is prepared, two restrooms, a private party room, a storeroom, and a small office. The public has unfettered access to just the dining room and the restrooms. Unless advanced arrangements are made and rent paid, the party room is not used. All other areas are off limits to the public. As a result, an agent may not gain access to those private areas without your consent or a court order. He does, however, have access to the public areas – the dining room and restrooms.

Let us again turn our attention to the regulation quoted above. Even if this regulation did impart some authority for an agent to enter your home, such authority is *conditional*. The regulation provides for a site visit to "establish facts that can *only be established* by direct visit." What facts relevant to your tax return can be verified only by a direct visit to and inspection of your home? *There are none!*

Even in the event that you claimed a home office deduction in connection with a home-based business, where the IRS may argue that a site visit is necessary to verify the existence of the home office, there are at least four alternatives to a site visit. The existence and use of a home office can be verified by: 1) photos, 2) drawings, 3) a videotape, and 4) the testimony of witnesses. I have used all four of these techniques in audit disputes over the business use of a home without allowing a site visit. Clearly, not even a home office claim is one that can be verified only "by a direct visit."

The bottom line here is that there is no legal or tactical reason an IRS agent should ever be in your home. In fact, under ideal circumstances, the entire audit should be conducted through the correspondence process to avoid the pitfalls of a face-to-face confrontation.

HOW TO PROVE YOUR BUSINESS IS LEGITIMATE

PLEASE RECALL THAT IN CHAPTER 5, I IDENTIFIED the most common ways the IRS attacks small business tax returns, in particular, Schedule Cs filed by sole proprietors. With staggering consistency, the IRS claims that upstart businesses showing a loss in the early years of operation are not legitimate businesses at all. Rather, the IRS claims that the activity is not engaged in for profit and as such the activity is classified as a "hobby." In that case, all the expense deductions are disallowed and in turn, you are asked to pay taxes on all the receipts without the benefit of any deductions.

This happens for two reasons. First, the IRS regularly misstates the applicable rules of law that control the issue. Secondly, most citizens facing this problem do not know or understand either the rules of law or the burden of proof on the issue. The result is the IRS takes unfair advantage of ignorant citizens. For these reasons, I address both of these issues in this chapter.

The Rules of Law Regarding Business Expense Deductions

Expenses that you incur in connection with activities carried on primarily for sport, hobby or recreation are non-deductible personal expenses. To be considered deductible business expenses, the activity must constitute a business operated for the purposes of earning income. That is to say, the activity must be engaged in *for profit*.

At the outset of this discussion, it is important to understand that there is *no* legal provision requiring you to earn a profit in a set number of years for the activity to be considered a business. This runs contrary to popular belief but it is nevertheless true. There are, however, two specific provisions of law we must address to understand the issue. Let us turn to them now.

The first is code section 162. This is the principal code section authorizing deductions for business expenses. It reads, in pertinent part as follows:

> There shall be allowed as a deduction all the ordinary and necessary expenses
> paid or incurred during the taxable year in carrying on any trade or business.

Two rules emerge from this. First, expenses are deductible only if they are "ordinary and necessary." Second, they are deductible only if incurred while carrying on a "trade or business." Expenses not related to a trade or business operated for profit are considered non-deductible personal expenses.

The second relevant statute is code section 183. It is the source of the confusion for taxpayers and deception by the IRS. Section 183(a) reads, in part,

> In the case of an activity engaged in by an individual or an S corporation, if such activity is not engaged in for profit, no deduction attributable to such activity shall be allowed except as provided in this section.

As if to re-state the general rules of section 162, section 183(a) provides that if you are not engaged in operating a trade or business for profit, you may not deduct the expenses incident to that activity. But if your activity is engaged in for profit, the related expenses are allowed as deductions. That might seem simple, but the confusion arises after reading section 183(d). That section reads as follows:

> If the gross income derived from an activity for 3 or more of the taxable years in the period of 5 consecutive taxable years exceeds the deductions attributable to such activity . . . then, unless the Secretary establishes to the contrary, such activity shall be presumed for purposes of this chapter for such taxable year to be an activity engaged in for profit.

Section 183(d) creates a presumption. The *presumption* is that the activity is *in fact* engaged in for profit if it produces profit in any three of five consecutive years. In that case, all proper deductions are allowed under code section 162.

That is what the law *says*. Now let us look at what it *does not* say.

It *does not* say that if no profit is realized in three of five years (or any other window of time), you are not entitled to claim deductions. Rather, if you fail to earn profit in at least three of five consecutive years, the *presumption* of a profit motive dissolves. That means you must *prove* a profit motive. And as long as you can prove a profit motive, you can lose money ten out of ten years and still claim your deductions. For example, in *Scheidt v. Commissioner*, T.C. Memo. 1992-9 (Jan. 6, 1992), the taxpayer lost money in consecutive years from 1980 to 1987 and yet the losses were allowed as business expenses.

The reason is the tests in both sections 162 and 183 for allowing deductions have nothing to do with whether your business *actually* earns a profit. The tests focus on whether you engaged in the activity with an *honest objective* of making a profit. It boils down to a question of intent. Did you undertake to earn a profit or did you intend to play and have fun? If the former, you are entitled to the deductions. If the latter, you may not be.

Moreover, the expectation of profit need not be *reasonable*. That is to say, your activity need not necessarily be a smart or savvy business move. Instead, you need only have a good faith objective of making a profit. The question of intent is subjective as to your beliefs, not measured by what some other person might have done under similar circumstances. The question is what did you intend? When a good faith profit motive exists, you are entitled to your deductions even if actual profit does not.

How to Prove a Profit Motive

The question for taxpayers in these cases is "How do I prove a profit motive?" The IRS cannot look into a person's head to see what he was thinking when he undertook his business activities. For that reason, the IRS has established regulations that guide the analysis. Revenue Regulation section 1.183-2(b) identifies several objective criteria used to evaluate your profit motive. As you review these, understand that your personal intent is *subjective* but it is measured by the following *objective* elements. Let us discuss them.

1. How you carry on the activity. Carrying on the activity in a "businesslike manner" indicates a profit motive. The following practices are considered businesslike operations:

- Keeping careful books and records,

- Adopting new operating techniques to replace non-profitable ones,

- Emulating the practices of profitable businesses,

- Seeking to improve and upgrade the quality of your product or service, and

- In general, cutting costs to improve income and hence, profit.

When you regularly follow one or more of the above practices to regulate and improve business operations, as opposed to operating by the seat of your pants, you are more likely to demonstrate a profit motive. Be prepared to describe exactly how you carried out the above tasks.

2. Your personal expertise or that of your advisor. Venturing into an area of business in which you have absolutely no expertise may indicate the lack of profit motive. But if you pursued a given hobby for years, you might reasonably convert that hobby to a profitable business. The law recognizes several means by which you can educate yourself. They include:

- Self-education through the study of books and periodicals,

- Attendance at seminars, trade meetings and shows,

- Memberships in trade organizations and associations, and

- Consultation with known experts.

3. The time and effort you spend in the business. This is an important factor. A profit motive is definitely indicated when you spend substantial time carrying on the day-to-day affairs of the business. This is particularly true if you quit a steady job to pursue your business. Spending full time in the operation, either personally or through employees, is strong evidence of a profit motive.

I once had a client who operated a photography business out of his home. The IRS tried to call his business a hobby and disallowed all his deductions. In addition to the other factors discussed here, we focused on this element to prove his profit motive. He spent full time in his business and in fact, it was the sole source of his income. He worked ten-hour days, six days a week and traveled throughout the state to photograph weddings and other events. Given the time spent and his reliance on the business for his livelihood, it was irrational to suggest he was doing it for the "fun of it."

4. The expectation that business assets will appreciate. Some businesses require a substantial investment in assets. While there may be no profit realized in the yearly operation of the business, a profit motive exists if you actually and honestly expect to earn profit through the appreciation of assets.

An example is the rental real estate business. Many rental properties actually lose money due to high maintenance costs, mortgage interest and real estate taxes. But at the same time, rental property can appreciate substantially, outpacing the negative cash flow over time. The anticipated appreciation of assets evidences a profit motive.

I had a client who operated a farm in Iowa. He made substantial improvements to the property and established, in addition to cash crops, a wildlife preserve in which he operated private, guided hunting trips for deer and pheasants. While the farming operation lost money, the value of the property increased substantially due to the wildlife and hunting elements. The increased value of the property more than offset the losses incurred in the farming operation.

5. Your success in carrying on past activities. The IRS looks to past success as evidence of intended success in the present undertaking. A history of success in your ventures weighs in favor of a profit motive.

6. The history of income or loss with respect to the activity. This sole element is chiefly responsible for the IRS's view that the lack of any actual profit indicates the lack of a legitimate profit motive. The IRS says a "continuing lack of profits, other than in the initial stages of a venture, *may indicate* that an activity is not engaged in for profit." Ibid, section 1.183-2(b)(6).

Note that the regulation *does not* state that the lack of any actual profits "proves" the lack of a profit motive. The courts have long recognized that lack of profits in the start up stages of an operation does not evidence the lack of a profit motive. New businesses need time to develop and mature before realizing consistent profits.

You must also consider whether unforeseen and unfortunate circumstances negatively impacted profitability. These might include conditions such as the health of the owner or a key employee, disease (as in livestock), weather and other casualties, unforeseen market conditions or other elements over which you have no control. In the case of my Iowa farmer, we were able to prove that he would in fact have made profits in some of the years in question but for substantial property damage caused by a tornado, much of which was not covered by insurance. Moreover, the operation did turn a profit in years beyond the audit years.

7. The amount of occasional profits. Occasional profit earned in prior or subsequent years evidences a profit motive. Courts are impressed that profits, even small ones sufficient only to support your family, strongly indicate a profit motive. Standing alone, however, failure to establish this element does not tip the scale against you. When the other factors point to a profit motive, even the absence of profits does not tip the balance in favor of the IRS. The potential for future profits also indicates a

profit motive.

8. Your financial status. The IRS often argues that if you earn substantial and steady income from other sources, this indicates lack of profit motive. It does not necessarily follow that citizens with reliable income from other sources fail to meet the profit motive test. The courts recognize that independent wealth or income is almost a prerequisite to financing a start up business, especially one with heavy initial capital demands. This is especially true in today's financial climate where obtaining bank financing is at best, difficult.

9. The elements of personal pleasure or recreation. This is one of the most critical of the nine points. If the business affords opportunities for substantial personal pleasure, this can be strong evidence of lack of a profit motive. Take for example the airline pilot who purchased a small airplane for use in his airplane rental business. He lost money in the rental business but regularly used the plane for his own recreational purposes. Of course he deducted all the plane's operating expenses and depreciated the plane. The IRS predictably did not find any profit motive in that business.

On the other hand, if the asset is seldom or never used for personal purposes, that weighs in favor an honest profit motive. Lack of personal use or pleasure, combined with the businesslike manner of the operation, weighs heavily in defeating the IRS's claim that an asset was purchased only for personal use. Moreover, it is not a requirement of law that you cannot enjoy your work. Just because you might derive some personal pleasure, enjoyment or satisfaction from your work does not mean you have no profit motive.

10. Other factors. In addition to the nine factors presented above, court decisions add additional factors to the list that are evaluated on a case-by-case basis. They are:

- Methods of advertising and promotion. When the business is advertised and promoted in a businesslike manner, this is strong evidence of a profit motive.

- A business plan. A clear business plan or design to build profitability is also strong evidence of a profit motive. Consideration is given to how the plan is carried out. However, the lack of a written business plan does not in itself suggest the lack of a profit motive.

- Use of a hired manager with profit sharing. Courts have recognized a profit motive when the citizen hired a manager who participated in a profit sharing arrangement. This indicates that at least one other person believes in the business's profit potential. I once had a client who hired a business manager away from a successful competing company to run my client's startup business. While my client's business lost money, the fact that he was able to persuade an experienced manager from a competing company that my client's vision had merit was sufficient proof that my client had an honest intent to make a profit.

How to Present Your Evidence

Present your evidence in the form of a detailed affidavit with supporting documents. Your affidavit must address each of the elements discussed above to the extent that they are relevant to your case. You explanation must be detailed and specific, not vague. While it is important to affirmatively declare that you "honestly intended to make a profit," your bald declaration will not carry the day. You must buttress your statement with objective facts tied to the factors set out above to support the conclusion that you had a profit motive and document your claims to the fullest extent possible.

For example, if you have a written business plan and used it to seek financing (whether or not approved), these are important indicators of a profit motive. Provide a copy of your business plan as an attachment to your affidavit. While you may not have a written business plan, you may have proceeded systematically to advertise and market your business. In this case, document the steps you took and provide copies of your marketing tools. These might include print ads, a web site, other Internet advertising, phone directory ads, business cards and stationary, direct mail packages, etc.

By applying the above elements to your business in the context of your facts and circumstances, you can defeat an IRS claim that your business is merely a hobby. By doing so, you sustain your deductions and insulate yourself from a big tax bill.

Please recognize that not every one of the above elements applies to every business. They do not have to. No single element will tip the scales in one direction or the other and it is not a question of simply counting the number of factors in your favor and those against you like a kind of sports game. The issue is decided on the basis of a preponderance of all the evidence. The question is whether the facts and circumstances as a whole indicate a profit motive.

What if You Cannot Prove a Profit Motive?

Even if your business is determined to be a hobby, all is not lost. By making the IRS follow the law, you can defeat the potential negative effects of losing all your deductions. There are two critical rules that apply in this situation, both of which are often ignored by tax auditors. Let us examine them.

The first rule is that even if you lack a profit motive, you are entitled to deduct expenses that are legally deductible in any event, regardless of a profit motive. These expenses include state and local taxes and interest on a home mortgage. Also included are casualty and theft losses, non-business bad debts, worthless securities, tax counsel expenses, medical expenses and charitable contributions. Code section 183(b)(1). All these expenses are allowed under other provisions of the code without regard to a profit motive. Therefore, even if you are not in business to make a profit, you get the benefit of these deductions if you incurred them.

The second point is that even if the activity is not engaged in for profit, you are entitled to deduct expenses up to the amount of the income earned. This is where IRS often misleads people. When the IRS claims your business is a hobby, it disallows *all* deductions. The effect is to force you to pay taxes on 100 percent of the income from the activity. Keep in mind that all income is taxable, regardless of whether earned in connection with a formal business or any other activity.

However, the code clearly entitles you to claim otherwise deductible expenses up to the amount of gross income derived from the activity. Code section 183(b)(2). For example, suppose you earned $5,000 in income and claimed $7,000 in expenses, thus creating a $2,000 loss. If you are not in business for profit, you may nevertheless claim the $5,000 of expenses as deductions. This eliminates any tax on the income but prevents you from using the loss against other income (such as wage income) in the year the loss was incurred. However, you are allowed to preserve the remaining $2,000 of loss and carry it forward to subsequent years once there is profit. The carry-forward period for suspended losses is indefinite.

Just because you cannot prove a profit motive does not mean you must shoulder the burden of the tax on the income. By claiming the deductions up to the extent of your income, at least you avoid the additional taxes on the income. Do not be bluffed into paying taxes you do not owe just because you cannot prove a profit motive.

PART FOUR

TAMING THE IRS

The IRS's mission is to collect the proper amount of taxes at the least cost to the federal government and taxpayers. However, due to the complexity of the tax law and the conflicting incentives that IRS employees face in administering the law, it is impossible to determine the proper amount of tax that should be collected..."

**UNITED STATES GOVERNMENT
ACCOUNTABILY OFFICE**

Chapter Thirteen

APPEALING
TAX AUDIT DECISIONS

IF THE ABOVE STATEMENT WERE COMPELLING IN 1994 when published (and it certainly was), than it must be even more compelling today. Following the publication of that statement, there were three major tax reform acts passed during the three years from 1996 through 1998 that changed more than 750 code sections. That string of changes was capped off by the massive IRS Restructuring and Reform Act of 1998. Most people cannot even name the three acts, never mind any of the specific changes brought about by any one of them.

But Congress was just getting warmed up when it came to changing the law. According to the National Taxpayer Advocate's 2012 Annual Report to Congress, during the period from 2001 to December 2012 (the date of that report), there were more than 4,680 changes to the tax code, "an average of more than one a day." Ibid, pg 6. The frequency of tax law changes, coupled with the scope and complexity of the tax code, "inflicts significant, even unconscionable, burden on taxpayers..." Ibid, pg 4.

This is why "it is impossible" for the IRS to determine the correct tax owed and one key reason why auditors so often make mistakes in the audit process. This is also why it is critical to understand that a tax auditor's decision is *never* final. Too many people believe it is and end up paying taxes they do not owe.

The IRS's Appeals Office reviews audit decisions. The Appeals Office is separate from other enforcement functions, such as Examination and Collection. The express function of Appeals is to negotiate settlements with citizens who disagree with the decisions of enforcement officers, such as tax auditors.

In chapter 4 we learned that in 2013, 91 percent of all face-to-face audits resulted in a tax debt. The average tax debt thus generated was about $16,000. However, historically, only about 3 percent of people audited ever appeal their case. This testifies to the degree to which the IRS has people convinced they cannot win when challenging an audit decision. In fact, as the National Taxpayer Advocate pointed out in her 2013 Annual Report, most people do not even know what their rights are when it comes to challenging the IRS. Ironically, on appeal, well over 80 percent of all cases are settled satisfactorily each year.

The magnitude of errors committed by the Exam function is *shocking*, even to me. In one report on Appeals Office casework, the GAO tracked the changes made by Appeals to audits that taxpayers challenged. The GAO examined tax disputes involving fourteen of the most common code sections. Among them are sections 61, 162, 167 and 311, each of which I explain below. The GAO's independent report forms the basis of the claim that I have made for years—that IRS auditors are wrong 60-90 percent of the time in the audit decisions they make.

Code section 61 defines "gross income." That section is the touchstone from which all income tax assessments flow. If an item is not considered income, it is not taxed. When the IRS makes a claim of unreported income, it cites code section 61 for its authority. According to the GAO, Appeals cut Examination's claims of unreported income by about 57 percent—more than fifty cents of every dollar when citizens appealed. Unfortunately, the vast majority of citizens *do not appeal.* GAO, "Recurring Tax Issues Tracked by IRS' Office of Appeals," GAO/GGD-93-101, May 1993, pg 17.

I explained code section 162 in the previous chapter. It allows a deduction to businesses for all expenses incurred in earning income. If the expense is "ordinary and necessary," it is allowed. According to the GAO, the Appeals Office reversed *71 percent* of the business expense disallowances issued by Examination. Ibid, pg 15.

The depreciation expense deduction under code section 167 is another recurring issue tracked by the GAO. According to the report, the Appeals Office reversed audit decisions in this area by a factor of more than *99 percent!* Ibid, pg 19.

Still another recurring issue arises under code section 311, relating to the taxability of corporate distributions to shareholders. The Appeals Office reduced *100 percent* of those adjustments. Ibid, pg 31.

Let me reemphasize that these cuts occurred only for those who *appealed* their audits. The majority of citizens *do not* appeal. These facts should make it clear to even the most casual observer why so many people reach amicable settlements with Appeals whereas they cannot with Examination.

What can possibly account for this wild spread in the results between the two functions? For starters, never lose sight of the main purpose of the Examination function. As stated by the GAO, the main purpose of Exam is to "protect the government's revenue." GOA/GGD-94-70, September 1994, pg 4. Said another way, the job of tax auditors is to *get the money.*

On the other hand, the function of the Appeals Office is much different. As the GAO states, the key function of Appeals is to "resolve tax controversies without litigation to the extent possible while being fair and impartial to both the government and the taxpayer." Ibid. This attitude is best expressed by the language of Revenue Regulation section 601.106(f), which sets forth the rules of procedure for Appeals Officers. Rule I states:

> An exaction by the U.S. Government, which is not based upon law, statutory or otherwise, is a taking of property without due process of law, in violation of the Fifth Amendment to the U.S. Constitution. Accordingly, an Appeals representative in his or her conclusions of fact or application of the law, shall hew to the law and the recognized standards of legal construction. It shall be his or her duty to determine the *correct amount of the tax*, with

strict impartiality as between the taxpayer and the Government, and without favoritism or discrimination as between taxpayers. Regulation section 601.106(f)(1), Rule I (Emphasis added.)

As you can plainly see, Appeals Officers are under strict authority regarding the settlement of cases. They must not be driven by the desire to simply get the money. Rather, their function is to determine the actual facts of the case and correctly apply the law to those facts. This process usually leads to a correct determination, not a falsely inflated one designed only to fill the Treasury's coffers.

For this reason, I often say that the purpose of the Examination function is to *cause* problems with citizens, while the purpose of Appeals is to *solve* them. Which one would you rather deal with?

Too often, citizens fail to appeal because they believe it will only make matters worse. They believe an Appeals Officer might reopen issues previously accepted or not reviewed by the auditor, or worse, will start an audit for another tax year. However, Revenue Regulation section 601.106(d)(1) stipulates that Appeals Officers are not to either "reopen an issue" agreed on at the audit level or to "raise a new issue." Moreover, IRS Policy Statement 8-2 expressly states: "Appeals will not raise new issues." IRM section 1.2.17.1.2. And the Policy Statement further provides that Appeals will not "reopen an issue on which the taxpayer and the Service are in agreement." Ibid.

Thus, any concerns about making matters worse are simply unfounded. The fact is you are always better offer appealing a tax audit decision than agreeing to it. This of course assumes that the decision is not 100 percent accurate, which in my experience, they never are.

How to Appeal

In any tax audit case, you enjoy the absolute right to appeal an "unagreed" case. Revenue Regulation section 601.103(c)(1). You file an appeal by submitting a timely protest letter. While not all cases require that the protest be in writing, it is always best to make your request in writing, for two reasons. First, the procedure is very simple and requires very little effort. And second, it eliminates the potential for miscommunication.

The time for making the appeal is set by Revenue Regulation section 601.105(d)(1)(iv). It provides that when an examination is complete, the revenue agent must communicate his findings to the citizen in the form of a "revenue agent's report" (RAR). The worksheets presented with the RAR state the basis of the proposed adjustments. The RAR must be accompanied by a thirty-day letter. The regulation describes the thirty-day letter as "a form letter which states the determination *proposed* to be made." Ibid; emphasis added. The form letter is usually IRS Letter 950.

Notice that the thirty-day letter is *not* a final assessment. Rather, that letter is merely the process of communicating the reasons why the agent believes you owe more tax. The thirty-day letter must also inform you "of appeal rights available if [you] disagre[e] with the proposed determination." Ibid.

The thirty-day letter asks you to agree with the auditor's findings and sign the waiver included. The waiver is Form 870, *Waiver of Restrictions on Assessment and Collection and Acceptance of Overassessment*. As I explain in chapter 8, you have no legal obligation to sign it and the IRS cannot punish you if you refuse. If you do sign it, the IRS assesses the tax and proceeds with collection. Your right of appeal is not lost, but the manner of prosecuting it is significantly altered and generally requires that you first pay the tax in full. This option is simply not practical for most people.

If you disagree with all or part of the proposal, you are usually presented with three options. The first is to submit additional information relevant to the agent's findings. If you have additional data that has not been presented, now is the time to do so. The second option is to request a meeting with the agent's supervisor. This too can be helpful and should be considered. Note, however, that in most cases, an agent's manager has already reviewed a thirty-day letter before it was issued. It is not likely that you will achieve measurable results by meeting with a manager. The final choice is to submit a protest letter asking for an appeal. If you have exhausted all possible remedies at the Examination level, this is the course to pursue.

You have thirty days from the date of Letter 950 in which to submit your written protest. Drafting the protest letter is simple. The first step in the process is to identify the specific issues in question. To do this, carefully review two IRS forms that are provided as part of the RAR.

The first is Form 4549, *Income Tax Discrepancy Adjustments*. This is a two-page form that shows you exactly what the IRS did to compute the additional tax. Items shown on line 1 of that form are the adjustments to taxable income as computed by the agent. Any income added to your return and any disallowed deductions are identified in line 1 along with the amount of the adjustment. For example, if the agent disallowed $5,000 of mortgage interest deductions, the notation on line 1 will say something like "mortgage interest" and the corresponding dollar amount shown in the adjacent column will be "$5,000."

Income adjustments are shown in various ways, depending upon the situation. If you are self-employed, the adjustment will be shown as "Schedule C gross receipts." If you are a farmer, the adjustment will be shown as "Schedule F gross receipts." If the income comes from alleged unreported interest or capital gains, the entry on line 1 will so state. There may be more than one adjustment on line 1. In each case, a few words will identify exactly what was adjusted and the amount.

Line 4 shows the "corrected taxable income" per the adjustments. Line 16 shows the amount of tax you owe as a result of the adjustments. Line 17 identifies what if any penalties were added and the amounts. And line 19 itemizes the total owed, including penalties (from line 17) and interest. Line 19e gives the total amount owed.

The second form to review is Form 886-A, *Explanation of Items*. This form provides the agent's reasoning behind the adjustments. If the adjustment added alleged unreported income, Form 886-A explains the basis (such as it exists) for the decision. Likewise, the reasoning behind any disallowed deduction is stated on an item-by-item basis. In the case of disallowed charitable contribution deductions, for example, the explanation may be something like, "Taxpayer failed to provide sufficient proof of charitable contributions." By reviewing these two forms carefully, you will know exactly what the examiner did and why he did it. This gives you the tools you need to craft a proper protest letter.

Your protest letter should be set up in letterhead fashion, with your name, address, SSN, phone number and the date at the top. It should be addressed to the "person to contact" identified on the thirty-day letter you received. That person is generally the auditor who handled your case. Your letter should be laid out in paragraph format, with each separate paragraph corresponding to the following items:

1. A statement that you want to appeal the examination findings to the Appeals Office. This should be a one-line statement, in bold letters, centered across the page under the name and address of the agent to whom the letter is addressed;

2. The date and symbols from the thirty-day letter showing the proposed changes. The symbols come from the lower-right margin of the thirty-day letter. As stated above, the typical thirty-day letter carries the designation Letter 950. The date is found at the top of the letter;

3. The tax periods involved. These are shown on Form 4549, under the heading "Period Ended," which is found on line 1 of the form;

4. An itemized schedule of the changes with which you disagree. After carefully reviewing Forms 4549 and 886-A you will be able to see what the agent did and therefore decide exactly what you disagree with. You cannot simply say, "I disagree with the report." Rather, you might say, "I disagree with the decision to disallow my mortgage interest deduction." If there are several issues at stake, you can say, "I disagree with the following adjustments:" and list each one separately. If you agree with one or more adjustments, simply do not include any reference to them in your protest letter;

5. A statement of facts supporting your position on any issue with which you disagree. This statement must be sufficient to show the Appeals Office the basis of your case. This statement need not be extensive or elaborate, as you will have a separate opportunity to present detailed facts and evidence to support your position. The statement need only be sufficient to show the Appeals Office the factual basis for challenging the agent's decision.

6. A statement of the law or other authority on which you rely. Likewise, this does not have to be an extensive analysis of tax law. In most cases, simply referring to the relevant tax code section is sufficient. For example, if the IRS disallowed certain business expenses, you might cite code section 162 to support your claim that the code allows the expenses. If you are unsure which code section supports your deductions, do some research as I explain in chapter 6. Also refer to the IRS publication that addresses your issue. For example, in the case of mortgage interest, Publication 17, *Your Income Tax*, has a chapter that addresses the deduction for mortgage interest. While it is true that IRS publications are not law, they are sufficient authority

for purposes of your protest letter. You can search the IRS's web site for references to all of its publications. For more information on the appeals process, see IRS Publication 5, *Appeal Rights and Preparation of Protests for Unagreed Cases.*

Your protest letter must have a perjury clause above your signature. This clause states that the facts presented under paragraph 5 are true under penalties of perjury. Your perjury clause should read as follows:

Under the penalties of perjury, I declare that the facts presented in this protest letter are, to the best of my knowledge and belief, true, correct and complete.

Without such a declaration, your protest is considered inadequate. Your signature must appear below the perjury clause. Your protest letter is now complete and ready to go. You do not have to provide any documents or other proof with the letter. That will come later, during your conference with an Appeals Officer.

Mail the letter via certified mail, return receipt requested, to the "person to contact" identified in the thirty-day letter. Be sure to keep a signed copy of the letter and be sure to keep the postal receipts for certified mail showing when and where you mailed the letter.

The Appeals Conference

After lodging your protest letter, an Appeals Officer (AO) is assigned to work your case. Your first contact with the Appeals Office will be in the form of an acknowledgement letter from the AO assigned to your case. That is usually IRS Letter 4141. I call this the "handshake" letter. It cordially explains what the Appeals Office is, how the process works and what you can expect. It does not set any hard deadlines or make any demands. However, this is the time to begin getting your documents, evidence and explanations organized, as the next letter you receive from the AO will set a conference date. There is no fixed time between the dates of the two letters. Timing is controlled solely by the workload of the Appeals Office handling your case.

You have the option to meet with the AO face-to-face if: a) you believe that will be helpful in presenting your case, and b) the office is close enough to make such a conference practical. You have the right to request that your Appeals conference be held at the IRS office closest your residence. If you wish such a conference, you should notify the AO of this fact upon receiving Letter 4141. If necessary, he will then transfer the case to another Appeals Office.

The AO's next letter notifies you in writing of the Appeals conference date. This could be a face-to-face meeting or a telephone conference. The appointment letter explains that if the time set is not convenient, you can contact the AO to reschedule. Appeals Officers are generally very accommodating when it comes to setting a conference date. The appointment letter also advises you to provide your evidence and documents prior to the conference so the AO can review them. It is a good idea to do this but failure to do so does not mean you cannot provide information (or new information) later.

The conference is an informal meeting between you and the AO where you may present evidence, argument, legal authority or other support for your position. Appeals Officers are remarkably different than auditors in their approach. First, they are generally more knowledgeable about the tax law. Second, they have a far better capacity (or willingness) to apply the facts of your case to the applicable law in order to reach a proper conclusion. Third, in coming to a decision in the matter, one of the key elements they consider is the "hazards of litigation," i.e., the government's risk of losing a case should it maintain its posture, whereas auditors never consider that issue. And lastly, they are not under the same pressure to produce revenue. Appeals Officers are under pressure to settle cases. All this adds up to a person better able to determine the *correct* tax versus one trying only to *collect* tax.

Be prepared to take the AO by the hand through the RAR during your Appeals conference. Point out the specific errors the agent made in calculating your tax. Use the protest letter as your guide to the issues. Present your facts in the form of documents and affidavits. Argue the law from specific code sections, regulations or other authority (such as IRS publications) that support your claim. Be prepared to answer any questions the AO might have about what you did and how you did it. Likewise, be mindful of and prepared to address any shortcomings in your documents or evidence.

The Appeals conference is not a one-and-done situation. In fact, most appeals involve several conferences along with the opportunity to provide additional information, facts and documents to answer whatever questions the AO raises. This process often stretches over several months. Take your time to fully answer all of the AO's questions so you do not provide a reason for him to say "no" to your appeal. Since the burden of proof is you, the AO does not generally need a good reason to say "no." But he does need solid evidence to agree with you.

As the case progresses, you will likely come to amicable agreements on individual issues, but the greater number of issues that are involved the longer this might take. In the case of issues that are not clear-cut one way or the other, be prepared to negotiate partial concessions. For example, suppose your mileage log for business travel was not the best it could have been. The auditor disallowed all your claimed mileage. The AO is willing to allow some mileage but not the entire amount due to the imperfect log. You might offer to the AO that he allow 75 percent of the claimed deduction, thus conceding 25 percent of your deduction. He might respond by saying he will allow 50 percent. In this manner, you can go back and forth until there is a reasonable agreement. Keep in mind, however, that your offer should always be based upon some evidence that is in the record and not just numbers you throw out in the hope that the AO will bite on something. See chapter 14 for more discussion on this process.

One issue you should always address on Appeal is the question of penalties. Even if you end up owing some tax, you can reduce or eliminate penalties if you establish that you acted in good faith, and based on some reasonable cause for your actions. This is especially important for issues involving more technical legal questions, where you might not be expected to know the tax law completely. See chapter 16 for my discussion of penalties and reliance on counsel. You should always push for the elimination (or at least reduction) of penalties based upon your good faith attempt to comply with the law. For more details on penalties, see my book, *The IRS Problem Solver*, which addresses this issue in great detail.

Assuming you reach an agreement with Appeals, the case is closed by signing a consent form. By signing the consent, you agree with the amount of tax negotiated and you agree that the IRS can assess and, by extension, you agree that the IRS can collect the tax. Appeals commonly uses Form 870, *Waiver of Restrictions on Assessment and Collection and Acceptance of Overassessment*, to accomplish this. However, when you settle your case, insist on using Form 872-AD. The key difference between the two forms is that Form 872-AD contains a pledge against reopening the settled issues while Form 870 does not. This gives you the finality you want and need, to know that the case is closed once and for all.

The Right of Tax Court Review

Though a great many cases are resolved favorably at the Appeals level, not every case is settled satisfactorily. This is true for a number of reasons. First, the Appeals Officer may be unimpressed with the validity of your proof. Second, the law may be such that the AO believes you are not entitled to the benefits you claim. Third, and least likely, is the AO is really just another tax auditor wearing the hat of an Appeals Officer and is just trying to get more money.

The Appeals Office is not the final arbiter on whether you owe taxes. The Appeals Office makes the final *administrative* determination on the matter, but that is subject to review by the United States Tax Court. If you cannot reach an agreement with Appeals, the IRS must mail a Notice of Deficiency (NOD). An NOD is the letter transmitting the IRS's final determination on the case. The IRS typically uses Letter 531 as the Notice of Deficiency cover letter. The NOD also includes Forms 4549 and 886-A as drafted by the AO.

The NOD is often referred to as a "90-day letter" because it provides you with the right to file a Petition for Redetermination in the Tax Court within ninety days from the date on the letter. Code section 6213. This deadline is fixed by law and *cannot* be extended. Therefore, to appeal to the Tax Court, you must submit your petition *within ninety days*. In counting the time, include Saturdays, Sundays and legal holidays. Please note that the deadline is *not* three months, but rather, *ninety days*. Therefore, take into consideration the fact that some months have thirty-one days and February has twenty-eight (or perhaps twenty-nine) days.

Once it mails the NOD, the IRS is precluded from assessing any tax while the ninety-day waiting period is pending. Code section 6213(a). If a petition is filed within the deadline, the IRS cannot assess until the Tax Court's judgment becomes final. If no petition is filed within the deadline, the IRS can and will assess the tax shown in the NOD.

A Tax Court filing gives you two clear advantages. First, the case is reassigned to the Appeals Office for settlement consideration. The difference between the first Appeals trip and the second is significant. The second time through involves a *docketed* court case where the IRS is under pressure to settle.

Second, filing the Tax Court petition brings the IRS's Office of Area Counsel into things—the lawyers who represent the IRS in Tax Court. They have absolute settlement authority over cases pending in the Tax Court and they have the power to override Appeals Office recommendations to settle cases on terms they deem suitable. A Tax Court case therefore provides two bites of the settlement apple. Of course, if you are unable to reach an agreement with counsel, you have the right to present your case to a Tax Court judge.

You may believe that filing a Tax Court case involves considerable cost, time and complexity. While it is true that these cases can take some time to resolve, it is not true that they are necessarily expensive. The filing fee for Tax Court is just $60. As to the complexity issue, if your case involves taxes of less than $50,000, you can use the Tax Court's "small tax case" procedures. These simplified procedures transform the Tax Court into a kind of small claims court. In such a proceeding, the rules of procedure are relaxed and the rules of evidence do not apply. This gives the *pro se* taxpayer the opportunity to present his case fully and without fear of running afoul of complicated court procedures and courtroom technicalities.

In chapter four of my book, *Taxpayers' Ultimate Defense Manual*, I provide step-by-step guidance in drafting a Tax Court petition and walking a case through the Tax Court. You can also download my *Tax Court Trouble Shooting Guide*, a free research report that gives you insider tips and techniques for handling a Tax Court case. The report is available at my web site, www.taxhelponline.com. Go to "resources and publications" then "special reports."

What to Do if You Owe Some Tax

Not every adjustment made in every audit is wrong. Often, audits involve several adjustments to minor items and one or two major adjustments. Just as often, the IRS is correct about one or more of the minor adjustments. For example, I represented a client who faced a $500,000-plus adjustment for alleged unreported income for the year in question. In addition, the IRS disallowed several thousand dollars worth of business travel expenses and added to income an IRA distribution of about $8,000.

The IRS was right about the IRA distribution. My client simply overlooked it in the preparation of his tax return. However, the agent was dead wrong about the unreported income and while my client did carry out the business travel he claimed, some of his records were missing. Therefore, it was questionable whether we could sustain the entire deduction. The bottom line is we knew he would owe some taxes and interest, at least based on the IRA distribution. We filed a protest letter challenging the unreported income and the disallowance of the travel expenses. We did not contest the IRA distribution.

Next, I instructed my client to begin making voluntary, designated payments to the IRS to address the anticipated tax on the IRA distribution. Because an appeal can take many months, some times up to a year (even longer if a Tax Court appeal is involved), it did not make sense to wait until the audit was over to begin paying what we already knew he owed. Any time there is a delinquent tax debt, interest accrues even while the case is on appeal. By making payments right away, the interest is minimized.

You do not need the IRS's permission to make partial payments on any tax debt. Moreover, when you send a partial payment to the IRS in a disputed case and designate that payment to apply as a "cash bond" to a particular tax year or type of tax, the IRS must apply that payment as you designate, as long as the designation is in writing and submitted along with the payment. With this in mind, we made a rough estimate of the tax that would be owed given what we could not win. I then had my client begin making monthly payments in an amount he was comfortable with, expressly designated to apply as a "cash bond" to the tax year in question.

He did this by sending a letter with each check, addressed to the agent who did the audit, saying: "Please apply the enclosed payment of $_____ as a cash bond to tax year _____." This same language was entered on the memo portion of each check, along with my client's SSN. Each letter was mailed certified mail, with return receipt requested and we kept a copy of the letter and check for each payment.

This continued to the point where our estimated liability was paid. By the time the appeal was over (in which we prevailed on 100 percent of the unreported income issue and about half of the travel expenses), the remaining tax balance was just about paid in full. By following this procedure, we avoided any risk of enforcement action and paid the tax owed on our terms, not theirs. Please review my discussion in chapter 15, under the heading, *"If you pre-pay the tax, you can avoid interest."* This addresses the cash bond issue.

Reopening a Prior Audit

I say throughout this discourse that too many people fail to understand, or are misled concerning, their right to appeal audit decisions. As a result, the vast majority of those audited face assessments they do not legally owe. This begs the question, "What can I do if I was so victimized?" The answer is found in the audit reconsideration, the procedure whereby closed examination cases may be re-opened. Let me illustrate.

Steve received a notice from the IRS that his returns for three tax years were selected for audit. He promptly took the notice to his tax preparer for help. Steve left the preparer's office with the assurance she "would handle everything." Confident she was capable of fulfilling her promise, Steve forgot all about the audit.

In the following months, he received a few more letters and each time he took the letter to the preparer's office and placed it in her care. Each time, the preparer offered assurances regarding the progress of the case. Her unflinching representations left Steve with every reason to believe all was "under control."

One year later, Steve received a bill demanding full and immediate payment of over $10,000 in taxes for all three years in question. How could this be? The preparer was handling everything. Her repeated assurances indicated that the matter was under control. But after confronting the preparer, Steve learned she did nothing about the audit whatsoever. The notices he forwarded to her were filed and ignored. She did not attend the audit conference nor did she submit information to support any of the claims on Steve's tax returns.

When the thirty-day letter was issued, Steve did not avail himself of his appeal rights as he was unaware of them. The preparer ignored the paperwork. Next came the NOD, which was also ignored. It turned out that Steve defaulted the entire process and ended up with a substantial tax liability as a result. But it was the IRS's notices threatening enforced collection that got his attention. Because of the preparer's incompetence, Steve was deprived of both his right to present evidence and to appeal the auditor's decision. Steve needed the benefits of an audit reconsideration.

An audit reconsideration is available in any circumstance where "the assessment of any tax is in excess of the taxpayer's liability per code section 6404(a)." IRM section 4.13.1.6, citing Revenue Regulation 301.6404-1. Under such circumstances, the IRS has the discretionary authority to abate the assessment. The IRM lists three general reasons why the IRS will entertain the idea of reconsidering an assessment. They are:

1. The request is based upon information "not previously considered" but which if timely submitted, "would have resulted in a change to the assessment,"

2. An original return is filed by the citizen after an assessment was made under the Substitute for Return (SFR) Program, or

3. There was an "IRS computational or processing error in adjusting the tax." IRM section 4.13.1.7.

In Steve's case, he had proof of the validity of his deductions that was never submitted because of the incompetence of his preparer. Clearly, he was entitled to an audit reconsideration under this IRM provision.

Another common situation calling for audit reconsideration arises in tax return non-filer cases. When one fails to file a return, the IRS often prepares a return for him. This is done under the authority of code section 6020(b). The return filed on your behalf is known as a substitute for return (SFR). The SFR becomes the basis of the assessment, though it does not consider any deductions, exemptions, credits, etc., against the tax. Moreover, the income is usually grossly overstated. Because of that, SFR assessments are always excessive. By submitting a request for audit reconsideration, you can get erroneous SFR assessments corrected.

The manual provides that an audit reconsideration request must be submitted in writing. The request must seek abatement of the excessive tax. You must specifically explain why you were deprived of the ability to submit data or appeal the original audit decision. Illustrate how the data would have reduced your tax if presented at the time of audit. The IRS provides the following list of "some reasons" a citizen might seek an audit reconsideration:

1. You did not "appear at the audit," as was the case with Steve,

2. You "moved and did not receive" the IRS's letters,

3. You have "new documentation to present,"

4. You disagree "with an audit assessment,"

5. You disagree with an "SFR assessment," and

6. You were denied "tax credits during a prior examination." IRM section 4.13.1.3.

To the extent that these factors apply in your case, give facts to explain the circumstances. Include the following material with your letter:

1. A list of the prior audit issues and the reasons for the abatement request. Specifically explain why the assessment is erroneous;

2. A copy of the tax return in question. Be sure to include the forms and schedules so the return is complete and the return must be signed and dated;

3. A copy of the original examination report if available; and

4. Documents supporting your claim. Be sure to explain the documentation and point out how the material: a) supports your original return, and b) was not available or otherwise not presented in the original audit.

5. If you never filed a return (as in the case of an SFR assessment), you must submit an original signed return and documents to support it. Refer to IRS Publication 3598, *What You Should Know about the Audit Reconsideration Process*. Among other things, that publication shows you where to mail your audit reconsideration request. Be sure to send it using certified mail and keep a signed copy of your letter. Do not mail original documents to the IRS. Mail clear photocopies only.

When the evidence indicates that the underlying assessment is in error, the case is to be assigned to an auditor for reconsideration. The auditor is to review the evidence and make the necessary adjustments. Upon completion of the review, the examining agent may fully grant or deny your reconsideration, or partially grant your reconsideration. If you disagree with the determination, you have the right to appeal. Exercise that right by filing a protest letter as outlined earlier in this chapter. However, you have no right to a Notice of Deficiency if one was already mailed. You are entitled to just one NOD per tax year, unless the IRS failed to mail the NOD to your last known address. I discuss the last known address issue in chapter 14, under the heading, **Maintain a Current Mailing Address**.

By following this procedure, erroneous assessments can be corrected even though the ink on the examination report has long since dried.

The Offer in Compromise (OIC)

Code section 7122 affords the IRS the authority to "compromise" any outstanding tax liability. There are two common reasons why a liability may be compromised. The first is where there is doubt as to the IRS's ability to collect the tax in full. You prove doubt as to collectibility by showing that you lack the income and assets to be able to pay the bill in full. The second reason is where there is doubt as to your legal liability for the tax. You prove that by showing that the tax assessment is erroneous. The OIC affords a potentially effective avenue of review provided there has been no Appeals Office or Tax Court determination of your liability.

Whether to proceed with an OIC or audit reconsideration is a question that must be considered. The audit reconsideration is a simple process. The IRS must look at your case when you meet the various criteria set out above. However, sometimes audit reconsideration requests fall into a black hole. In that case, you have to push the Taxpayer Advocate's office for help in getting action on the matter.

On the other hand, an OIC generally receives faster action by the IRS. The reason is that code section 7122(f) provides that if an OIC is not specifically rejected within twenty-four months of filing, it is deemed accepted. Because the law simply does not allow OIC cases to linger indefinitely, the IRS works them aggressively.

The real negative aspect of filing an OIC is that the statute of limitations governing the IRS's right to collect the tax is tolled (that is, the clock stops running). The statute remains tolled during the time the OIC is pending, including appeals, plus thirty days. Normally, the IRS has just ten years from the date of the assessment in which to collect the tax. If they cannot collect within that time, the assessment expires and is no longer collectible. You toll that statute by filing an OIC. Thus, you must consider whether the benefits of the OIC (assuming it is accepted) outweighs the fact that the IRS will have more time to collect if the OIC is rejected.

The OIC is beyond the scope of this work. However, I address in great detail both aspects of the OIC as well as the collection statute of limitations in my book, *How to Get Tax Amnesty*. Review it carefully before submitting an OIC.

Chapter Fourteen

16 SECRETS TO EFFECTIVE COMMUNICATION

JOBS ARE LOST, MARRIAGES FAIL AND NATIONS GO TO
war over *mis*communication. To that list we can add the fact that IRS problems are often either caused or exacerbated because of miscommunication. That is why it is vitally important to understand not only who at the IRS you are dealing with, but how to communicate with that person.

What follows here is my list of specific tips, secrets and techniques for communicating with the IRS while your case is in various stages before the agency. Use this information to give yourself the greatest possible chances of a successful resolution.

1. Maintain a Current Mailing Address

This may seem simple but it is often overlooked. You cannot solve problems you do not know exist and you will not know they exist if the IRS is cannot reach you. The IRS's legal burden is to mail its notices to your "last known address." Unless you file the IRS's change-of-address form that I explain below, your "last known address" is the address shown on your most recently filed tax return. *Abeles v. Commissioner*, 91 T.C. 1019 (1988). If you move and do not notify the IRS, you may miss important communications, and thus lose the opportunity to challenge the IRS in the most effective forum because your appeal rights are time sensitive.

Keep in mind that an NOD and most other IRS notices mailed to your "last known address" are valid whether or not you receive them. However, if the IRS knows or has reason to know that such address is incorrect, the notice is invalid. *Gibson v. Commissioner*, 761 F.Supp. 685 (C.D. Cal. 1991). As a result, you have the burden to provide the IRS with notice of a new address.

Use IRS Form 8822, *Change of Address*, to communicate your new address to the agency between annual tax return filings. The form can be used for either individuals or businesses. Form 8822 should be sent by certified mail to the address shown in the instructions.

2. Take Delivery of all Certified Letters

I know people whose only defense to the IRS is that they refuse to accept the IRS's certified mail. Hiding from the IRS and ignoring its mail does not solve problems. In fact, the only thing you usually accomplish by ignoring IRS mail is losing your rights by default.

3. Respond in a Timely Manner

Nearly every IRS communication requires a response within a certain time frame established by law. Only by responding within the set time are your rights preserved. Some of the common time limits are:

File a petition with the United States Tax Court within ninety days of the date on a Notice of Deficiency – code section 6213(a),

Respond to an auditor's RAR within thirty days of the date of the letter – Rev. Reg. section 601.103(c).

Demand abatement within sixty days of the date of a notice that an assessment was made under the math error rules - code section 6213(b)(2), and

Respond within thirty days to a notice and demand for payment of assessed taxes - code section 6331. Notices and procedures regarding tax collection are discussed in *How to Get Tax Amnesty*.

4. Respond to the Appropriate Office

The IRS is a decentralized bureaucracy. As a case progresses from stage to stage, the file changes hands from one office to another. No function of the IRS knows or necessarily cares what the others are doing. If your case is before the Appeals Office, a response directed to the Examination function will fall on deaf ears.

IRS letters and notices usually indicate the particular function handling the case. By knowing which function generated the correspondence, you can do two important things. First, you know where your case is within the system. Second, you are able you to commence or continue negotiations under procedures appropriate to that function.

If a communication does not identify the function handling the case, the signature on the letter or the "person to contact" often provides the title of the person writing the letter. The typical titles and the function they correspond to are as follows:

Title	Function
Revenue Agent	Examination
Revenue Officer	Collection
Appeals Officer	Appeals
Special Agent	Criminal Investigation
Attorney	Area Counsel (IRS lawyers)

On the upper right corner of nearly every IRS letter or notice, you find the following information: 1) the year in question, 2) the date of the letter, 3) and the "person to contact." The left side of the letter gives you a return address and generally a "mail stop" or "room number." Your response should go to that person at the address shown.

5. Make all Communications in Writing

All communications should be in writing to the fullest extent possible. You must be able to document your communications if necessary. Mail your letters via certified mail with return receipt requested. Maintain a photocopy of the letter in your personal file. Attach a copy of the Postal Service receipt for certified mail and the card bearing the signature of the recipient. You can also use the Postal Service's web site to track and confirm your certified mail. Either way, secure proof that the IRS received the letter you mailed. That can be very important in many situations, such as when the date of filing a Tax Court petition is called into controversy.

6. Do Not Respond to Initial Verbal Contacts

It is not unusual for the IRS to initiate contacts via phone or through personal visits. For example, two revenue officers once appeared at the office of a local business. They barged into the room and demanded that the secretary point them to the file cabinet where they might find copies of federal tax returns. One agent flashed some kind of badge but was so quick about it the secretary was unable make it out.

The boss was out of the office but just happened to phone in at the instant this transpired. "Who are they? What do they want?" The confused and intimidated secretary had no idea. Either the agents did not make themselves very clear (possible) or the secretary was too shaken to make sense of it (probable). Her boss said simply, "Send them away and have them put whatever it is they want in writing. I will respond to them promptly." The fear-stricken secretary carried out the instructions.

To get to the bottom of what happened, I later questioned the secretary. "What were their names?" I asked.

"I don't know," she said. "They didn't say."

Surprised, I said, "Did you ask?"

"No. They just said they wanted to see the files."

"What files were they talking about?"

"I don't know," she said. "The one lady just kept saying something about tax returns."

"What type of returns she was talking about?" I queried.

"I don't know. She just kept telling me that the forms had to be mailed to her right away."

"Did you ask for her address?"

"No."

When I asked why she did not ask these basic questions, she squeaked defensively, "I didn't know I was supposed to. I didn't know what to do."

It is very easy to get scared and disoriented when IRS personnel appear unexpectedly making demands. For this reason, it is wise to know in advance how to handle it.

Since there was no tangible information upon which to base a reply, we decided to do nothing. What do you say when you have no idea who appeared or even why they appeared at your door? I believed that if the contact were genuine, the IRS itself would follow up with a letter. Please note that many phone contacts purportedly by IRS personnel are in fact, bogus. See my discussion of this in chapter 19, under the heading, **Avoid Phone and E-Mail Scams**.

A few days later, a letter appeared at the office. After calmly reading it, we saw that the IRS somehow processed the company's employment tax returns under an erroneous identification number. All that was necessary to settle the dispute was to supply copies of the requested documents with an affidavit verifying they were filed timely.

In retrospect, it was good the boss was not present. He may have provided all kinds of documents not having any idea where the inquisition was heading. The presence of mind to send the agents away with a request that they put their demands in writing helped in many valuable ways. First, and perhaps most significantly, it eliminated the tension of the moment. It allowed everybody involved, particularly the poor secretary, to catch their breath and actually think before reacting out of pure fear.

Secondly, it put the onus on the IRS to make a specific demand rather than continue the shotgun approach. That way, the IRS would not have unchecked access to "the file cabinet." Lastly, upon receiving the letter, we were able to analyze it and determine the best, most effective and least risky way to settle the dispute. None of this is possible when responding spontaneously to verbal demands made without warning.

I once asked a special agent why they routinely call on targets of criminal investigations *without* warning. For example, special agents arrive at one's home at 7:30 in the morning, just as the taxpayer is getting out of the shower. After reading a Miranda warning they begin asking questions about what took place three, maybe four years ago. "Why?" I asked. "Where is the sense of fair play in that tactic?"

The agent's response was that unannounced interviews "encourage spontaneity" and that "spontaneous answers tend to be more accurate." That answer may be sound impressive but my experience shows there is an ulterior motive. Consider this scenario. An IRS special agent surprises you quite early in the morning. You had no idea the IRS was even interested in you, much less concerned about potential criminal conduct. After hearing a Miranda warning at 7 a.m., you are bombarded with questions concerning transactions and events occurring years ago.

You have not given a moment's thought to any of the events since they occurred. You are confused. You are scared. You do not know why the IRS is asking these questions. The words "potential criminal prosecution" are ringing in your head. When you try to get a little information, the agents sandbag you. "We can't tell you that," they say. "We are asking the questions here."

The result is you likely make statements and give information which *is not* accurate. No other result could reasonably be anticipated under the circumstances. Later, after reviewing your records and consulting counsel, you find the statements were indeed wrong. The difficulty is that you can never *change* information previously given to the IRS. All you can do is *supplement* it and update it with information you believe is correct. Remember the old saying, *you cannot unring the bell.*

What is important is *not* that the latter material is indeed accurate, but rather, that it *contradicts* your initial responses. Contradictions do not bode well with the IRS. I have therefore concluded that this tactic is deliberate and carefully calculated, not to obtain correct information, but rather to cause the citizen to make contradictory statements.

For these reasons, I strongly recommend that all substantive information be provided to the IRS in writing, and only in response to a written request for such information. If the initial contact is made via phone or in person, politely send the agents away asking that they follow up with a written request. Keep in mind that the IRS will *never* make contacts via e-mail. As I explain in chapter 19, if you get an e-mail contact purportedly from the IRS asking for money or bank account information, the chances are overwhelming that it is a fraudulent attempt to steal financial information.

7. Take Careful Notes During Face-to-Face or Phone Discussions

Some verbal conversations are unavoidable, as in a face-to-face audit or telephone appeals conference, and unless you are an extremely unusual person, it is difficult or impossible to recall all the points raised during such conferences. Therefore, make careful notes of the conversation. Keep the notes in the "I said — he said" format. The notes should also bear the time and date of the conversation together with the names of the parties involved. You can be sure the IRS will have such notes.

Use your notes for: a) a follow up letter summarizing the points of the conversation, and b) a reference from which to reconstruct obligations made and agreements reached. The notes can also serve to contradict inaccurate IRS statements about the substance of the conversation.

In audit cases, agents regularly request additional information or further proof of certain items. In one audit we needed additional proof of business miles, uniform deductions and rental property expenses. I did two things to protect the citizen's interests. First, I took careful notes, recording the items that we verified and those needing additional documentation. Secondly, I asked the agent to provide an Information Document Request for the additional items, "so there is no confusion."

I compared the agent's IDR with my own notes. This allowed me to not only verify the items needing more proof, but also to verify those we did prove. When mailing the supplemental proof, I sent a cover letter itemizing the documents contained in the package. Based upon my own notes and the IDR, I itemized the issues already proven. This prevented the agent from later saying those items were still in question.

8. Be Sure You Are Always Dealing With a Person

Millions of times each year the IRS sends computer notices lacking a person's signature. I have yet to meet a person who is able to successfully negotiate with a computer. When it comes to an audit, respond to unsigned communications promptly but ask that a living person be assigned to handle your case. I once worked with a man who received a letter from the local IRS office. The letter requested he appear for audit on a certain date, "between the hours of 8:30 a.m. and 4:30 p.m." There was no name on the letter. He was to see the "appointment clerk."

I wrote a letter with a simple request, "Please assign an agent so that pre-conference discussions might resolve as many issues ahead of time as possible." In a subsequent conversation with the appointment clerk, the clerk said, "We will not be assigning an agent until the taxpayer comes into the office."

"You may have misunderstood my letter," I replied. "We won't be coming into the office until an agent is assigned."

Rather huffy, she explained, "Our policy here is not to assign an agent until the taxpayer arrives."

"I have several good reasons why an agent should be assigned now," I stated. "For example, the audit notice does not indicate which specific items are in question. I must speak with an agent to see what proof we need to prepare before our meeting. Secondly, it is my policy to at least talk with the agent before the meeting to establish the ground rules under which the audit will proceed. I will not be coming into the office before the assignment of an agent with whom I can discuss these matters."

She agreed to consider my request. I wrote a follow up letter based upon my notes of the conversation. The letter summarized the facts and restated my reasons. I repeated my specific request for an agent and informed the clerk that we would not be appearing without one.

Eventually I received a phone call from a revenue agent who was assigned to the case. We discussed the audit and agreed on the procedures for handling the case. Again, I followed up the conversation with a letter to verify the agreements reached.

9. Establish Ground Rules Before Your Meeting

Never walk into an IRS meeting blind. The advantage is decidedly with the IRS if you are ignorant as to the purpose of the meeting. For your own good, establish the ground rules beforehand.

For example, I was involved in an audit that raised questions surrounding equipment purchases and installation. The IRS contended the equipment did not qualify for certain business deductions and credits. During the audit, we intended to do two things the IRS generally looks on with disfavor. We intended to bring witnesses to testify about the nature and use of the equipment and we intended to record the audit so the testimony could be used later if necessary.

My "ground rules" letter informed the agent that we would present witnesses and that we would have IRS Form 8821, *Tax Information Authorization*, available for each witness to avoid disclosure problems. As required by law, I also informed the agent of the fact that we would record the audit. See my discussion of recording conferences in chapter 8, under the heading, **The Right to Record the Audit**.

Specific items that may be addressed in a ground rules letter include:

- The time and place of the meeting,
- The presence of witnesses,
- The specific issues in question,

- What will and will not be discussed,
- The nature of evidence for and against you,
- Disclosure of appeal rights,
- The use of tape recording devices,
- Disclosure to you of documents or statements already in the IRS's possession,
- Representation by counsel,
- The probable result of failure to cooperate,
- Third-party contacts,
- Whether a criminal investigation is pending or contemplated,
- The IRS's legal authority to demand the meeting or the records sought, and
- The uses to which information they obtain from you could be put.

This list is not exhaustive. It varies depending upon the facts and circumstances of each case. By setting ground rules ahead of time, you accomplish two very important goals. First, you reduce or eliminate surprises. You learn the exact reason for the meeting and the circumstances under which it will be conducted. And, you learn—indeed help to establish—the latitude each party is permitted.

Secondly, by setting ground rules, you communicate the important message that you are an informed citizen with a full understanding of your rights. As such, the IRS is less likely to attempt to take advantage of you.

10. Do Not Ask Questions, Make Demands

The IRS is quite effective at dealing with requests. They usually just say "no!" That is why I have long since abandoned the idea of making *requests*. It is far more effective to make specific *demands*, but do so politely and professionally. For one thing, when you affirmatively state your position, there is no question about what you want. If your position is not clear, it is more difficult for the IRS to understand your needs.

One example of where the "request" operates to your disadvantage is with the IRS's so-called math error notice. Under section 6213(b), the IRS is allowed to recalculate your tax bill if there is a math error in the return. However, if you object in writing within sixty days of receiving the notice, the IRS is obligated to abate its assessment.

However, people typically respond by writing and *inquiring* about the bill. "Please tell me what error I made. I do not understand why you penalized me." This is not a specific demand and the IRS is not obligated to take any action.

The following statement is much more effective:

I reviewed your notice dated _____ (copy enclosed) and I disagree with the amount you claim I owe. Please abate the tax immediately. If you believe I owe it, I demand a hearing.

This very specific statement is impossible to misunderstand.

Another example involves getting more time from an auditor to provide additional documents. The auditor might set a deadline of three weeks to produce the information. As the deadline approaches, you realize that you cannot get the documents organized, copied and sent to the agent within that time. Rather than asking for more time (which might well be denied), you simply send a letter to the agent stating that it will take more time to get the records and that you will produce them by X date. In this way, you do not ask for an extension. Instead, you effectively give yourself an extension.

11. Do Not Provide Information that is Not Requested

One mistake people consistently make with the IRS is they talk too much. By that I mean, they provide information that is not requested, yet often fail to provide information that is needed to prove their case. To avoid this problem, listen carefully to what the agent asks. Make sure you understand the question. Then answer only the question that was asked.

If you do not understand the question, ask for clarification. Do not guess at what you think that agent might mean. Do not assume the agent means one thing if he says another. Do not guess or speculate at your answer. If you cannot answer accurately on the spot, state that you need time to review your records and will get back to the agent with an accurate answer. Provide accurate information but only the information that is requested and that you are required to provide. No more.

A former client was involved in an audit in which he was represented by his accountant. The accountant had no experience dealing with audits or auditors. As the audit progressed, the agent asked for information about the client's home office, his business expenses and the manner of operating the business. One issue was the client's home office, which happened to be on his boat, which is where he lived. The agent argued that the boat could not be a home office.

The client provided all the details regarding the business use of a portion of the boat along with the information on the costs related to the boat. The agent did not ask for any information about how the boat was purchased. He only wanted to know its purchase price and the expenses of maintaining it such as were relevant to the home office deduction. All that material was provided.

As the audit wrapped up, the agent allowed the business expenses. However, he disallowed many of the deductions associated with the home office. In his conversation with the agent as they discussed the report, the accountant went over the issues. The agent confirmed that he intended to deny several of the boat's costs, but said, "otherwise, everything else is okay."

The accountant should have left it at that and appealed the decision. But he did not. Instead, he said, "So you don't have any questions about the cash used to buy the boat, right?"

Wait, what? What cash? Where did that comment come from?

As it turns about, my client made the down payment for the boat with $30,000 in cash. The agent never asked one question about that. He only wanted to know: a) what the boat cost, b) how it was used for business, and c) what the costs were of maintaining the boat. Why would the accountant offer up the fact that the down payment was made using cash, then ask the agent whether he had any questions about that?

As you might imagine, the agent suddenly had all kinds of questions about an issue he was not even concerned with until the accountant opened his mouth. And it was not like the accountant answered a specific, pointed question, which he might well have been obliged to do. He simply offered up the fact from left field, without any prompting whatsoever. This is exactly the wrong thing to do in any conversation with the IRS. The lesson is this: provide only the information required to carry your burden of proof – and no more.

12. Focus on Agreements, Not Disagreements

An Appeals Officer once told me, "If we can agree on the major issues, the small ones have a way of falling through the cracks." This is to say that some issues are "litigation points" and others are "bargaining chips." Litigation points are the issues neither party wishes to concede. Bargaining chips are those one is willing to concede if it means prevailing on a litigation point.

From your perspective, litigation points are the issues that most profoundly affect your pocketbook and where the law and facts are clearly on your side. It is with respect to these issues that you want to remain most tenacious. However, it is possible to reduce the number of issues you must sacrifice as bargaining chips in order to make a deal. In the ideal negotiation, *none* of your bargaining chips are surrendered. In the realistic negotiation, some (but not all) of your chips are surrendered in exchange for success on the litigation points. The extent to which you are successful depends largely on technique.

The best way to bring about agreement in a tax dispute is to start by discussing the agreements that already exist on the minor points. This has a profound psychological benefit and many practical ones.

Psychologically, the audit environment is often quite adversarial. When the typical person walks into an IRS office, he is usually raving about the ridiculous bill he received or the arbitrary way he was treated in an audit. Although some may doubt this, IRS agents are human and human tendency is to defend one's actions—right or wrong—in the face of an all-out attack. Consequently, when you begin negotiations by attacking, the auditor immediately alerts his defense mechanisms and he goes to "battle stations." You are faced with a bitter fight on each point. Before you know it, you may stand to lose all the issues.

On the other hand, if you begin with a less acrimonious attitude, you are less likely to meet with resistance on all fronts. This creates a less adversarial environment. It naturally becomes easier to reach agreement on critical issues. I am not saying to be milquetoast or to simply cave in. On the contrary, my formula *creates* the circumstances that dictate the overall direction of the negotiations, rather than merely reacting to them.

I begin by identifying all the issues in question. This simple technique prevents you from overlooking important elements of the case. Review the issues by reference to your ground rules letter, the audit notice, the RAR or your protest letter. Now proceed issue-by-issue seeking the agent's agreement that such point is an issue in the case. By the time you reach the end, you have not only gotten the agent to agree with you several times (creating a positive atmosphere), but you also accomplished the important task of fixing the points you must now address one at a time.

Starting with the first issue, begin by discussing the aspects of the issue to which there is or can be no reasonable disagreement. Focus upon the agreements, not disagreements. Let me give you an example of how it works in practice.

I once helped Marilyn remove a federal tax lien from a home she and her husband were selling. The IRS had a large tax assessment against her husband. However, the assessment was not against Marilyn. She owed nothing.

The revenue officer was quite belligerent. She would not allow the sale to close without full payment. The tax was in excess of $22,000 and the equity was just $18,000, half of which belonged to Marilyn. The revenue officer convinced the title company that the entire lien had to be paid before the title could be transferred. Marilyn's position was that the most the IRS could get was one-half the equity. Marilyn's interest in the home could not be touched since she owed no tax. Furthermore, her money could not legally be seized to satisfy her husband's debt.

When I contacted the revenue officer, her opening words were, "What do you want from me?" Clearly, she was uninterested in resolving the problem. After a couple of minutes I determined this "hard case" would have to be taken very slowly and deliberately. I began to focus on the most basic points on which I knew we could agree.

I took a deep breath and began. "Pat," I said, "you will agree with me, won't you, that there is no assessment against Marilyn?" She did.

"And you will agree, won't you, that without an assessment, the IRS cannot file a lien against Marilyn?" She did.

"And you will also agree, won't you, that without a valid assessment, the IRS cannot collect any money from Marilyn?" She did.

"And you will also agree, won't you Pat, that before the IRS can get an assessment, certain administrative procedures have to be followed?" She did.

"Now Pat, you will follow all of the IRS's administrative procedures with regard to Marilyn, won't you?" Of course, she agreed with that.

"Then you must also agree that you cannot legally seize any of Marilyn's money from the sale of the house, don't you?" She did.

Having gotten her agreement on the basic underlying facts, I moved the revenue officer into a position where it was impossible for her to disagree with me on the ultimate issue. The next question I asked was, "Then there is no legal reason not to lift the lien and allow the home to be sold, is there?" Based upon the previous agreements, she was forced to accept this premise. I followed up the conversation with a letter and the sale went ahead as scheduled. Marilyn got her full share of the money and the buyers got a clear title.

It is usually not necessary to resort to such basic statements of fact in order to get an agreement from the IRS. What is necessary is that you begin with the simpler issues, moving up to the more difficult or controversial issues. Proceeding in this fashion enables you to: a) obtain as many agreements as possible before reaching the pivotal issues, and b) having reached the litigation issues, you surrender as few bargaining chips as possible.

When moving backwards, the agent has the ability to negotiate your litigation issue by cashing in some of your bargaining chips. Since I do not like to surrender points, I do not move backwards. Also, by moving from lesser points to litigation issues, it becomes more difficult for the agent to retract a previous agreement in order to negotiate a litigation point. He becomes more or less committed to previous concessions.

Let me illustrate. Rowena was involved in several farm-related businesses. One concerned a mechanical heating system that enabled farmers to capture body heat from animals and use it to heat barns. My client purchased the system from the manufacturer and leased it to several veal producers in Wisconsin.

Rowena received an NOD covering the years the business operated. Many of the points raised in the NOD were minor items, but a major issue revolved around the leases. The IRS took the position that Rowena purchased *paper* (written lease contracts) from the manufacturer. Rowena insisted that she purchased *equipment*, not paper, and in turn leased the equipment to farmers. The difference was substantial. If the IRS prevailed, Rowena would lose thousands of dollars in investment tax credits since they applied only to equipment.

In our negotiations, the Appeals Officer made it clear he was willing to surrender on several of the lesser issues in exchange for the major lease question. Having foreseen this, I determined to head it off at the pass. Just as I described above, I presented proof to the Appeals Officer on each of the minor points. One at a time, we offered canceled checks, receipts and testimony to prove the issues. After presenting proof on an individual item, I was careful to seek and obtain agreement that such proof was sufficient to eliminate contention on that point. If there were further questions, they were resolved before moving on. This went on until I reached the lease issue.

As I anticipated, we could not reach an agreement on the question. The AO held to his view and we stuck to ours. The result was an impasse and each party threatened to go to Tax Court. But the AO stated, "All bets are off if you litigate," meaning that the agreement we just reached on all other issues would be pulled off the table. Expecting this ploy, I pointed out that he *just agreed* we were entitled to those items as a matter of law. "You cannot, in good faith," I asserted, "litigate issues you already agreed were proven as required by law."

After some bantering, he agreed that if we were to litigate, the only point of the trial would be the matter of the leases. This worked to carve tens of thousands of dollars worth of bargaining chips out of the case, in turn allowing Rowena to make the decision to litigate based solely upon the probability of success on the key issue alone without losing the lesser issues.

13. Negotiate the Deduction, Not the Tax

One of the biggest mistakes a person can make is to attempt to negotiate non-negotiable points. After receiving a bill for $1,700, a man once asked me if he could "just offer 'em $850 to settle the whole thing?" Believe it or not, neither the Examination function nor the Appeals Office is concerned with collecting taxes. Their function is merely to determine the *correct tax due*. It does not matter to them whether the correct tax ever gets paid, as long as the correct tax gets assessed. Therefore, auditors are unimpressed with offers to settle a case "for half what you say I owe." (Note, however, that once a tax liability is assessed, the Offer in Compromise can be used to settle for less than you owe if you qualify. See: *How to Get Tax Amnesty*.)

This gives us a major clue as to *how* to approach auditors and Appeals Officers. As I said, their job is to determine *liability*. They do it by considering total gross income and all applicable deductions, credits and exemptions. If one's income is increased or a deduction, credit or exemption is deceased, the final tax liability goes up. The process is that simple.

So, rather than negotiating the bottom line tax liability, negotiate the added income or disallowed deduction that created the liability. For example, suppose you claim a $5,000 charitable contribution deduction. Suppose the agent disallows the entire deduction. When presented with the RAR, you are asked to pay $1,500 in taxes, plus penalties and interest.

To negotiate the deduction, you might approach the problem this way. "Mr. IRS Agent, I claimed $5,000 on the return. You disallowed the entire amount. But surely my receipts prove I gave $2,500 to charity. I believe this evidence entitles me to at least half the deduction, or $2,500." Provided you prove at least $2,500 in contributions using one or more of the techniques we discussed in chapter 6, the agent must oblige. The result is that the ultimate tax is cut in half.

14. Do Not Negotiate Based on Nuisance Value

Litigation is expensive, both for the government and private citizens. In cases not involving the government, litigants routinely settle cases based upon their "nuisance" value. The nuisance value is the cost a party faces if the case goes to trial, whether or not he wins. In that regard, the settlement of litigation becomes a business decision.

Citizens have a tendency to bring nuisance values into tax negotiations believing the IRS is interested in keeping its costs down. But the IRS does not consider settlement offers based on a case's nuisance value. Appeals Rule II, Revenue Regulation section 601.106(f)(2). Said another way, the IRS never has to make the business decision to settle a case because of the potential costs of litigation.

Audit and Appeals decisions must be based upon the law and facts of the case. They must represent a good faith effort to settle the case in a manner that fairly represents the interests of both parties. For this reason, any offer of settlement must be buttressed with solid references to the facts and applicable law.

On the other hand, the Appeals Office regularly settles cases based on the "hazards of litigation." That is to say, Appeals considers the risks of losing the case and creating a negative precedent. As such, the dollars and cents do not matter as much as a negative legal precedent. Therefore, in you settlement discussions, emphasize the hazards of litigation by reminding the IRS of: a) the facts and evidence supporting your position, and b) the law, regulations, court decisions or other authority that support your position. By marshalling this material, you demonstrate that the IRS faces some risk of losing the case, which in turn justifies a negotiated settlement.

15. Always Ask for a Conference

Always demand a conference (or hearing) on the merits of your claims. An example is where you submit a written protest letter in response to a thirty-day letter. The conference allows you to present evidence and testimony to prove your case. Absent a request for a conference, your case might not be assigned for one. Your conference can be either face-to-face or by telephone. In either event, press for the opportunity to argue your case and be heard.

16. Enlist the Aid of Outside Offices

In stalled negotiations, the lines of communication can sometimes be re-established by appealing to one of two "outside" offices. The first is the Office of the Taxpayer Advocate (TA). The TA is charged with the duty of getting to the bottom of and sorting out disputes when normal channels fail.

The TA helped in a case where a citizen filed a claim for refund. The revenue officer to whom the claim was submitted sent it to a service center for processing. Thereafter, nobody in either the local office or the service center could find it. After several months of waiting, we wrote a letter to the TA seeking assistance in tracking it down. Within a matter of days, the TA located the refund claim. Once we knew where it was, we were able to correspond directly with the persons responsible for making a decision.

The TA also has the authority to *stop* the IRS from taking action that may result in causing a "significant hardship" to the citizen. Code section 7811. Such hardship generally grows from enforced collection action. More details on this process are provided in *How to Get Tax Amnesty.*

The second outside office that can sometimes assist is that of your Senator or Congressman. In some circumstances, determined prodding by a conscientious representative may lead to favorable results. But a problem that hampers congressional inquiries is that the IRS is forbidden from releasing tax return or return information to unauthorized persons. Senators and Congressmen are no exception. To avoid this problem, sign and submit to your representative Form 8821, *Tax Information Authorization.* The representative can then submit it to the IRS together with the request for help or action.

Not all congressional inquiries obtain results. To increase your chances, submit a written description of the problem, citing tax code sections and where appropriate, case authorities. This eliminates the need for your representative to do any research on the legal aspect of the problem. If such information is not provided, I do not believe you can expect your representative to seek it out. Next, prepare a detailed written procedural history of the case. This evidences that you pursued and exhausted all administrative remedies without satisfaction.

Once a congressional inquiry begins, the IRS responds in writing to any letters and generally sends a copy to the citizen. In the final analysis, the effectiveness of this appeal is directly related to your ability to provide ammunition to your representative. Therefore, quickly respond to IRS letters. This gives the representative something tangible with which to fight.

CHAPTER FIFTEEN

13 BLUFFS AND INTIMIDATIONS AND HOW TO COUNTER

IN TESTIMONY BEFORE THE SENATE FINANCE Committee in 1969, former Senator Henry Bellmon of Oklahoma told his colleagues:

> In a recent conversation with an official of the IRS, I was amazed when he told me, "If the taxpayers of this country ever discover that the Internal Revenue Service operates on 90 percent bluff, the entire system will collapse."

Not much has changed since that statement was uttered. The art of bluff and intimidation is an integral part of IRS training and practice, though its employees and manuals never admit it. History speaks plainly, however. It is clear that without bluff, in many cases, the IRS just would not collect money.

Sometimes the bluffs are subtle. In one case, an IRS agent explained that he would hate to see the citizen "run up all kinds of legal fees fighting a case he couldn't win." By not taking the bait the citizen did fight, and did win—without running up "all kinds of legal fees."

Other times the bluffs are not so subtle, unless you think a train wreck is subtle. An example is a doctor who was harassed to within an inch of his life by the IRS. After the auditor made literally hundreds of thousands of dollars in mistakes and lost the doctor's receipts, the case went into collection. The IRS demanded he pay over $550,000 in back taxes "now." After listening to the doctor's explanation that he did not have the money to pay "now" and pleas for time to raise the funds, the revenue officer told him, "Our experience with doctors who say they don't have the money is, if we just squeeze them hard enough, the money they don't have just seems to come from someplace."

Whether subtle or bold, the success of a bluff depends on two things. The first is that the individual will not recognize it as a bluff. The second is that his own lack of confidence moves him off his position and into the mental state necessary to accept the "bad news."

In this chapter I identify some of the more common tactics the IRS uses to get money that is not owed. I break them down into three general categories: 1) bluffs used by examiners in the audit process, 2) bluffs used by Appeals Officers, and 3) bluffs used by the IRS in the automated collection process.

By understanding these bluffs and how to counter them, if you end up paying money, it will be because you owe it not because you were bluffed out of it.

Bluffs Used in the Audit

1. The Bluff: *"You must appear at the audit when told."* In chapter 8, under the heading, **The Time and Place of the Audit,** I discussed your rights under section 7605 to set a "reasonable" time and place of your audit. I shall not restate my case here, but will emphasize a few points.

This law is clear that you cannot be pushed into an audit for which you are unprepared. Since the burden of proof is on you, fundamental fairness mandates you be afforded reasonable time to prepare. This includes time to gather, organize and if required, reconstruct records.

Often an agent presses the issue by claiming that if you do not appear on "X date" or if records are not produced by "X date," all of your deductions will be disallowed. However, agents have no unilateral authority to disallow your deductions. The agent can only *propose* a disallowance which is subject to your right of appeal. See chapter 13.

2. The Bluff: *"You must submit to a 'line audit'."* For years, the IRS used the highly invasive, costly and cumbersome Taxpayer Compliance Measurement Program (TCMP) audit to build its statistical database. In turn, that database is used to select the majority of returns audited. In chapter 4, under the heading, **How Returns are Selected for Audit,** I explained the process. I also explained that due to my testimony to Congress, the planned TCMP sweep for 1995 and 1996 was de-funded. About six years later, Congress resurrected the program under a new name, the National Research Program (NRP).

Because NRP audits are "research audits," they are, in the truest sense of the phrase a "fishing expedition." The manner of selecting returns is wholly arbitrary, other than perhaps your return may have common attributes with others in the target universe. For example, the IRS may target partnership tax returns with just two partners and income under $500,000. Likewise, the audit may involve a grueling line-by-line examination or it may focus on a more limited target, such as Schedule C deductions.

While the NRP is a research tool, it is unquestionable that the IRS uses it to get more money. Because the IRS often fails to identify the items in question, the agent may feel free to create problems as the audit develops. The citizen must then react to on-the-spot demands and questions, something most people find difficult to do. Combine that with unreasonable time constraints on producing data and you have a recipe for abuse.

The NRP audit can be neutralized with a little forethought and the understanding of your right to appeal audit decisions, as discussed in chapter 13. Let me put this into perspective.

In an ordinary audit, a person produces his records, and if the IRS has its way, he ends up with a tax bill. The Appeals review is *limited* to whether the examiner correctly computed the tax under all of the facts of the case. Now let us work this knowledge to our advantage. Suppose you do not produce records in a NRP audit. What would be your reasons for not doing so? What would be the IRS's likely reaction to your stance? And what would be the consequences? The following hypothetical dialogue answers these questions.

AUDITOR: Good morning, Mr. Smith. My name is Revenue Agent Jim Henderson. Thank you for coming this morning. Let's get right down to business. Did you bring all of your books and records for 2010? I would like to go through them.

MR. SMITH: Well, Jim, before we go in to any of that, tell me, what part of my return is in question?

AUDITOR: The entire return. This is a NRP audit. We look at each item.

MR. SMITH: Why?

AUDITOR: To see if the return is correct and to help the IRS keep accurate statistics for future audits.

MR. SMITH: Is there a specific entry that caused this audit?

AUDITOR: Well, no, not exactly. We want to look at each item.

MR. SMITH: Are you saying there is no one particular entry that caused my return to be kicked out?

AUDITOR: No. Your return was selected at random just to review it. That helps us make adjustments to our database and to more accurately select other returns for audits in the future.

MR. SMITH: Why should I go to all this hassle if there is nothing wrong with my return?

AUDITOR: You have to. When your return is called into question, you have to verify all items claimed.

MR. SMITH: You just said there's nothing on my return that has been called into question. You said this audit is random to help you build your database.

AUDITOR: Look, if you don't want to produce your records, I will just have to disallow all your deductions. Then you will have a bill to pay, with interest and penalties.

MR. SMITH: Are you saying I don't have any right to have your decision reviewed? Are you the one and only person I'll ever deal with here?

AUDITOR: Of course not. But if you don't produce records, the Appeals Office will uphold my decision every time.

MR. SMITH: I am perfectly happy to verify anything you feel may be out of line. But I am not going to waste my time going through this hassle just so you can beef up your computer system. Just tell me the item you think is out of line and we'll talk about it.

AUDITOR: I just explained I must look at each item. We can take them one at a time if you like but I must have proof for each item. If you don't want to cooperate, I'll just disallow your deductions and you can go from there.

MR. SMITH: I just told you I'm willing to verify my return if there is something wrong with it. But you keep saying there's nothing wrong with it. Then, in the next breath, you tell me I have to produce every scrap of paper I own to prove it. That doesn't make sense. So unless you just tell me what's wrong, I guess I will take it to Appeals.

Later on, at the Appeals level:

APPEALS OFFICER: Mr. Smith, we are here to review the determination made by Examination that you owe additional taxes. It appears from the file your deductions were disallowed because you refused to cooperate. Apparently, you refused to turn over your records. What is your contention here?

MR. SMITH: First of all, I didn't refuse to cooperate. I told the agent again and again I would produce any records he asked for if he would just tell me what was wrong with my return. He wouldn't — so I didn't.

OFFICER: Well, my job is to decide whether the determination is correct. It appears to me that it's just a matter of verifying what you've claimed. If you're willing to cooperate, it'll be just a simple matter. If not, there's nothing I can do. In the absence of records, we just can't allow any deductions. Are you willing to do that?

MR. SMITH: Yes. I was willing to do it at the audit, but the examiner would not cooperate with me. Let's just take the items one at a time. We can begin with . . .

What do you accomplish? The case is transferred to Appeals, responsible for *solving* problems, and away from Examination, responsible for *creating* them. You may ask, "How have I helped myself? I still have to produce records. Why didn't I just give them to the auditor and be done with it?"

The auditor's job is to find ways to collect more money. In a wide-open NPR audit, he could have found any number ways to do that. By contrast, the Appeals Officer only determines whether the auditor's actions are justified. At that point, it is simply a matter of *verifying* deductions by producing records. Since the auditor made a blanket disallowance, the resulting tax bill is overcome by record production at the Appeals level. The Appeals process changes the environment radically and the advantage swings in the citizen's favor.

You should note, however, auditors enjoy the right to summons records under code section 7602, as I discussed in chapter 7. This power is not often used to procure records from an individual regarding deductions (because the burden of proof is on the taxpayer) but it can be and the instances in which they do are growing. Usually, summons are used to obtain records from third parties such as banks and employers. If the agency uses a summons against the citizen, the law generally requires you to provide the records.

3. The Bluff: *"Your proof for this deduction is not sufficient."* The most common audit bluff is for an examiner to attack your form or method of proving deductions. Agents claim canceled checks are no good. They often ignore receipts and even year-end statements. Of course, most agents never accept testimony despite the rules I teach in this book.

The "Your Proof is No Good" bluff works only if you believe you have no recourse to contest the auditor's decision. However, when your proof meets one or more of the criteria set out in chapter 6, there is no need to fall victim to this bluff.

4. The Bluff: *"No witnesses are allowed in the conference."* It is not unusual to require the presence of one or more witnesses at an audit conference to present evidence on a claimed deduction. One example is the case of Paul who claimed travel expenses for a trip to California. He brought a friend with him. The two traveled to California to research a possible investment the second man contemplated making in Paul's business.

The audit called these deductions into question. To establish the business purpose of the trip, I intended to bring Paul's travel companion to the conference. I intended to present his testimony regarding the purpose, length and nature of the trip.

Upon walking in the door with our witness, we were met with immediate opposition from the revenue agent. "These conferences are confidential," she said. "I cannot permit unauthorized persons to be present." I explained that the man's presence was for the limited purpose of offering testimony on the travel expenses. Once that is concluded, the witness could be excused. That way, he would not be privy to anything else.

"I'm sorry," she responded. "The law is quite clear and I just can't allow it."

The law is code section 6103. It forbids the IRS from releasing any confidential "tax return or return information" to any "unauthorized person." The intent of the law is certainly noble. However, auditors deliberately use it as a sword, not a shield. Without the testimony of Paul's witness, we could have been at a decided disadvantage. The agent knew this and that is exactly why she flexed the section 6103 muscle.

However, I anticipated the objection. To counter, we prepared in advance IRS Form 8821, *Tax Information Authorization*. Its purpose is to permit the citizen to give his written consent to the IRS so it may release otherwise confidential information to any person.

With Form 8821 in hand, the agent had no legitimate cause to exclude our witness and his important testimony. See chapter 8, under the heading, **The Right to Present Evidence,** for more on Form 8821.

5. The Bluff: *"You must sign this waiver."* At the conclusion of an audit, the agent presents the RAR. If tax is owed, the citizen is asked to sign Form 870, *Waiver of Restrictions on Assessment and Collection of Deficiency.* Form 870 permits the IRS to assess the tax and begin collection immediately.

Of course, signing the form is not mandatory. Moreover, the IRS is powerless to force a signature. If you do sign, however, your only appeals recourse is to pay the tax in full, and then file a claim for refund. To talk with the IRS, though, you would believe that unless you sign the form, "bad things will happen."

Years ago, Bud came into my office looking for help with his audit. He already went through several conferences with the auditor, his lawyer and accountant. The IRS questioned the sale of some real estate. Due to a mistake, the sale was not reported on the tax return. The agent analyzed the sale, made some adjustments and computed a new tax. The agent presented Bud with a bill for about $14,000, before interest. Bud was told he must pay it. The agent also demanded that Bud sign Form 870.

But Bud did not agree with the figures and had no intention of paying the tax if he could help it. The agent gave Bud no alternative. "Sign it," he said. "If you don't, I'm going to write it up just the way it is." Exactly what he meant by "I'm going to write it up" was never explained. The implications were left solely to Bud's imagination.

Bud turned to his lawyer and accountant for help. The accountant's advice was profound. "We've done all we can do. Looks like you're gonna have to pay."

The lawyer's observation was even more compelling. "You haven't paid much taxes in the past four years anyway—might as well just give 'em the money."

Great advice, don't you agree? The best part is Bud paid for that advice.

Now let us understand something important before we go any further. The agent's computation was dead wrong. He computed important aspects of the sale improperly and he overlooked several thousand dollars in deductible expenses. In addition, he asserted a penalty that was totally out of line. I pointed out the errors to Bud and sent him back to the agent with the new ammo.

Bud returned two days later. He got nowhere. He sadly reported that the agent just repeated his demands or he would "close the case." The unmistakable impression left by the ultimatum was if Bud did not voluntarily sign the waiver, the IRS would just collect the tax anyway.

I explained the appeals process to Bud, a fact ignored by the agent. "Hey Bud," I said, "If you don't agree, let him 'write it up.' All it means is that you have the chance to take the case to Appeals and then to the Tax Court. You have a right to trial before you have to pay a dime. If he won't bend, that's fine. Go over his head."

"No kidding," replied Bud. "He never said I could do that."

"Of course not," I observed. "You might actually take him up on it."

Bud asked for another meeting and the agent agreed to look at the evidence more carefully. Bud left the meeting discouraged. The agent remained unimpressed. Again he demanded Bud sign the 870 or he would "write it up." Now that Bud knew what "write it up" meant, he challenged the agent. "Fine, write it up," he said. "I will just appeal."

Rather astonished, the agent replied, "Appeal? You will appeal?"

"That's right," pushed Bud, more confident now. "I disagree with your figures and I made a counter-offer that's correct. And if you don't accept it, I'm going to appeal!"

Apparently pushed into a corner, the agent said, "Fine. Appeal it. I'll issue the notice."

Bud left the office. Not more than three hours later the agent called Bud at home. It seemed he reconsidered. It seemed the case was not worth hassling over any longer. It seemed his computations indeed overlooked several items and he was willing to settle the case as Bud proposed.

That saved Bud over $8,000. And all it really took was the intestinal fortitude to say "no" and stick to it. With just a little information, Bud was not bluffed into paying thousands in taxes and penalties he did not owe. Chapter 13 explains how to exercise the right of appeal.

Bluffs Used in the Appeal

1. The Bluff: *"If you pre-pay the tax, you can avoid interest."* At the conclusion of an audit or appeal, expect the IRS to ask for payment of the additional tax owed. The pitch generally goes something like is, "If you pre-pay the tax, you can stop the interest from running and save yourself a lot of money. You can maintain your objections, but at least the interest stops." Like a broken clock, this statement is both correct and incorrect. Pre-paying a tax liability does indeed stop interest from running, a major consideration when fighting the IRS.

However, keep in mind that you owe interest only to the extent that you owe the tax. In Bud's case, for example, he did not owe any interest on the erroneous tax cut from the bill. Moreover, it is misleading to claim that after paying, you can "continue to object," because taken out of context the statement creates a false impression. Under ordinary circumstances, the IRS cannot collect a dime without an assessment. It cannot obtain an assessment without issuing a Notice of Deficiency. Upon receiving an NOD, you have the right to petition the Tax Court before paying. See chapter 13 for details.

The IRS mails an NOD only if there is a tax "underpayment." Code section 6211(a) states that a deficiency is *reduced* by the amount of tax collected by the IRS. Consequently, if the IRS determines that a $2,000 deficiency exists, and you pay $2,000, the IRS *will not mail an NOD*. Consequently, you *will not* have an opportunity to petition the Tax Court for redetermination of the bill.

After paying the tax, the only way to continue the battle is to file a claim for refund. But the IRS does not explain that fact when requesting pre-payment. As a result, a person writes his check then waits for the next letter. But the next letter never comes. It never comes because the burden is now on the citizen to file a claim for refund, something he either does not know or does not know how to do. The result is the IRS gets more money with less fight.

Before making a decision to pre-pay taxes, carefully and objectively weigh the chances of success. Do that by considering all the facts of the case and the governing law. Next, if you decide to pre-pay as I discuss in chapter 13, under the heading, **What to do if You Owe Some Tax,** do it in such a way as to preserve all possible avenues of appeal. Designate the payment *in writing* as a "deposit in the nature of a cash bond." Never say you are "paying the tax." The deposit not only stops the interest to the extent of the payment, but it ensures you will be mailed a Notice of Deficiency, thus preserving your right to a Tax Court appeal.

2. The Bluff: *"All bets are off!"*

An Appeals conference involves a process of give and take designed to reach an agreement. As you move through the points of contention, the goal is to narrow the scope of the dispute as much as possible. That way, if a trial becomes necessary, it will involve as few issues as possible. Narrowing the disputed issues is the purpose of any pre-trial negotiation. This is desirable for a number of reasons. Most notably, you reduce the inherent risk of litigation and greatly reduce your burden should the case go to trial.

The process of give-and-take negotiations eventually leads to one party making an offer of settlement. Suppose your audit involves the following issues:

1. $1,500 in travel expenses disallowed,

2. $2,500 in home office expenses disallowed,

3. $1,000 in charitable contributions disallowed, and

4. 20 percent in penalties added to the bill.

After reviewing your evidence, the Appeals Officer makes this offer: "I will allow all the contributions. I will give you $1,000 in travel expenses. And, I will allow one half of the office-in-home expenses." He makes no specific mention of penalties. Thus, as far as he is concerned, the penalties remain in the case as part of the deal.

You respond: "I don't like it. I want the penalties out of there. I believe the facts justify removing them."

The Appeals Officer is firm on his position. "I don't think you've shown the good faith required to remove the penalties."

Unwilling to budge, you are now faced with a decision: either you take the deal offered or you litigate the issue of the penalties. Comfortable with the figures offered on the tax issues, you state, "I'm willing to settle on the basis of the deductions offered, but I want the penalties out. If you are not willing to bend, I want to litigate the penalties."

The Appeals Officer responds with the bluff. "Okay, then all bets are off. I will withdraw my offer to settle the deductions and you will have to litigate *everything*. The offer I made is to settle the case. If you don't want to settle the case, I withdraw the offer."

Your blood runs cold. At least with the offer you have a bird in the hand. If it is withdrawn and you are forced to try each issue in court, you stand to lose that bird in the hand. What to do?

I follow a two-step process. The first is rather simple. Elicit an admission that his offer of settlement is based upon the proof that you provided. You could ask, "You would agree, wouldn't you, that the reason you're allowing $1,000 in travel expenses is because I proved $1,000 in travel expenses?" When he says, "yes," ask the same question as to the other issues. After eliciting affirmative responses each time, proceed to the second step.

Step two is to refer to Appeals Rules of Practice. I quoted Rule I early in chapter 13. Please recall that Rule I prohibits any settlement not based on the law and facts of the case. Rule I presents a stiff admonition against making or withdrawing offers solely on the basis of discouraging litigation on a legitimate issue.

Moreover, Rule II provides that Appeals Officers are to give serious consideration to any taxpayer proposal which:

> fairly reflects the relative merits of the opposing views in light of the hazards which would exist if the case were litigated. However, no settlement will be made based upon nuisance value of the case to either party. If the taxpayer makes an unacceptable proposal of settlement under circumstances indicating a good-faith attempt to reach an agreed disposition of the case on

a basis fair to both the Government and the taxpayer, the Appeals official generally should give an evaluation of the case in such a manner as to enable the taxpayer to ascertain the kind of settlement that would be recommended for acceptance.* * * Rev. Reg. section 601.106(f)(2), Rule II.

Based on the above, I approach the matter with three carefully worded questions.

1. "You of course recognize your obligation to resolve this case on the basis of the law and facts as they exist in the case, do you not?" Do you think he will say no? Next question.

2. "And the offer you made to settle the deductions is based entirely on the law as you understand it and the facts as they exist, isn't it?" What do you think his answer will be? Next question.

3. "So if you withdraw your offer and force me to litigate issues which you already agree have been proven, your case is no longer based on the law and facts, is it?" What can he possibly say? And when he agrees with you, he is finished!

Using this technique allows you to carve problem issues out of the case yet remain strong on those where the law and facts are behind you. At the same time, you have substantially reduced the "hazards of litigation." Review chapter 14, under the heading, **Focus on Agreements, Not Disagreements.**

3. The Bluff: *"Just file an offer."*

This is a last resort plea to induce a settlement in a case involving big numbers. Of course, the single largest factor for citizens in deciding to accept a settlement is the bottom line. "How much will I owe if I accept this deal?" You must ask this question or you are cheating yourself. After all, tax disputes are about money.

The bluff refers to the Offer in Compromise (OIC) provided for by Code section 7122, which I mentioned briefly at the end of chapter 13. The OIC allows the IRS to reduce a tax bill if you either do not legally owe it or cannot pay it.

If your liability is ultimately determined by Appeals, you eliminate one ground upon which an OIC can be based. The IRS will not consider an OIC based on liability if that question was previously determined by the Appeals Office or a federal court. See my book, *How to Get Tax Amnesty* 8.

On the other hand, an OIC based upon doubt as to collectibility involves a lengthy and detailed income and asset investigation. The IRS wants to ensure that you are unable (not just unwilling) to pay the debt. If you have the income and assets to satisfy the bill, regardless of how excessive it may seem, you are expected to pay it. Your OIC will be rejected.

Do not fall into the trap of accepting an otherwise unacceptable proposal simply because the OIC carrot is dangled under your nose.

4. The Bluff: *"We will add a $25,000 penalty if you litigate."* This bluff is used when one is determined to take an issue to trial in the Tax Court. In that case, the IRS sometimes threatens to apply for the $25,000 penalty provided for under code section 6673. The idea behind the bluff is that if one loses a case in Tax Court, not only is he required to pay the

tax but he is responsible for an additional $25,000 penalty to boot. This, of course, is very dissuading to a would-be litigant. However, the penalty is not automatic.

Under the law, the Tax Court has just three reasons to impose a penalty of up to $25,000 (or a lesser amount, at its discretion). The conditions are if: a) your legal position is "frivolous or groundless," b) the proceeding was instituted "primarily for delay," or c) you unreasonably failed to pursue "available administrative remedies." Code section 6673(a)(1).

The penalty is avoided: a) if your legal claim has not been specifically rejected as frivolous by the Tax Court in previous cases, or b) if, based on the applicable law and facts, the court is able to find in your favor (in whole or in part), thus reducing the alleged deficiency. When either of these conditions is met, you face virtually no risk of the penalty. As long as you act in good faith and for the purposes of resolving the dispute, and not merely delaying the inevitable, the penalty does not apply. The penalty is to punish those who abuse the system, not those who use it to legitimately redress improper IRS decisions.

The third condition of the statute makes it imperative that you do all you can to exhaust administrative remedies before petitioning the Tax Court. Code section 6212(d) relates directly to this issue. It gives the IRS the authority to rescind a Notice of Deficiency, thus treating it as if it were never mailed. This eliminates the need to file a Tax Court petition at all. IRS Form 8626, *Agreement to Rescind Notice of Deficiency*, is used for this purpose.

Once both the citizen and the IRS sign Form 8626, the NOD is treated as though it never existed. If the agreement is not accepted, you must petition the Tax Court within the ninety-day grace period. Simply requesting the IRS to rescind its NOD does not extend the time for petitioning the Tax Court. The rescission is not effective unless the IRS signs the form prior to the expiration of the ninety-day period. If the IRS fails or refuses to rescind, you have exhausted your administrative remedies prior to filing a Tax Court Petition, thus substantially reducing your risk of a penalty under section 6673. Please see *Taxpayers' Ultimate Defense Manual*, chapter 4, for a full discussion of Form 8626.

5. The Bluff: *"There is a 90 percent chance we will win the case."* After all other inducements to settle have failed, expect the Appeals Officer or Area Counsel attorney to inform you of your chances of prevailing on the merits of the case. Glibly, he claims the government's chances of prevailing are high, perhaps as high as 90 percent. "There really isn't much sense in going forward," he reports. "I can tell you what the court is going to say about this. There is a 90 percent chance this is going to go our way. I don't see what you have to gain by pursuing this."

Anybody with any experience in trial work can tell you that the only thing certain is that the outcome is *uncertain*. The one aspect of litigation universally recognized by trial lawyers is that the risks are high. For that reason, our judicial system has been almost completely transformed into a forum for arbitration and settlement. Maybe that is good; maybe not. The point is, except in very unusual cases, seldom can one accurately predict the outcome of a trial. IRS lawyers, while they often pretend to be capable, are no exception.

It is true that certain cases present attributes making them more or less likely to meet with success. An example is the so-called "tax protester" case. Over the years, people have challenged the constitutionality of the tax laws on several grounds. Almost without exception, the courts reject the claims as meritless. But not every tax issue has a record paved with the defeats of predecessor cases and without some case history to go on, an attempt to handicap the chances of success or failure on the merits of a given case is, at best, a shot in the dark.

One case in which I dealt with an IRS attorney involved a deduction for $12,000 of fees my client paid to a return preparer/business manager. The IRS offered to allow just $4,000. Our position was that as a business manager, the preparer performed services to the company on an ongoing basis. The services were essential for maintaining the profitability of the company. In addition, a portion of the services was attributable directly to tax return preparation and bookkeeping services, which are deductible expenses under code section 212.

Early in the negotiations, the IRS held firm on its offer. Both the attorney and Appeals Officer were convinced the IRS had a "95 percent chance" they would be successful if we litigated the question.

I phoned the attorney to discuss the matter. "Mike," I asked, "on what do you base your statement that there is a 95 percent chance the IRS will win?" He answered quickly, "You haven't shown that all of the consultant's work was directed at earning income for your client."

Pointing to the evidence we submitted, I countered, "All of the consultant's time sheets detail with particularity the work he did. You heard the testimony of my client concerning his work. This evidence clearly satisfies the requirement."

Mike's only retort was, "Well, I don't think it does."

There was no question that the attorney was firm in his position, but I also knew he had no tangible legal authority to back him up. So rather than attack his position, my tactic was to make him *argue* his position, as strongly as he could. Knowing his stance was weak, I believed the most effective way to convince him of that was to allow him to convince himself.

I asked, "Mike, I want you to talk me out of litigating this case. What do you have in the way of case authority to dissuade me from taking this any further?" He responded flatly, "I don't have any."

Not surprised, I asked, "Well then, what specific facts are you going to rely on to support the notion that we are not entitled to the whole deduction?" Smelling my approach, he got defensive. "Hey," he snapped, "you have the burden of proof. I don't have to prove anything."

"That's true," I replied calmly. "And my proof consists of the unrefuted testimony of my client and that of the consultant himself. You heard what each had to say. You are not saying these people are liars, are you?"

More reserved now, he said, "Of course not."

Pushing a little more, I asked, "In fact, Mike, you would have to agree that they are both quite believable people, wouldn't you?"

The attorney was no dummy and knew exactly what I was doing. He just could not prevent it. He said, "If you are asking me whether I think the court will find them to be believable, yes, it probably would."

My last question spelled the end of the fight. "Well then," I said, "what is there in your case to justify your hard-line position?" In light of all the previous admissions, he was forced to come to grips with the weaknesses and surrender.

The bluff works when a citizen has no idea what the prevailing state of the law is on the issue or simply has no evidence to back up his factual assertions. But when you have a grip on each of these two things, the bluff means nothing.

Bluffs Used in Automated Collection

1. The Bluff: *"You owe penalties."* The tax code contains over 140 different penalties the IRS uses with reckless abandon. Because citizens have the burden to prove the penalty *does not* apply, the IRS asserts them without regard to the facts and often without even an investigation. This happens not only in audits but as an integral part of the IRS's computer notice program. In 2013 alone, the agency assessed over 37.9 million penalties against individuals and businesses, most through the mail. A notice simply declares you owe a penalty and demands payment. If you do not pay, the notice threatens "enforced collection action."

Every penalty section contains a good faith or reasonable cause provision. It means simply that the penalty does not apply when the citizen acts in good faith and with a reasonable cause for his actions. The good faith provision is to ensure penalties are issued only against a deliberately negligent citizen—one who takes affirmative steps to improperly avoid paying the correct tax or who intentionally fails to carry out his legal duties.

Examples of good faith and reasonable cause include, *but are not limited* to:

a. Adverse financial conditions brought on by circumstances over which you had no control,

b. Medical factors leading to the inability to meet your tax obligations,

c. Reliance on the advice of qualified counsel (which I discuss in detail in chapter 16), *or the IRS*, which turned out to be in error,

d. Reliance on IRS statements or publications which either turned out to be wrong or which you in good faith misunderstood or misapplied, or

e. Simple ignorance of the law or requirements in a particular area, where you demonstrate that you made at least minimal efforts to ascertain your responsibilities.

These ideas are not intended to be exhaustive. See chapter 16 for details.

Most penalties are assessed at the service center level and communicated by letter. Often those trying to deal with penalties are told by IRS employees, "The penalty is automatic. You just have to pay it." Nothing could be further from the truth. You have the right to the cancellation of any penalty on the premise of good faith when you prove your case.

To meet the burden, make a written request for abatement of the penalty. Support it with a sworn statement to establish all the facts. Provide copies of all relevant documents such as medical records, etc. Offer sufficient detail to support the contention that you acted in good faith and based upon a reasonable cause for your actions. Failure to provide detail is the most common error I see with failed penalty cancellation requests. The facts should contradict the legal presumption that the penalty applies. Mail your request to the office that issued the penalty using certified mail, return receipt requested. In the context of the tax audit, the same rules apply, though you merely present your request to the auditor or the Appeals Officer handling your case.

Historically, the IRS has used penalties both as a means of raising revenue and to pressure citizens to accept audit findings they did not otherwise agree with. Agents often threaten to load more penalties onto the bill if their unreasonable demands are not met.

As far back as 1992, the IRS adopted a Policy Statement expressly *abandoning* this practice. The policy declares that penalties are to be used only for their "proper purpose;" that is, when one deliberately disregards or disobeys the law. Specifically, penalties are not to be used "as bargaining points in the development or processing of cases." IRS Policy Statement P-1-18, May 19, 1992. Use this to prevent the auditor from threatening penalties if you do not accept an erroneous determination.

Chapters 4 and 8 of my book, *The IRS Problem Solver,* is probably the most thorough, definitive discussion ever written to the public on techniques for winning abatement of penalties. Anyone setting out to challenge tax penalties must read that analysis.

2. The Bluff: *"You owe more taxes."* For decades, the IRS has used a blizzard of computer-generated contacts claiming citizens made mistakes on their returns and thus, owe more tax. One of the most common such notices is known as a "math error" notice. I call it the "arbitrary notice." With no explanation, the notice claims that some additional amount is due. Just like the penalty letter, it states that unless you make immediate payment, "enforcement action" will be taken. This correction program is responsible for generating billions in additional revenue each year. Since we know from GAO studies that IRS computer notices are wrong about half the time, people pay a fortune in taxes they do not owe. The plot unfolds this way:

After receiving an arbitrary notice, the victim phones the IRS's toll free "help" line and talks to an IRS representative.

"I got this notice," he says. "It claims I made a mistake on my return and I owe $650. I don't understand. It doesn't even say what the mistake is. I asked my accountant and he is sure the return was prepared correctly."

The friendly voice says, "I'll bring up the account. What is your Social Security Number, please?" After giving the number, the caller hears the sound of computer keys being skillfully punched. Soon the voice says, "Yes, here it is. Your return was corrected due to an error. You owe $650."

"I know that," the caller chirps. "But why? My accountant says the return was done correctly." Responding abruptly, the voice says, "I don't have that information in my computer. The account only shows an assessment. When may we expect payment?"

Frustrated, the caller barks, "I don't even know if I owe this and you can't tell me why. Why should I pay it?"

Firm now, the voice threatens, "Sir, if you don't pay promptly, we can take enforcement action. That includes filing tax liens and levying your wages, salary and bank accounts."

If the citizen writes a letter expressing his concern, he gets a form letter in response that reads simply:

> We are giving special attention to your inquiry about the tax account identified above. We will write you again within 45 days to let you know the action we are taking.

After some time, the next communication is the levy or lien mentioned by the Voice. By then, it is just a matter of biting the bullet and paying the tax. The bluff is successful if one does not respond to the initial letter properly.

Code section 6213(b) allows the IRS to automatically correct "mathematical" and certain other tax return "errors" without having to first mail a Notice of Deficiency. But the law also expressly states that a citizen:

> [M]ay file with the Secretary within 60 days after notice is sent. . .a request for an abatement of any assessment specified in such notice, and upon receipt of such request, the Secretary *shall abate the assessment.* Section 6213(b)(2) (A); emphasis added.

Provided you respond timely and properly, the IRS has no choice but to abate the tax. Moreover, if the IRS is convinced the assessment is correct, it must mail a Notice of Deficiency in accordance with section 6213(a). That gives you a right to be heard in Tax Court before paying a dime. See chapter 13.

Any response that is: a) not in writing, b) does not demand immediate abatement of the tax under section 6213(b)(2)(A), and c) is not made within sixty days, renders the tax subject to enforced collection. I provide details on the abatement process and many other computer notices in *The IRS Problem Solver.*

The Unspoken Bluff - "You will go to jail!"

One of the most heinous elements of the IRS's 1984 Strategic Plan was that calling for the agency to "create and maintain a sense of presence" in America to "encourage and achieve the highest degree of voluntary compliance" possible. There is little doubt the IRS was aspiring to be the American Gestapo. And if you think all the "reform" legislation passed since 1984 must have fixed that problem, consider that IRS's the most recent five-year plan released in 2014 addresses this same point, saying:

> Additionally, we recognize that widely publicizing timely enforcement actions can have a deterrent effect, preventing taxpayers from becoming

noncompliant in the future. IRS Strategic Plan, 2014-2017, pg 31.

Ask anyone you see on the street what will happen if you cheat on your taxes. Their answer is likely, "You will go to jail." To ensure this attitude prevails, the IRS does its best to prosecute a token number of carefully chosen targets each year. Is it mere coincidence that the majority of indictments and sentencings take place in the spring, on the threshold of the tax return filing deadline? For example, after being convicted of tax fraud, New York real estate mogul Leona Helmsley was ordered to report to prison on April 15. The federal judge who sentenced her said he did it to "send a message."

In other cases, newspaper headlines shout, "Man Charged With Tax Fraud - Faces 15 Years."

"Fifteen years?! *Good Heavens!* Why didn't the idiot just pay the stupid tax?"

Americans bombarded with this propaganda not only have the poor stooge convicted even before a trial, but they are themselves convinced that when you mess with the IRS, you can look forward to exactly the same fate. It is appalling that a very large segment of the population believes you run a risk of jail just by *speaking out* against the IRS.

What has the IRS become if it commands that kind of respect? More importantly, what has it done to *earn* that kind of respect?

I believe it is high time we end the *myth* about jail. The reality is that not all so-called tax cheaters go to jail. And as hard as the IRS strives to achieve ubiquitous power, it is not there yet.

The criminal investigation and prosecution statistics tell the real story. According to the Internal Revenue Service's 2013 Data Book, Table 18, there were 5,314 total criminal investigations undertaken that year—typical for a given year. About 33 percent (1,753) involved "illegal source" crimes, such as drug dealing, identify theft, illegal gambling, extortion, etc. Identity thieves are the among the highest profile targets for the IRS these days. Right out of the chute your chances of being implicated in a tax crime are automatically reduced by a third if you do *not* earn income from an illegal source.

Please also keep in mind that in 2013, about 146 *million* individual income tax returns were filed. When that figure is compared to 5,314 criminal investigations, you quickly realize that you have a better chance of being eaten by a shark than you do of being implicated in a criminal tax investigation.

Also note that while 5,314 investigations were undertaken in 2013, only 3,865—about 73 percent—ran their full course resulting in full scale, liberty-threatening criminal prosecutions. Even at that, just 2,253 citizens were actually sent to prison in 2013. And 40 percent of those people were involved in crimes related to *illegal source* income.

Of the total number of people sent to jail in 2013, just 1,086 were sentenced to jail time as a result of what you might call typical tax crimes. When you divide that number by 146 million (the number of individual returns filed), you find the true statistical probability that any one citizen will ever do time because of a tax crime. It is about *7/10,000ths of a percent*. Honestly, who is kidding whom?

The reality is, even with all its computers and its "everybody-on-the-block-is-a-spy attitude," the IRS is not capable of prosecuting every person who fails to dot an "I" or cross a "T." I do not say this to encourage cheating. On the contrary, the point is, honest citizens *need not* be terrified simply because a few tax cheaters and identify thieves are convicted of crimes each year. Honest citizens need not be afraid to speak out against IRS abuses or unjust collection practices, or challenge erroneous audit decisions on the vague threat of jail.

In *How to Get Tax Amnesty*, chapter 3, I explain in detail the IRS's burden of proof in criminal cases. It is much different than in civil cases and that difference explains why so few people are convicted of tax crimes.

When is the IRS NOT Bluffing?

It is critical to recognize not only when the IRS is bluffing, but also when it *is not* bluffing. Even though many IRS demands have no legal basis, some threats are backed with awesome power.

So make no mistake about it. The IRS's Collection function has staggering powers and too often a twitchy trigger finger. Its lien, levy and seizure arsenal make it the most powerful government agency. And this fact is exploited by the IRS. It cleverly uses publicity generated by its own, sometimes-tyrannical collection practices to create a condition of fear. This helps keep people whipped into shape. The IRS calls this "encouraging voluntary compliance." It goes hand-in-hand with high-profile criminal prosecutions.

Everybody has heard an IRS horror story—one that makes your blood run cold. There have been countless books, articles and news accounts written of how the IRS seizes businesses, homes, bank accounts and autos in what seems like almost indiscriminate abandon. The impact of these stories is profound. People are convinced that if you do not turn out your pockets when asked, your house will be seized—or worse, you will go to jail. The stories have emasculated the public. An overwhelming fear of our own government causes many to seek refuge in blind obedience to every demand, regardless of its legality.

Each year, the IRS issues between three and four million wage and bank levies and files approximately one million federal tax liens. On top of that, thousands of people lose homes and businesses. Tax delinquencies are growing fast and the IRS enforces collection in the most oppressive ways. To make matters worse, most of these actions are carried out through the automated process, without personal oversight.

The bottom line is simple. The Collection function does not bluff. When it states that "enforced collection action will be taken," that is exactly what it means. Enforced collection includes liens, levies and seizures of property. Therefore, all correspondence from Collection must be taken seriously and dealt with promptly.

Anyone facing a back tax debt must consult my book *How to Get Tax Amnesty*. Since its initial release in 1992, it has helped hundreds of thousands of people avoid enforcement and settle tax debts they might never have otherwise settled. The strategies I discuss in the book will ensure that you never fall victim to an IRS levy or seizure.

CHAPTER SIXTEEN

HOW TO GET THE MOST OUT OF YOUR RETURN PREPARER

PAID TAX PROFESSIONALS PREPARED JUST OVER 60 percent of the 146 million individual tax returns filed in 2013. Most people trust that they are getting the full benefit of all available tax breaks and have full confidence that their pro can handle any IRS situation. Unfortunately, the facts indicate something entirely different. Most tax pros know what they are doing but those who do not can cause serious problems. Here are some tips to help you get the most out of your tax pro and protect yourself from penalties if things do not go right.

Not All Tax Preparers Get it Right

I have written extensively about GAO studies proving that millions of people overpay their taxes. You might think that you do not have to worry about overpaying if you use a paid professional. However, according to the GAO, *half* the citizens who overpay their taxes use paid professionals. What is more troubling about this finding is the fact that the GAO's studies typically focus on just one area—itemized deductions—which happens to be one of the simplest areas of the tax code. What kind of mistakes do preparers make in more complicated areas that might cost you big money every year?

20 Ways to Get the Most Out of Your Tax Preparer

There are a number of reasons tax preparers might make errors or omissions on tax returns that cost you money. Some are the fault of the preparer but, frankly, much of it can be attributed to you. After all, if you never brush and floss your teeth, you can hardly blame the dentist for the fact that you have cavities and gum disease.

You must take responsibility for what is in your tax return. Even if you do not like the sound of this admonition, the legal reality is that once you sign the return, even if a paid professional prepared it, you are on the hook for *all* of its claims and omissions—period.

That said, let us examine twenty ways to get the most out of your tax preparer.

1. Be systematic about keeping records. As I pointed out in chapter five, two key reasons people lose their deductions is either that they do not keep proper records, or their records are in disarray. You cannot scramble around at the last minute looking for records and you cannot expect your tax pro to manufacture records to support what you believe to be deductible expenses. If nothing else, you need affidavits to support claims,

say, of the business use of your home or auto. Get into the habit of making, organizing and keeping these records on a systematic basis. The sooner you start, the more likely you will benefit.

2. Provide actual records to the preparer. Many preparers use a questionnaire or other worksheet to gather the information needed to complete the return. That is fine, but in my experience, many people fail to complete the questionnaire fully or properly, or do not understand all of the questions. For this reason, you should be proactive in requesting that your tax pro actually review your documents or at least those you are unsure of, to determine whether you have overlooked something important that could save you money. If you do get a questionnaire, be sure to complete it with all the details of your financial situation taken from your own record keeping system.

3. Your tax pro should talk with you. To provide the most thorough preparation service possible, the tax pro should know about you, your business and a bit about your lifestyle. This way, he knows better what to look for in the way of deductible expenses. A simple example is a tax pro who does not know you are a traveling salesperson. He may look at your travel expenses as nothing more than excessive, non-deductible personal vacation expenses. This would cost you dearly in overpaid taxes. Look for a tax pro who is willing to spend some time getting to know you and what you do for a living. This will save you money.

4. Do not be afraid to ask questions to be sure all areas of potential tax deductions are captured. Just because you are not a tax expert does not mean you do not have the right to question what is in your return. After all, you are the one ultimately responsible for the bill. If you cannot find where a certain deduction is claimed on your return, ask. If the item was not claimed, make sure you get a satisfactory explanation of why. Likewise, if you see an entry that seems large or unusual, question it until you understand the claim.

5. Stay involved with your tax pro. As I said earlier, if you have bad teeth, you cannot blame a dentist if you either failed to follow his advice or failed to consult him for advice in the first place. The same is true of a tax pro. You have to stay involved by consulting him from time to time as issues arise.

6. Review your W-4 Form. About 70 percent of all citizens get a tax refund annually. Most refunds go to wage earners and most get the refund because they did not correctly adjust their *Withholding Allowance Certificate*, Form W-4. There is no legal reason to pay more taxes than you owe and there is no financial reason to allow the IRS to hold your money for more than a year without paying you a nickel's worth of interest. Your tax pro should review your withholding situation annually—more often if your circumstances change. This review should take place no later than after the completion of your tax return. A better time to do it is at the end of the year. Say, sometime in December. This way you can go into the next year with the correct withholding right from the start. See chapter 19, under the heading, **Stop Lending Money to the IRS.**

7. Look for a tax pro who educates you on the law. It is a lot easier to comply with record keeping and reporting obligations if you understand the law you are trying to comply with. The more you understand, the better you can provide relevant information and interact with your preparer. Your tax pro should be willing to spend time briefing you

or providing written guidance on relevant areas of law so you can better comply. This will help tremendously to save time and money in the long run.

8. I do not recommend using a part time tax pro, one who prepares tax returns three months out of the year and sharpens saws the other nine. These people tend simply to be form filler-outers and, while there are always exceptions, they tend not to keep up on substantive law changes at a depth sufficient to help you in the planning process. Seek out a fulltime preparer with a commitment to staying current on the legal issues and helping you cut your taxes and stay in compliance.

9. Use a tax professional who has experience in the particulars of your financial life and in the job or business that you are in. Many preparers pound out thousands of returns annually precisely because the forms are short and easily produced in a virtual assembly line fashion. Such a preparer may not have experience in, say, small business tax returns.

10. Be aware of changing circumstances. The circumstances of your business and personal life change often. You buy or sell a house. A child is born or one moves away from home. You get married or divorced. You buy a business or dispose of one. You move to a new town or get a new job in the same town. The list goes on. Do not carry out these substantial changes in a tax vacuum. Be aware of your changing circumstances and get guidance from your pro—preferably *before* the changes are final—as to their impact on your tax bill. Very often, a tax pro can help arrange your affairs to reduce the tax bite or increase the tax breaks incident to the change.

11. Beware of a tax pro who ignores your information. You should seriously question the thoroughness of a tax pro who does not consider all your facts and circumstances. If a tax pro is non-responsive to your questions, ignores relevant information, overlooks obvious factors such as your marital status or the number of dependent children, or worse, ignores or is non-responsive or vague about IRS notices you received, you might be dealing with somebody who is unsure of what he is doing. This is especially true in the arena of tax law enforcement. Often, tax pros who are perfectly fit to prepare returns are hopelessly lost when it comes to dealing with penalties, improper computer notices, audits and, especially, delinquent collection accounts.

12. Beware of a tax pro who recommends shelters. For at least the last twenty-five years, countless thousands of people have been sucked into bogus tax shelters and offshore tax saving strategies. Some were outright scams hustled by con artists, but some appeared to be legitimate transactions and were recommended and supported by reputable accounting firms. The IRS is *very* aggressive about cracking down on what it calls "abusive tax shelters" and those with offshore investments. The agency makes it a priority to review the records of accounting firms whose clients were sold tax shelter strategies. Over the past five or so years, the IRS has essentially broken the wall of secrecy that previously existed with offshore banks and investment companies. If your tax pro recommends a shelter or offshore strategy of *any kind* as a means of cutting your taxes, you will do yourself a *huge favor* by getting a second opinion from an experienced tax pro entirely *unrelated* to the firm or individual making the pitch. If you are already involved in a shelter or offshore strategy, consider getting a second opinion

right away on the merits of what you have done, and if necessary how to correct it.

13. Go over your return before signing it. You are ultimately responsible for what is in your return, regardless of who prepares it. You should ask questions about it and make sure you understand what the preparer did before signing and mailing it. If you are uncomfortable, do not file the return. If necessary, get a filing extension and seek a second option.

14. Be wary of paying for unnecessary services. This can be more difficult for the non-tax expert to ascertain, but is not impossible. Tax preparers often charge by the tax form. The more forms you file, the higher the fees for the return. And this is fine, as long as the pro is not building unnecessary work into the process. Get an explanation from the preparer in advance as to what forms and schedules you need and why. He should be able to tell this to a near certainty after interviewing you. If he proposes what seem like unusual forms, schedules or other items for which additional fees are charged, get details on the reasons and consider a second opinion.

15. Do not get a Refund Anticipation Loan. Referred to as RALs, these are loans arranged by a tax preparer, issued by a financial institution and secured by your tax refund. These loans are sold on the idea that you will get your money in two to ten days, rather than having to wait weeks or months for the IRS to send a check. But these loans do not come cheap. Often, the combined fees paid to the preparer and the lending institution, including interest on the loan, can range from $300 to $500. Considering that the typical tax refund is about $3,000, this translates to an effective annual interest rate approaching *one hundred percent* on these loans. The better plan is to work with a reputable preparer who will ensure that you do not overpay your taxes in the first place.

16. Watch for clear signs of fraud. Even if you are defrauded by a tax pro, you are still on the hook for the taxes and interest, even if you are successful in getting the IRS to cut the penalties. As I mentioned in chapter 15 with respect to reasonable cause, the good faith reliance on counsel can be grounds for canceling penalties. I discuss this issue more specifically later in this chapter. So do yourself a favor and keep an eye out for clear indications of potential fraud or mistakes just waiting to happen. Here are some things to watch for:

- A preparer who seeks a fee based on the percentage of the refund on your original return. Besides being a violation of IRS procedures, this is too often a means by which dishonest pros falsely increase your deductions just to boost their fees.

- A pro who asks you to write a check for your taxes directly to him, not the government. Never write a tax check payable to your tax pro. Always make the check payable to the U.S. Treasury. This eliminates any temptation for the pro to deposit the money in his account.

- A pro who claims to "have friends on the inside" who can offer "under the table" help or support to move things along, whether in the case of audits, delinquent returns, collection issues, penalty abatement or other problem areas. Most often, this is just a ruse to persuade the client that the pro has good connections and is therefore better able to get the job done. But in the worst case, there could in fact be a criminal conspiracy existing between the pro and somebody within the IRS.

- A preparer who asks you to sign blank tax forms. Make sure your return is completed properly before you sign it and, as outlined above, go over the return with your preparer before filing it.

- A preparer who promises to mail your tax returns for you. Do not leave the pro with the added task of mailing your return. In the first place, the majority of paid professionals are required to e-file the tax returns they prepare. You must sign Form 8879, *IRS e-file Signature Authorization*, and provide it to your preparer. Upon e-filing the return, the preparer receives from the IRS either an acknowledgement that the return was accepted, or a rejection stating that there were errors in the return. In either event, you have to be notified by the preparer and you should obtain confirmation for your records that your return was in fact accepted (after errors were corrected, if necessary) for filing. In the second place, even if a return can be mailed through the Postal Service, anything can happen (and often does), which might then leave you in a situation where your return goes unfiled. The fact that you left your return with a tax pro for filing might not be a defense to non-filing penalties.

- All "untax" scams. *Avoid them like the plague.* Any program that promises to get you out of the system and end your obligation to file returns and pay taxes—for *whatever* reason—cannot and will not work. You will just end up in trouble at some level. Not only will you owe the back taxes plus the usual penalties and interest, but also expect the IRS to assess an additional $5,000 penalty for making a "frivolous submission." Code section 6702. For more details on tax scams, see my special reports, *The Untax Promise* and *Why Trusts Don't Work*, both of which are available free of charge on my web site, at www.taxhelponline.com. On the home page, click on "resources and publications," then on "special reports." For the IRS's current published list of frivolous positions that could lead to a $5,000 penalty, go to the IRS's web site and search for "frivolous positions."

- Offshore trusts, banks or other foreign investment or savings strategies that promise to allow you to move income offshore, not declare it on your tax return, and yet enjoy the benefits of it by repatriating the money through credit cards, debit cards, loans, the use of trusts, corporations or any other devices. These are under systematic attack by the IRS and they will not work. You should avoid all of them no matter what the promises of the promoters may be.

- Generally speaking, be overly cautious of tax pros who promise the moon when it comes to cutting your taxes or solving delinquent tax problems. Very few strategies in the tax world can be considered "slam dunks" for citizens. Such solutions exist, but the more probable scenario is that the strategy has risks or a downside that *must* be explained honestly and evaluated before you can make an informed decision on how to proceed. In this regard, do not ever be afraid to ask questions and seek legal authority for any proposed strategy.

17. Your tax pro will be working under deadlines. Therefore, you must provide all requested information in a timely manner.

18. Have a clear fee agreement. Make sure you understand your obligation for fees and costs and the tasks your representative will perform. Do not be afraid to ask for this in writing. This is especially important if your tax pro is representing you in a problems resolution situation. Such cases can take substantial time and effort and costs can escalate. Make sure you know going in what the potential cost will be for professional services.

19. Do not give your original documents to your tax pro. Provide clear photocopies only unless originals are needed for trial (which is rare). If there is ever a problem in your relationship with your tax pro and you must change counsel you will need to have access to your records. I am personally familiar with more than one horror story about tax pros who suddenly retired, moved out of state or worse, died, leaving clients with little hope of carrying on their cases because they gave up their original documents.

20. If you are involved in a problems resolution matter such as an audit, appeal or collection case, do not expect miracles. Problems resolution takes time, mostly because the IRS moves like a glacier and does not care about your life. But it is reasonable to expect and obtain updates as your case progresses.

If you are uncomfortable with your current tax pro or are in the market to hire one for the first time, contact one of the members of my Tax Freedom Institute. This is my national association of attorneys, accountants and enrolled agents dedicated to preserving taxpayers' rights and reducing your tax bill to its lowest legal level. You can find a list of the current members by going to www.taxhelponline.com, and clicking on the Tax Freedom Institute logo.

What to Do if You are the Victim of a Tax Scam

For as long as there have been taxes, there have been tax scams. Today, there are hundreds of people promoting dozens of different ideas calculated to "legally reduce or eliminate" you tax debts.

Some are promoted as tax shelters by reputable accounting and law firms. Some are outgrowths of the so-called tax protester "untax" movement, which generally argues that the tax laws are unconstitutional or voluntary. Some scams involve complicated entity structures, such as domestic and offshore trusts, corporations or other business entities. Some involve sending "demand letters" or complicated legal arguments to the IRS claiming that you are not a U.S. citizen or that you did not receive taxable income in exchange for your labor.

Regardless of the means of carrying them out, they all seem to have one common attribute: they do not work. And the citizens who are swept up in the programs end up facing substantial tax assessments and a mountain of penalties, including very often the frivolous submissions penalty. To illustrate how bad this can be, consider Jack and Deb. They were the victims of a scam in which they were advised to submit amended tax returns for the past three years and a current return asserting an argument based upon a frivolous position. They were *both* assessed the $5,000 penalty for *each* amended return as well as for the current return. That is eight $5,000 penalties, totaling $40,000. And that did not even include the income taxes.

As I stated in chapter 15, the IRS rarely makes clear the fact that all penalty provisions of the tax code can be canceled. Some of the most common penalties assessed in tax scam cases include the accuracy penalty (code section 6662), failure to pay taxes (code section 6651(a)(2)), failure to file returns (code section 6651(a)(1)) and failure to pay estimated taxes (code section 6654). I mentioned the frivolous submissions penalty (code section 6702) earlier. In some of the more egregious cases, the IRS might even assess the civil fraud penalty (code section 6663). Let us discuss penalty abatement more generally.

Managing Tax Penalties. Virtually every penalty provision of the tax code contains some clear authority allowing for the cancellation or non-assertion of the penalty. This means very simply that if one meets the statutory conditions, the penalty does not apply. The most common statutory condition justifying abatement is the reasonable cause standard. For example, the failure to file penalty, code section 6651(a), provides that the penalty applies unless the citizen proves that the failure is attributable to "reasonable cause and not willful neglect."

The Supreme Court defined the phrase "willful negligence" as a "conscience, intentional failure or reckless indifference." *United States v. Boyle*, 469 U.S. 241 (1985). Implicit in this definition is the idea that the citizen failed to take reasonable steps to determine the legitimacy of his actions or to otherwise ascertain and meet what he understands to be his legal obligations. The idea of reckless indifference is the opposite of the action taken by a person operating under a compliant spirit. Such a person undertakes to ascertain his legal duties and then moves systematically to discharge those duties. Such conduct—even if erroneous—is not willfully negligent nor attributable to reckless indifference.

Common Attributes of Tax Scams. The vast majority of tax scams marketed today share various common attributes. First, they are marketed as a perfectly legal means of reducing or eliminating one's income taxes. The marketing materials offered by promoters in almost every case include a detailed explanation of the proposed structure as well as a lengthy discussion of the statutes, regulations and court rulings that purportedly support the legal conclusions advanced by the promoters.

Secondly, either the promoter himself or somebody closely associated with him holds himself out to be a tax professional with specialized training in the subject matter covered. For example, trust promoters are often attorneys or CPAs, or are aligned with attorneys or CPAs. The promoter argues that by virtue of his specialized skill and training, or that of his close associates, the participants in his program are assured the best possible legal and accounting advice and by extension—protection.

Third, promoters offer some type of IRS correspondence or documentation that purports to show IRS acceptance of the plan. The documentation is often a featured aspect of the presentation since it speaks to the one question all potential participants have: "What does the IRS say about this?"

Fourth, a promoter's package consists of testimonial letters or statements from "satisfied customers" who purportedly followed the advice of the promoter and achieved the results advertised. Often, the package includes copies of IRS refund checks or other correspondence intending to lead one to conclude that the IRS ruled favorably in that specific case.

The preponderance of the evidence amassed by promoters and presented in the fashion outlined above can be very compelling, especially when presented by a competent speaker. To the untrained eye, it can appear very clear that the claims made by various promoters and repeated by their clients are indeed true.

Reliance on the Advice of Counsel as a Defense to Penalties

Given the supposed "evidence" amassed by the promoters and the "expertise" they claim regarding the subject, how can those factors be turned to the advantage of a citizen victimized by a promoter's lies? One way to accomplish this is to use the promoter's own evidence as a means of establishing your "reasonable cause" as a defense to penalties. One factor recognized as reasonable cause is one's good faith reliance upon the advice of counsel. As the Supreme Court stated in the *Boyle* case,

> When an accountant or attorney advises a taxpayer on a matter of tax law, such as whether a liability exists, it is reasonable for the taxpayer to rely on that advice. Most taxpayers are not competent to discern error in the substantive advice of an accountant or attorney. To require the taxpayer to challenge the attorney, to seek a "second opinion," or to try to monitor counsel on the provisions of the Code himself would nullify the very purpose of seeking the advice of a presumed expert in the first place. Ordinary business care and prudence does not demand such actions.

Courts generally require a citizen to show three elements to establish reliance on counsel as a defense to tax penalties. They are:

- The citizen is unfamiliar with the tax law,

- The citizen made full and truthful disclosure of all relevant facts to the tax pro, and maintains contact with the tax pro from time to time during the administration of the case, and

- The citizen otherwise exercised ordinary business care and prudence. *Rohrabaugh v. United States*, 611 F.2d 211 (7th Cir. 1979).

The IRS's Penalty Handbook also recognizes the fact that reasonable reliance upon the advice of counsel is a defense to penalties if that advice is related to a technical or complicated issue. IRM section 20.1.5.6.3, "Experience, Knowledge, Sophistication, and Education of Taxpayer," reads as follows:

(1) Circumstances that may suggest reasonable cause and good faith include an honest misunderstanding of fact or law that is reasonable in light of the facts, including the experience, knowledge, sophistication and education of the taxpayer. The taxpayer's mental and physical condition, as well as sophistication with respect to the tax laws at the time the return was filed, are relevant in deciding whether the taxpayer acted with reasonable cause.

(2) If the taxpayer is misguided and unsophisticated in tax law, but acts in good faith, a penalty is not warranted.

For example, questions regarding trust structures, estate planning strategies, the taxation of offshore entities, tax shelter strategies, exotic refund scenarios and corporate income taxes are questions the complexity of which go well beyond garden variety tax law. An inexperienced or unsophisticated person has the right to rely on counsel in such a matter. IRM section 20.1.5.6.4, "Reliance on Advice," provides as follows:

(1) Reliance upon a tax opinion provided by a tax advisor may serve as a basis for the reasonable cause and good faith exception to the accuracy-related penalty. The reliance, however, must be objectively reasonable. For example, the taxpayer must supply the advisor with all the necessary information to assess the tax matter. Similarly, if the advisor suffers from a conflict of interest or lack of expertise that the taxpayer knew about or should have known, the taxpayer might not have acted reasonably in relying on that advisor. The advice also must be based on all pertinent facts, circumstances and the law as it relates to those facts and circumstances.

(2) The advice must not be based on unreasonable factual or legal assumptions (including assumptions as to future events) and must not unreasonably rely on the representations, statements, findings, or agreements of the taxpayer or any other person. For example, the advice must not be based on a representation or assumption which the taxpayer knows, or has reason to know, is unlikely to be true, such as an inaccurate representation or assumption as to the taxpayer's purposes for entering into a transaction or for structuring a transaction in a particular manner. Similarly, the advice must not be based on an assumption that the transaction has a business purpose other than tax avoidance.

Citizens typically seek professional guidance in areas of the law that are unusual. This includes the areas of estate planning, tax shelters, trusts and other complicated entities designed to reduce or eliminate taxes. These are the very areas where unscrupulous tax professionals victimize citizens. The problem is that the typical citizen is in no position to know where or how the recommendations of their tax counsel may fail. Only those with experience in a particular area can advise an unwitting citizen that the proposed arrangement is destined to fail.

The Fact that the Advice was Incorrect Does Not Matter. The IRS's Penalty Handbook describes the purpose of tax penalties and explains the kind of people against whom they should be assessed. At IRM section 20.1.5.1, "Penalty Policy," the manual plainly states that the purpose of penalties is to "encourage voluntary compliance" with the tax system. When you make a good faith effort to meet your tax obligations, compliance is achieved, even if you fall short. At section 20.1.5.6.2, "Taxpayer's Effort to Report the Proper Tax Liability," the IRM states as follows:

> (1) Generally, the most important factor in determining whether the taxpayer has reasonable cause and acted in good faith is the extent of the taxpayer's effort to report the proper tax liability.

Even though mistakes may have been made in connection with determining and reporting your tax liability, when the mistakes are not deliberate or willfully negligent, no penalties should be imposed. When the mistakes are due entirely to your good faith reliance upon tax advisors who provided erroneous advice on matters of a highly technical and complex nature, your good faith reliance insulates you from penalties. In the context of that advice, you acted conscientiously in an effort to "meet the tax obligations" imposed by law.

How to Prove Reliance

The key to success with a reliance defense is to prove that the reliance was "reasonable." It is not reasonable to rely on your babysitter for advice about your federal tax matters. On the other hand, it is reasonable to rely on the advice of a trained, experienced professional who holds himself out to the public as qualified to give tax counsel. This may be somewhat problematic when dealing with some tax scams because often, the promoters are *not* tax professionals. Instead, they are merely slick conmen.

Thankfully, the standard for reasonable reliance is not whether *in fact* the promoter is trained, educated, etc., but rather, whether you reasonably believed him to be a trained professional, based upon all the information available to you. In this regard, it is very important to offer proof of the biographical information presented to you by the promoter. As explained above, the public representations made by these people regarding their training, experience, skill and expertise seem quite impressive—at least on paper.

The IRS often counters with a simple question: "Did you seek a second option?" Other times the agency questions whether you challenged the conclusions of the promoter in any way or otherwise did independent research regarding their claims. If you in fact did so, this is very helpful in proving that you acted reasonably and exercised due diligence in researching the promoter's claims.

In one case, Joann got involved in a trust scheme but ran the idea past her own accountant prior to buying the trust package. In truth, the accountant did not know one thing about trusts but was hesitant to reveal his ignorance to his long-time client. Rather than admit he did not have a clue, he tacitly endorsed the idea as having some validity. In Joann's mind, this was the equivalent of the gold standard and sealed her reliance defense.

On the other hand, in cases where the promoter is a bona fide licensed professional such as an attorney or accountant, seeking a second option is not required. As the Supreme

Court stated in *Boyle*, the idea of requiring an uninformed citizen to second-guess an attorney, obtain a second opinion or otherwise monitor the attorney in the performance of his duties, nullifies the "very purpose" of seeking counsel in the first place. Anybody capable of knowing whether the advice of a trained, licensed professional in a given area of complex tax law is actually correct probably does not need counsel.

Once you prove that your position was based upon the advice of counsel, you must prove that you disclosed all relevant facts to counsel and in fact, took the steps advised by counsel. It is no defense to blame counsel for bad advice that you never followed or to blame counsel for rendering a bad opinion if you failed to provide all the correct, relevant facts. This is not difficult in most tax shelter or other complicated entity structure cases, where the promoter provides a thick package of documents and all you do is add water. Not many people deviate from the precise instructions given them in these cases.

You must prove that you are ignorant of, or at least unfamiliar with the tax laws that govern the subject matter in question. For most people, this is not difficult to do. There is a massive body of law on the question of tax shelters, trusts in general and use of trusts and other entities in the area of estate planning in particular. In fact, estate tax law and planning is one of the most litigious areas of the tax law. When you are not familiar with the law, you have a right to seek and rely upon the advice of counsel.

To be successful, you do not have to prove a negative. Simply establish where your field of expertise lies. In Joann's case, she had no training in tax law or accounting. She ran a retail jewelry business. Her training and experience was limited to the areas of retail sales, marketing, diamonds and colored gems. She sought professional counsel to enable her to discharge her legal duties vis-à-vis income tax return filing and general tax law compliance.

Finally, you must show that you otherwise exercised reasonable business care and prudence. In this regard, it is very helpful to show that you engaged in an exit strategy as soon as you became aware that the scheme would not work. That is to say, you must abandon the improper structure under which you are operating. The sooner you do, the better your chances of proving good faith. On the other hand, continuing down the path after becoming aware of the shortcomings of your plan—or worse, switching to some other avoidance scheme—only strengthens the IRS's baseline proposition that you got involved in the scheme merely as means of cheating on your taxes.

The Frivolous Submissions Penalty

As I already explained, code section 6702 gives the IRS the authority to assess a penalty of $5,000 against any person who files a "frivolous submission." A submission can be a tax return, claim for refund, *Offer in Compromise* (Form 656), *Request for Collection Due Process Hearing* (Form 12153), *Installment Agreement Request* (Form 9465) or *Request for a Taxpayer Assistance Order* (Form 911). For a detailed discussion of what is considered a "frivolous submission," see my *Tax Amnesty Supplement*, chapter nine.

Code section 6702(d) provides discretionary authority to the IRS to reduce or eliminate the penalty. That section reads:

The Secretary may reduce the amount of any penalty imposed under this section if the Secretary determines that such reduction would promote compliance with and administration of the Federal tax laws.

As you can see, there is no specific "reasonable cause" language in this provision. For that reason, the IRS often takes the position that the typical reasonable cause grounds generally do not apply to a request for abatement under section 6702(d). However, the IRS adopted a "one-time" reduction policy, allowing the IRS to "reduce all section 6702 penalties assessed against that person to $500." Revenue Procedure 2012-43, 2012-49, I.R.B. 643, section 5.

The policy was adopted in November 2012, and applies to all frivolous filing penalties assessed that have not been paid. The reduction is available as long as you seek the reduction before the IRS files a lawsuit in federal court to "reduce any assessment of the penalty to judgment." Ibid, section 4.02. Such a suit is very rare.

To qualify for the one-time reduction, in addition to the timing issue mentioned above, you must comply with all the following requirements:

1. Submit the request for reduction on Form 14402, *IRC 6702(d) Frivolous Tax Submissions Penalty Reduction*, which must be signed under penalty of perjury;

2. The $500 reduced penalty must be paid by submitting at least $250 with Form 14402, and either: a) paying the balance upon abatement, or b) paying the balance in connection with an installment agreement (already in effect) for the payment of the income tax assessments. If the installment agreement covers the $5,000 penalty assessment, and you have already paid more than $500 toward the penalty, you do not have to pay anything additional to qualify for the reduction;

3. You must be in full compliance with all tax return filing requirements;

4. You must have fully paid all income taxes (but not the frivolous filing penalty) or have made arrangements to pay in full through an installment agreement. You must be current with all obligations under the installment agreement; and

5. If the person making the request is an employer, all employment tax deposits must be current for at least the past two quarters. Rev. Proc. 2012-43, section 4.01-4.04.

When all the above requirements are met, the IRS will reduce the total of all $5,000 frivolous submission penalties to just one $500 penalty. This procedure takes the sting out of the frivolous submissions penalty if you are otherwise in compliance with your filing and payment obligations.

Understand that in the final analysis, the duty to file a correct tax return on time is non-delegable. That means you bear the ultimate responsibility for filing a correct tax return and for filing it on time. But the complexity of the law demands that we seek counsel in our efforts to comply with this duty. In light of the risks, be sure the tax pro you work with is competent and capable of handling your specific tax situation.

CHAPTER SEVENTEEN

STAYING AHEAD
OF THE IRS

WHAT WOULD IT BE WORTH TO YOU TO KNOW IN advance whether your tax return was selected for audit? Clearly, that advanced knowledge gives you a host of advantages, not the least of which is the ability to prepare an airtight package of documents necessary to prove your income and deductions long before being contacted. The best part is that it does not take a brother-in-law working for the IRS to get it done.

The IRS maintains a computer file on every tax return, both business and individual. The file is known as a Master File. For 1040 filers, the file is referred to as an Individual Master File (IMF). Business tax return information is organized in a Business Master File (BMF). Each file constitutes a statement of account and record of all relevant activity for that tax year. For example, the date of filing your return is shown in the IMF for a given year. So is the tax assessment date, the amount of tax assessed, whether interest and penalties were added and in what amounts, and what notices were sent regarding the account, etc.

All activity is reported using what the IRS calls transaction codes (TC). A three-digit code represents a given transaction. For example, the filing of a return and the corresponding assessment of tax is shown with a TC 150. When a return is initially flagged for review and potential examination, a TC 420 shows up in the Master File. If after a preliminary review of the return the IRS determines that the return has no potential for change, a TC 421 is entered, reversing the TC 420. That ends the matter. On the other hand, if the return is handed off to a local office for examination, the Master File shows a TC 424.

It generally takes several months to complete the first review process before a decision is made whether to pass a case on for a full-scale audit. From that point, it takes several more months before a case is assigned to an examiner. In turn, it takes a few more months before an examiner sends a notice informing you of the audit. In the meantime, however, the various codes are entered in the IMF. When you know how to obtain it, you have wonderful advanced warning of the gathering storm.

In addition to the IMF and BMF, the IRS maintains a similar computer file for information returns. It is known as a Wage and Income Transcript, sometimes referred to as an Information Returns Master File (IRMF). This file is crosschecked with other computer records to see whether citizens receiving Forms 1099 and W-2 timely filed tax returns reporting all income reflected in those forms.

Wage and Income Transcripts are particularly helpful to non-filers working to file missing tax returns. If you have no records of your income, these transcripts give you all the information the IRS has regarding your reported income for a particular year. You can see who paid you, how much, for what years and whether any federal or state income taxes were withheld. This information goes a long way in helping you reconstruct your income.

Wage and Income Transcripts are a fruitful source of data for those needing to confirm whether and to what extent any information returns were filed. Monitoring this data helps to avoid costly confrontations should an errant W-2 or 1099 appear in the system, or if you are an ID theft victim. Please recall that citizens have the burden to "fully cooperate" with the IRS in cases of errant information returns. See my discussion of code section 6201(d) in chapter 10, under the heading, **How to Dispute Erroneous Information Returns.** When you do cooperate, the IRS bears the affirmative duty to present "reasonable and probative information" relative to the document. The agency cannot simply rely blindly on the data contained in the information return.

Accessing this data puts you into a commanding position with regard to that duty. Keep track of the information returns submitted on you and be aggressive about correcting erroneous forms long before the IRS comes knocking on your door. This may be one of the surest ways to keep the burden on the IRS regarding errant information returns.

How to Get Into the IRS's Files

The Freedom of Information Act (FOIA) provides access to all of these IRS files and more. Under the FOIA, you have the right to receive any material the IRS has compiled with regard to your personal tax matters. There are some narrow exceptions for records relating to national security and ongoing law enforcement matters. However, all of the Master File records discussed here are available and easily obtainable under the FOIA.

Moreover, records generated by an auditor or Appeals Officer in connection with your case are likewise obtainable. And if your case involves a collection matter, the records of a revenue officer are available. Available records include an agent's work papers, case activity reports, collection activity reports, examination reports, information obtained from third parties, etc. Such material often proves tremendously valuable when defending an audit or prosecuting an appeal, especially if the IRS is relying on third-party information otherwise unknown to you. The IRS will not, however, release informant statements or identities in connection with a criminal investigation.

To obtain Master File records, make a written request under the FOIA to the applicable Disclosure Office. The addresses of the various Disclosure Offices change frequently. The most recent addresses can be found by searching the IRS's website.

In order to win release of your Master File records, you must establish your identity and right to receive the material. Do that by submitting an affidavit attesting to your identity and providing a photocopy of a picture ID bearing your signature. A driver's license or other government-issued ID works well.

The request must be specific as to the documents sought. Identify Master File records by the tax period and type of tax return in question. For example, to obtain your IMF for

2014, request the "Individual Master File Statement of Account relative to Form 1040, for tax year 2014." A Business Master File may use different tax periods. For example, when requesting the BMF relative to employment tax returns for 2014, you must specify all four quarters since each quarterly Form 941, *Employer's Quarterly Federal Tax Return*, is subject to a separate BMF record. A business income tax return, such as Form 1065 or 1120, is also recorded in a separate BMF.

To obtain records relevant to an ongoing audit or collection action, use care in specifying the documents sought. The FOIA does not require the IRS to guess at what you seek. The agency is required merely to provide specific documents not otherwise exempt under the law. What is more, the FOIA does not require the IRS to answer questions. If you are seeking data relative to a particular issue, phrase your request in terms of seeking the production of documents, rather than stating a question.

For example, suppose you need information relative to the filing date of your return. Do not ask the IRS, "What is the date of filing my 2014 income tax return?" Instead, ask the agency to "Produce documents which reflect the filing date of my 2014 income tax return."

The FOIA is stringent about how the request must be styled. The guidelines say the request must:

1. Be in writing and signed by the person making it;

2. State that it is made under the FOIA;

3. Be addressed to the IRS's Disclosure Office;

4. Reasonably describe the records sought. When you know what you are after, as in a Master File, state your request with precise clarity. When you do not know the name of the specific document, give as much detail as possible;

5. Establish your identity and right to receive the material. Do this with a photocopy of an ID bearing your photo and a declaration that you are the person making the request;

6. Provide an address where you can be contacted;

7. State that you wish to have the documents mailed to you;

8. Agree to pay the costs of searching for and reproducing the documents, although the first one hundred pages are provided free. Since there are usually about three to five pages in a typical Master File Transcript, most FOIA requests fall well short of the one-hundred-page limit. For more information, see my *Freedom of Information Act Request Kit.*

When requesting Master File records, ask the IRS to provide a copy of the latest version of its *Transaction Codes Pocket Guide*, IRS Document 11734. It shows the translation of the three-digit transaction codes used to signify each account action. Without it, you will be lost in interpreting the IMF or BMF. For more help in reading and interpreting your Master File records, see my *Freedom of Information Act Request Kit.*

By keeping close tabs on your Master File, you can always be one step ahead of the IRS. I recommend that you obtain your IMF (or BMF) records for the past three years. As I explained in chapter 8, under the heading, **Freedom From the Audit—The Statute of Limitations,** the IRS typically has three years from the date a return is filed in which to audit that return. Beyond three years, it is highly unlikely that the IRS can or will initiate an audit. By getting transcripts for the past three years, say on an annual basis, you can keep careful track of what the IRS is doing in your case.

If you are dealing with the IRS in a collection case, these transcripts are vital. They will tell you exactly what tax years you owe for, how much, when the taxes were assessed and the extent to which penalties and interest were assessed. The assessment date is critical since the IRS's statute of limitations on collection (which is ten years from the date of the assessment) begins running with the date of the assessment. There is no reliable way other than through Master File transcripts to ascertain the assessment date. For more on the collection statute of limitations, see *How to Get Tax Amnesty.*

Finally, monitoring your Master File records can tip you off as to whether any ID theft issues are present in your case. This is especially true with Wage and Income Transcripts, since ID thieves often fabricate fake W-2 Forms to generate bogus tax refunds. For more on ID theft, see chapter 19, under the heading, **How to Detect and Solve Identity Theft Problems.**

People regularly ask me whether seeking a Master File somehow "raises a red flag," thus calling undue attention to yourself. The short answer is no, it does not. In more than thirty years of practice, I have seen no case where merely requesting Master File records triggered an IRS audit or other action. The key reason is that the Disclosure Office is independent of all IRS enforcement functions. The job of Disclosure Officers is limited to fulfilling FOIA requests and that is what they do all day long. Your particular request would be no more interesting to a given Disclosure Officer than any of the rest of the hundreds he deals with regularly.

But even if the IRS was somehow more compelled by your request than any of the others, the information you learn from these files is so important as to outweigh the potential risks associated with making the request. This is most certainly true in collection cases, since there is no other way to get the critical information needed to defend your self. Moreover, if you owe the IRS money you cannot pay, the red flag is already raised high and flapping in the breeze. You cannot make matters any worse by submitting an FOIA request.

Chapter Eighteen

HOW TO RECOVER FEES AND COSTS WHEN YOU WIN

TOO MANY PEOPLE GIVE UP AND PAY THE IRS JUST because they think it will cost too much to fight back. This is one reason the IRS routinely asserts unreasonable positions in cases, at least at the audit level. But as with so many taxpayers' rights, people just do not realize that specific provisions of the tax code allow you to recoup all or part of the costs of battling—and beating—unreasonable IRS claims. What is worse, most tax professionals are equally ignorant of these remedies.

I have long taken the position that it is cheaper to win when doing business with the IRS than it is to lose. In the first place, when you cave in to an improper claim, you agree to pay taxes, interest and penalties you just do not owe. Those assessments almost always exceed the cost of fighting back. But beyond that, by rolling over you send the message that you are an easy target. That opens you up for further audits and possible future assessments. The fact is, by caving in you actually make it harder on yourself than if you fight back and win.

You must recognize that like you, the IRS does not have unlimited money and manpower with which to fight its battles. This is one reason the IRS uses bluff and intimidation when dealing with the public. Like the schoolyard bully, the IRS often prevails largely because it goes unchallenged, not because it is unbeatable.

Still, there is no getting around the fact that fighting can be expensive. That is why you must understand how to recover the costs of fighting. What follows is my analysis of the two provisions of law that allow you to make the IRS pay when you prevail in your fight against improper or unlawful claims.

Making the IRS Pay—The Easy Way

Code section 212(3) provides an itemized deduction for the fees and costs you incur in fighting the IRS. The law provides as follows:

> In the case of an individual, there shall be as a deduction all the ordinary and necessary expenses paid or incurred during the taxable year—

(3) in connection with the determination, collection, or refund *of any tax*. (Emphasis added.)

Rev. Reg. section 1.212-1(1) offers specific guidance on what items are covered by this deduction. It reads in part:

Expenses paid or incurred by an individual in connection with the determination, collection, or refund of any tax, whether the taxing authority be Federal, State or municipal, and whether the tax be income, estate, gift, property, or any other tax, *are deductible*. Thus, expenses paid or incurred by a taxpayer for tax counsel or expenses paid or incurred in connection with the preparation of his tax returns or in connection with any proceedings involved in determining the extent of tax liability or in contesting his tax liability *are deductible*. (Emphasis added.)

Without question, the deduction is available for fees paid to a tax professional to prosecute or defend your case. Such fees include tax return preparation fees, representation fees paid to an attorney, an accountant, appraiser, or other tax practitioner in connection with your case. Out-of-pocket expenses (other than professional fees) are also deductible under this provision. Examples include court or administrative filing fees, duplicating costs, postage, witness fees and their travel expenses, transcript costs, your own travel or mileage expenses, parking fees and similar disbursements.

From the moment you become embroiled in a dispute with the IRS, begin counting the costs of battle. Keep receipts for parking, track your mileage, log the number of photocopies you make, save postage receipts, and otherwise record and be prepared to prove the amount and nature of all your expenses. While the cost of paying a professional is deducible, the value of your own time is not.

The deduction under section 212(3) is not limited to just the cost of battling the IRS. I already mentioned that tax preparation fees are deductible, but the benefit goes even beyond that. Also deductible are the costs of purchasing educational material designed to provide tax advice. Under this category, text material used or useful in the preparation of your tax return is deductible. In addition, any material you purchase that is used or useful in connection with the determination, collection or refund of any tax is deductible. As such, all material published by Winning Publications, Inc., *including this book*, is tax deductible since it is designed to provide help and guidance in connection with the "determination, collection or refund of any tax." The expenses are deductible in the year paid.

The deduction under code section 212(3) is considered a miscellaneous itemized deduction. To claim it, you must file a Schedule A with your Form 1040. Miscellaneous itemized deductions must exceed 2 percent of your adjusted gross income. For example, if your adjusted gross income is $25,000, you are entitled to deduct miscellaneous expenses exceeding $500 ($25,000 x .02). So, if you incur $2,000 in fees and costs fighting the IRS, you are entitled to deduct $1,500 as miscellaneous expenses (subtracting the first $500), in addition to whatever other miscellaneous itemized deductions you have for the year in question.

Making the IRS Pay—The Complete Way

Code section 7430 goes far beyond the scope of section 212(3). Section 7430 allows you to recover fees and costs when you prevail against the IRS, whether in an administrative proceeding or litigation in any court. Stated more simply, section 7430 forces the IRS to reimburse the expenses you incur in fighting under certain circumstances. I examine those circumstances here.

In order to recover fees and costs, the following elements must be established:

1. You must be the "prevailing party" in litigation or in an administrative proceeding with the IRS. Section 7430(c)(4)(A) defines "prevailing party" as one who has "substantially prevailed with respect to the amount in controversy, or has substantially prevailed with respect to the most significant issue or set of issues presented."

2. The IRS's position in the case must be substantially "unjustified" based on the law and facts of the case. Code section 7430(c)(4)(A). To be justified, the IRS's position must have a reasonable basis both in law and fact. When the IRS cannot satisfy a reasonable person as to the validity of its position, the position is unjustified. The burden of proof is on the IRS to establish that its litigation position was substantially justified.

3. You must have exhausted all administrative remedies and must not have unreasonably protracted the proceedings. Code section 7430(b)(1) and (b)(4). If you "unreasonably protracted" portions of the proceeding, you cannot recover costs as to that portion. However, you may still recover costs for the portion you did not protract. Rev. Reg. section 301.7430-2(d).

4. You must establish the nature and extent of the fees and costs incurred. This is done through an affidavit presenting testimony as to the nature of the fees and the purpose of the expenses. Code section 7430(c)(1).

5. You must establish eligibility under the Equal Access to Justice Act, Title 28 U.S.C. section 2412. Under the Act, a person whose net worth is in excess of $2 million, or a business with net worth exceeding $7 million or having more than 500 employees cannot recover fees or costs under section 7430. The only option is to deduct the expenses under section 212(3).

Case Studies on Recovering Fees and Costs

Since section 7430 was added to the law by the Taxpayers Bill of Right Act in 1988, there have been hundreds of cases awarding fees and costs to citizens. These cases deliver a decisive blow to the IRS's arbitrary actions. These cases, more than anything I can say, perfectly illustrate the point I have made for years, that when you know your rights and understand the IRS's limitations, you never have to become a tax collection statistic. The cases also illustrate the point I made above, that it is indeed cheaper and more beneficial to win when dealing with the IRS than it is to lose.

Case Study No. One – *Abernathy v. United States,* 150. B.R. 688 (U.S. Bankruptcy Court, ND IL 1993).

Faced with tens of thousands of dollars in growing tax assessments they could not pay, Bill and Peggy Abernathy filed a Chapter 7 bankruptcy petition in June 1986. In October 1986, the Bankruptcy Court issued a discharge order, thus eliminating all the taxes they owed for the years 1979 through 1982. (Yes, tax debts are dischargeable in bankruptcy in certain cases. See: *How to Get Tax Amnesty*.) Despite the discharge order, the IRS continued to send collection notices and continued its annual practice of seizing tax refunds and applying them to the discharged taxes.

By September 1988, they had enough of the IRS's disregard of the court's order. They filed a separate proceeding to enforce the order. Amazingly, the IRS's deliberately wrongful collection action continued even after the proceeding was filed. In an effort to stop the IRS, the court entered an order holding the agency in contempt for violating the discharge order. The contempt order was entered in June 1989, but even that did little to slow down the IRS's illegal actions.

In June, November and December 1991, more collection notices were issued, threatening further enforcement action if the discharged taxes were not paid. In February 1992, the IRS seized their 1991 refund and issued yet another levy notice. The IRS's actions can only be described as bureaucratic madness, for even while the Abernathy's motion for fees and costs was pending, the IRS issued *yet another* collection notice. In January 1993, while the court was considering the motion, the IRS seized their 1992 refund.

As you might hope, the court was incensed by the IRS's bold, defiant actions of violating not one, but two court orders. The court observed:

> In its more than two decade-long involvement as a practitioner, professor and judge in the bankruptcy court system, this court has never encountered a more egregious flaunting of the bankruptcy system as that which it has seen by the IRS in this case. For some five years, the constant position of the IRS has been that it is free to ignore the Debtors' bankruptcy discharge of certain taxes as it sees fit. However, the IRS *cannot act with impunity*, like a rogue elephant. It is not free to simply proceed as if the taxes the Debtors owed the IRS had never been discharged in bankruptcy. The IRS, like any other person or entity involved in a bankruptcy case, must obey the rule of law in this bankruptcy case, which is that the income taxes it seeks to collect have been discharged in bankruptcy and that the IRS is enjoined from trying to collect the taxes, period. (Emphasis added; footnotes omitted.)

The court found that "without a doubt," the IRS's position was arbitrary and unjustified. If fact, the court pointed out that the IRS's position was not just substantially unjustified, it was "completely unjustified." The court found that the Abernathys were entitled to recover all the fees and costs they incurred because of the IRS's continued willful, arbitrary and defiant disregard of the bankruptcy discharge.

Case Study No. Two – *Christensen v. United States*, 815 F. Supp. 786 (U.S. District Court, DE 1993).

Jim Christensen operated a construction company in Colorado that failed in 1983. After a perfunctory employment tax audit in 1986, the IRS determined that Jim paid employees a total of $424,000 in wages and failed to withhold or pay any of the required employment taxes. As a result, the IRS assessed a Trust Fund Recovery Penalty against Jim in the amount of $91,946.

There was one glaring problem with the IRS's determination: Jim had no employees whatsoever. The IRS never completed a proper examination of Jim's business. Instead, the agency made an arbitrary determination of his alleged payroll. Subsequent to the assessment, the IRS seized refunds and applied them to the assessment. In October 1991, Jim filed a suit in the United States District Court seeking the return of his seized refunds, and a determination that he was not liable for the assessment. Eventually, the government conceded that Jim was not responsible for the assessment. The government agreed to abate the assessment and refund $4,837. Jim then filed a motion seeking attorney's fees and costs.

In opposition to the motion, the IRS argued that it secured the "actual payroll records" from Jim's company. According to the agency, those records constituted the evidence supporting its claim. From such evidence, the IRS contended that its position was "substantially justified" and therefore it was improper to award fees and costs.

The court pointed out that to be substantially justified, the government's litigation position must be based upon information that "would satisfy a reasonable person to go forward with the proceedings." In other words, the government's evidence cannot be concocted or imagined. The position does not necessarily have to be correct, but it must have substance and the evidence must be capable of persuading a reasonable person as to its merits. Upon careful examination of the IRS's evidence, the court found government's case entirely lacking.

For example, the documents did not identify the number of employees Jim allegedly had, or their names and addresses. Thus, the IRS was unable to show that Jim actually paid a dime in wages to any person. Most importantly, however, the government's claim that the company's payroll was gleaned from its records was simply incorrect. The audit report stated that "actual payroll records" were obtained but in fact, as the court noted, "there are no payroll figures in the record." In reality, the government had absolutely no evidence upon which to support its claim. Therefore, the court held that the government's evidence "does not show that the position of the IRS was justified to a degree that could satisfy a reasonable person."

The court ordered the IRS to pay attorney's fees in the amount of $10,741 and costs in the amount of $238.40. What began as claim against Jim for $91,900, ended up costing the IRS $15,816, including the money it agreed to refund.

Case Study No. Three – *Kreidle v. Department of Treasury, Internal Revenue Service*, 145 B.R. 1007 (U.S. Bankruptcy Court, CO 1992).

Jim Kreidle operated a number of businesses. He was liable for about $8 million in non-tax partnership debt and other personal guarantees. Because of this debt, his creditors forced him into an involuntary bankruptcy. After some negotiation, all agreed that Jim would be given a crack at a Chapter 11, Reorganization.

In October 1986, subsequent to the agreement to file under Chapter 11, the clerk of the bankruptcy court inadvertently issued an Order for Relief under Chapter 7. That order gave the appearance that a Chapter 7 liquidation proceeding was pending, rather than the reorganization as agreed. The IRS received the Order for Relief but never acted on it. In addition, the agency never made any appearance in the case whatsoever.

Shortly after discovering the erroneous order, the clerk corrected the mistake. The IRS was notified of the correction. Later, it was given notice of all relevant events as the Chapter 11 progressed. At no time did the IRS participate in the process. In November 1987, the court confirmed Jim's Plan of Reorganization. He was on his way to getting out of financial trouble.

In the meantime, Jim and his wife filed their personal tax returns in a timely manner and paid their tax. From 1987 to October 1990, Jim made his bankruptcy plan payments and everything progressed smoothly. He was, however, being audited for 1986, 1987 and 1988.

The trouble began in October 1990, when the IRS issued a Notice of Deficiency for the years mentioned. The IRS alleged that Jim owed $1.5 million in taxes due to unreported income. The unreported income was based upon two theories. First, the IRS claimed that Jim improperly filed an election that entitled him to terminate his tax year as of the date of filing Chapter 11. That effectively pushed income out of 1986 and into 1987. If the IRS was correct, Jim had substantially more income in 1986 than he reported.

Second, the IRS contended that Jim realized income from the discharge of indebtedness. Initially, the IRS claimed the amount was $5.3 million but later, reduced the claim considerably. Still, the agency maintained that Jim realized substantial unreported income from canceled debt. A tax auditor made these determinations and issued the Notice of Deficiency. Neither was reviewed for correctness. As it happens, both were grossly erroneous.

As to the first issue, the IRS maintained that Jim's election was filed late. However, the IRS used as its starting point for determining timeliness the date the bankruptcy clerk erroneously issued the Chapter 7 order. Remember, this was not a Chapter 7 case. It was a Chapter 11 reorganization. All parties, including the IRS, knew the Chapter 7 order was erroneous yet the auditor used that date to calculate the deadline for filing the election.

There were two glaring problems with the second issue. First, Jim did not realize any income from the discharge of indebtedness because he filed a Chapter 11, not a Chapter 7. Next, even if substantial debts were canceled by the bankruptcy, code section 108 expressly excludes from income all debts canceled through a bankruptcy case. The IRS attorney later admitted that this code section was "overlooked."

After trial on the issues, the court found that Jim did not owe the $1.5 million sought by the IRS. In fact, Jim was owed a refund for both years. Jim then submitted a motion for fees and costs. The IRS asserted its position was reasonable, but the court rejected that contention, saying:

> [The] IRS's failure to confirm the accuracy of its audit before trial supports
> a finding of unreasonableness. Overall circumstances, including the IRS's
> unfavorable settlement during trial on the amount of cancellation of debt

income, also demonstrate the unreasonableness of the IRS position on this issue. The IRS was not substantially justified in its position on the amount of cancellation of debt income.

Both the auditor and the IRS's attorney "overlooked" a key provision of the tax code when issuing the Notice of Deficiency. That happens so often that I have come to believe that most tax auditors do not know or care about the tax law. They want only to collect more money. In this case, however, the IRS was forced to pay the price for its actions. The court ordered the IRS to pay Jim's costs and fees, in the combined amount of $192,817.23.

Case Study No. Four – *Powers v. Commissioner,* 100 T.C. 457 (U.S. Tax Court 1993).

Melvin Powers was a real estate developer in Houston where he owned and operated five office complexes. The IRS audited Mel's tax returns for the years 1976 and 1977. It also looked at his returns for 1978 and 1979 but made the decision not to audit those years. Despite this fact, the IRS asked Mel to sign a Form 872 for both years, waiving the time limit on the assessment statute of limitations. See my discussion of this form in chapter 8.

Mel agreed to sign the forms. What he did not know, however, is that the IRS already made the decision *not to pursue* 1978 and 1979 if he refused to sign the waivers. Thus, if Mel refused to sign the waivers, he would have had no problems with the IRS. After obtaining the waivers, the IRS did nothing for three years. In March 1986, Mel's attorney counseled him to terminate the waivers in order to get the matter closed and behind him. Mind you, Mel and his attorney still had no idea the IRS made the decision *not to pursue* the matter. As of March 1986, there was no effort made whatsoever to audit Mel for the two latter years. Neither did the agency make any contact with him.

After Mel terminated his waivers, the statute of limitations was to expire in June 1986. In April 1986, the case was assigned to an auditor who discussed it with the attorney representing the IRS in the 1976-1977 audit appeal. The auditor proposed to disallow all Mel's deductions in excess of $9,000. The agent's reasoning was because of the "lack of time on the statute." The agent claimed to be protecting "the government's interest" by disallowing all deductions. The IRS's attorney reviewed the agent's proposal and approved the issuance of a Notice of Deficiency. This was done despite the fact that an earlier decision was made *not to pursue* Mel for those years. Furthermore, there was "nothing in the file suggesting that (Mel) had improperly claimed deductions." In fact, IRS counsel knew better because of his involvement with the appeal on the two earlier years.

Nevertheless, the IRS issued a Notice of Deficiency and Mel ended up in Tax Court. Subsequent to filing the petition, another agent was assigned to assist in reviewing Mel's records. By the time the case was called for trial, Mel and the IRS agreed that he was entitled to all deductions as claimed and that he owed no taxes or penalties for either 1978 or 1979. Mel then filed a motion seeking an award of fees and costs under code section 7430.

The IRS opposed the motion, claiming its position was substantially justified. The counsel attorney asserted that because a Notice of Deficiency is, under the law, "presumed correct," such presumption by itself constitutes "substantial justification."

The Tax Court disagreed. To be substantially justified, a legal position must have "substantial evidence to support it." In this case, there was no evidence at all. Furthermore, the IRS made no effort to gather any evidence. During the three-year period in which the assessment statute was suspended, the IRS did nothing. They failed to act because of an administrative decision specifically not to act. Still, they asserted in a Notice of Deficiency that Mel was not entitled to any of his deductions. In rejecting the IRS's claims, the court declared:

> In the instant case [IRS's] position had no factual or evidentiary basis. If some relevant evidence is required [to support a claim] *then none is surely not enough.* In addition to having no relevant evidence about the case, [IRS] had specifically decided not to contact [Mel] to seek any. It has been held that the Government does not have a reasonable basis in both fact and law if it does not diligently investigate a case. (Emphasis added; footnotes omitted.)

The mere fact that the IRS may assert a claim in a Notice of Deficiency does not make it immune from an award of fees and costs under section 7430. It is true, the Notice of Deficiency is presumed correct, but that presumption merely places the burden of proof on the citizen. It does not allow the IRS to make unreasonable, arbitrary and meritless claims with impunity. As the court observed:

> The fact that the Commissioner has the right to maintain a position does not bar a taxpayer from receiving an award for litigation costs if the position is unreasonable.

The IRS makes a practice of disallowing all deductions on a tax return simply because the assessment statute is about to expire. This means that even when the IRS has absolutely no evidence to support its disallowance, the citizen is placed in the position of having to prosecute a Tax Court case to prove his innocence. In Mel's case, it came back to haunt the IRS in a big way. Mel was awarded attorney's fees, accountant's fees and related costs to the tune of $55,707.

My list of case studies on section 7430 could go on and on. The courts have spanked the IRS for years, but only when citizens specifically seek such relief. Courts hammer the IRS when it pursues a course that is unreasonable, unfounded, arbitrary or without justification. Code section 7430 is an important right, but you cannot exercise that right if you are ignorant of it.

As evidenced by the case studies discussed above, the IRS is simply not at liberty to arbitrarily harass and intimidate you. But you must take advantage of code section 7430.

Procedures for Recovering Fees and Costs

There are two forums available for making a claim for the payment of fees and costs. The first is the administrative forum. This involves a case before the IRS that did not go to court. The second is the judicial forum. This involves a case, such as those cited here, that did wind up in court. I address each one individually.

The Administrative Claim for Fees and Costs. Under Revenue Regulation section 301.7430-2(c), an application for fees and cost must be made in writing and sent to the IRS personnel who have jurisdiction over the case. For audits, jurisdiction lies with the

Examination function. Appeals cases are controlled by the Appeals Office.

The request must contain the following information:

a. A statement showing that the underlying tax liability issues have never been presented to a court. If a court decided the tax issues, the same court must decide the question of fees and costs;

b. A clear and concise statement as to why you believe the position of the IRS was not substantially justified. The position per se lacks substantial justification if the IRS's failed to follow its own published guidance on a particular matter. Published guidance includes final or temporary regulations, revenue rulings, revenue procedures, information releases, notices, announcements, and, if issued to you specifically, private letter rulings, technical advice memoranda and determination letters;

c. A statement showing that you substantially prevailed in the case, either with respect to the amount in controversy or with respect to the most significant issue or set of issues in the case;

d. A statement showing that you did not unreasonably protract the portion of the proceeding for which you are seeking costs and fees;

e. A detailed statement showing the nature and amount of fees and costs you incurred;

f. An affidavit stating you meet the net worth requirements as outlined above;

g. Copies of any bills, receipts or other documents evidencing your claim for fees and costs; and

h. The address at which you wish to be notified of the ruling on your claim. Your claim must contain a declaration that it is made under the penalty of perjury. See: Rev. Reg. section 301.7430-2(c)(3)(i), (ii) and (iii).

The timeliness of the claim is very important. Under section (c)(5) of the above-cited regulation, the claim must be made within "90 days after the date the final decision" covering all underlying issues is either "mailed, or otherwise furnished" to the citizen. The IRS has six months to rule on your application. If the application is either denied or no action is taken within that time, you have the right to appeal to the Tax Court. Failure to respond within six months is tantamount to a denial.

Appeal by filing a petition with the United States Tax Court. Rev. Reg. section 301.7430-2(c)(6) and (c)(7). For more information, see chapters 4 and 7 of my book *Taxpayers' Ultimate Defense Manual*.

The Judicial Claim for Fees and Costs. When a court, such as the Tax Court, passes upon the correctness of the IRS's claims, only that court has the authority to decide an application for fees and costs. For example, suppose the Appeals Office rules against you, then issues a Notice of Deficiency. You in turn file a petition in the Tax Court and eventually win your case. Under that scenario, you must file your application directly with the Tax Court.

When a judicial application is made, the rules for making the claim are the same as those outlined above, with one important exception. Under code section 7430, you must file the claim within thirty days of the court's final decision on the merits of the case. Chapter 7 of the *Defense Manual* offers more information on the application itself, including a sample application form.

That form can be adapted for use either within the IRS or the Tax Court. When adapting the form for use within the IRS, be sure to meet the content requirements of Rev. Reg. section 301.7430-2(c)(3), which are set forth above.

One way to stop IRS abuse—especially in your own personal case—is to make them pay for their improper or abusive tactics. Using the two techniques discussed above, you can both recover the costs of fighting abuse and send a clear message to the IRS in the process. The message is simply that we will not tolerate the agency's illegal actions.

CHAPTER NINETEEN

10 WAYS TO PROTECT YOURSELF FROM THE IRS

By wisdom a house is built, and by understanding it is established;
By knowledge the rooms are filled with all rare and beautiful treasures.

Proverbs 24:3-4.

1. Protecting Future Returns
Against Claims of Unreported Income

IT IS POSSIBLE TO TAKE WHAT WE LEARNED, ABOUT a) how returns are selected for audit, b) tax audit defense techniques, c) your responsibility to make and keep records which "clearly reflect income," and d) the IRS's burden of proof, and blend them into an elixir that prevents face-to-face audits in the first place. Not only would this prevent the damaging results of audits in the general sense but it would avoid altogether the trauma of the economic reality audit.

The process starts with recognizing the reason so many people have inadequate records of income. About 85 percent of Americans work for an employer and receive W-2 Forms at the end of the year. W-2s report wages paid and taxes withheld. Most W-2 employees generally do not keep independent records of income. Instead, they rely on employer-provided W-2s. For a number of reasons, this is a critical error. For starters, employers make mistakes and the errors are not isolated.

Secondly, some people file fraudulent information returns in a deliberate effort to get others into tax trouble. This is so widespread that Congress added section 7434 to the code, allowing those harmed by such acts to sue the perpetrator.

The third problem is that companies go out of business and fail to issue information returns. If you do not have independent records of your income, you might not notice that a form is missing, especially if you changed jobs often. However, the IRS notices the unreported income if it obtains your bank records or otherwise discovers the data in some other way.

The fourth and most compelling reason to make independent records of your income is simple. A Form W-2—however accurate—does not speak to what you earned elsewhere working a second job. It addresses only what you earned from the company making the report. An agent may say, "Sure, the W-2 proves what you earned from the ABC Company, but it does not address what you earned working on the side." This is an attempt to box you into proving a negative.

On the other hand, independent income logs, such as those made by Judy and Ramon that we analyzed in chapter 10, give you just such an advantage. As I explain in detail in chapter 10, your logs form the foundation of an airtight package of documentation that can defeat any unfounded claim of unreported income. My strongest recommendation, therefore, is that you begin documenting your income through your own independent logs for all future returns. See my book, *How to Double Your Tax Refund*, for more details on creating logs.

2. Audit-Proofing and Penalty-Proofing Your Tax Return

The next step is to use your logs to audit-proof and penalty-proof your tax return. Recall from our earlier discussion how returns are selected for examination. The majority is flagged on the basis of the Discriminate Income Function (DIF) scoring process. Each line of your return is compared to averages for persons in your same income bracket, geographic location and profession. If any line of your return is at variance with the averages, the difference is scored. The higher the DIF score, the greater the chances of audit.

My audit-proofing techniques are based on that idea. To audit-proof a return, provide information with the return to answer any potential questions raised in the return. To audit-proof your income, provide copies of your independent logs and an affidavit to support them.

This audit-proofing process is tied together with IRS Form 8275, *Disclosure Statement,* which is specifically designed for augmenting returns. It notifies the agency of an issue that may be questionable, and allows you to provide the answers with that return. This prevents the need for a lengthy and costly examination.

Moreover, you give yourself two clear advantages. First, we know that the IRS has nowhere near the manpower to audit everybody in a face-to-face encounter. Therefore, such audits must focus on returns with the most potential for change, which is usually measured by DIF scores. Returns with little potential for change are generally not questioned. By using a Disclosure Statement in combination with information that answers potential questions in your return, you send the clear message that your return holds little promise of increased revenue.

The second advantage is that in the event you do make an error (people make honest mistakes), you avoid penalties by making full disclosure of the facts at the time of filing. Recall that penalties are pointed at people who are "willfully negligent" in complying with the law. Penalties are not intended for those who do their best to comply, but through no fault of their own, make an honest mistake. Penalties cannot apply to those who act in good faith and based on a reasonable cause for their actions. Using a Disclosure Statement evidences good faith and reasonable cause on the front end. More details on audit-proofing and penalty-proofing tax returns are presented in *The IRS Problem Solver.*

3. How to Detect and Solve Identify Theft Problems

Identity theft is a growing problem in America. Identity (ID) theft occurs when someone uses your personal information such as your name, Social Security number (SSN) or other identifying information without your permission to commit fraud or other crimes. In the context of the IRS, ID thieves mainly use your personal information to file tax returns claiming fraudulent refunds, which are directed to an address where the thieves obtain and cash the check. One of the most common areas of criminal investigation and prosecution by the IRS is that of ID thieves.

Because of the pervasiveness of this problem, you need to always be aware of your return filing and tax refund status with the IRS. In chapter 17, I talked about the importance of obtaining and monitoring your Individual Master File and Wage and Income Transcripts for audit purposes. Another reason to do this is to look for signs that you might be the victim of ID theft. Of course, unauthorized credit card spending is a key sign, as well as notations in your credit report showing new accounts that you did not authorize.

Where the IRS is concerned, signs of ID theft generally show up in the way of a notice or letter from the agency claiming one or more of the following:

- More than one tax return was filed for you in a single year,

- You have a balance due, refund offset or collection actions against you for a year you did not file a tax return or for which you paid in full at the time of filing,

- You were the victim of employment related identity theft,

- Wages were reported to the IRS from a company you did not work for,

- You received a Form W-2 or 1099 from an employer for whom you did not work,

- Your annual *Notice of Earnings* statement from the Social Security Administration shows more income than you earned in one or more years, or

- Your Social Security benefits were adjusted or even denied because of wages that you did not earn.

If you are or believe you might be the victim of identity theft, take affirmative action as quickly as possible to mitigate the damages. Consider one or more of the following actions:

a. In response to any letter or notice from the IRS, reply in writing to the "person to contact" at the address on the notice. Explain specifically the discrepancy and provide whatever documents or other proof is necessary to support your position. Keep careful records of what you send to the IRS.

b. If you do not have an IRS notice but believe there may be ID theft issues, call the IRS at 800-908-4490. The IRS can flag your account to watch for potentially questionable activity.

c. Fill out and file Form 14039, *Identity Theft Affidavit*, as instructed in the form. The form allows you to, 1) reply to an IRS notice or letter regarding questionable action on your account, and 2) alert the IRS that there may be questionable activity on your account due to another event that may lead to IRS-related ID theft.

d. File an online complaint with the Internet Crime Complaint Center (IC3) at www.ic3.gov/complaint. IC3 is a partnership between the FBI and the National White Collar Crime Center. IC3 sends every complaint to the appropriate law enforcement or regulatory agencies with jurisdiction over the matter.

e. File a report with your local police department.

f. File a complaint with the Federal Trade Commission (FTC). Do this if you have specific information about a specific business that used your personal data in some unauthorized manner. File a complaint in one of the following three ways:

> Over the Internet: www.ftccomplaintassistant.gov

> By telephone: 877-438-4338

> Through the U.S. mail: FTC Identity Theft Clearinghouse, 600 Pennsylvania Avenue NW, Washington, DC 20580

g. Place a fraud alert on your credit reports by contacting any one or all of the three credit reporting companies. Do this either online or through their toll-free phone numbers as follows:

> Equifax: 888-766-0008 – www.equifax.com

> Experian: 888-397-3742 – www.experian.com

> Trans Union: 800-680-7289 – www.transunion.com

h. If you received a Form W-2 from an unknown employer or the wages reported by the Social Security Administration on your earnings statement shows more than you earned, contact the Social Security Administration at 877-438-4338. Provide whatever documents are necessary to show your correct information.

i. Contact your banks and other financial institutions to close any accounts that were used improperly, somehow tampered with or opened without your permission. Open new accounts with new account numbers. Do this with your credit card accounts as well.

Keep in mind that while you have an open identity theft case with the IRS, you still need to file future tax returns on time. You may not be able to file electronically because someone already used your SSN on a fraudulent return or the IRS placed an ID theft alert on your account. In that case, mail your return using certified mail with return receipt requested. Keep your postal receipts in your file along with a signed and dated copy of the tax return itself. Use the Freedom of Information Act to monitor your Master File and Wage and Income Transcripts to keep abreast of all developments. See chapter 17.

4. Guard Your Social Security Number

ID theft would not be possible if the thieves were unable to obtain your SSN. An SSN is needed to file a tax return, open a bank account or credit card account, get a loan, and do just about anything else that involves financial matters. This is highly ironic given that when the SSN was created in the 1930s, it was *not* to be used for identification purposes. In fact, early Social Security cards declared right on their face that the number was not to be used for identification. Now the use of SSNs is so pervasive they are in fact assigned to children *at birth*.

The IRS implemented new regulations allowing the filers of information returns to use truncated identification numbers as a means of combating ID theft. See: Treasury Decision 9675, July 15, 2014. Under these rules, unless specifically prohibited by other rules, your employer can mask all but the last four digits of your SSN (i.e., xxx-xx-1234) to minimize the risk of publishing the full number. Talk to your employer about implementing this policy if it is not already in place.

Get in the habit of questioning the legal requirement to provide your SSN to non-tax government agencies and private businesses that ask for it. You will find that most likely have no authority to require you to produce it. Most companies and non-tax agencies merely have become accustomed to people providing SSNs without question.

With regard to private businesses, unless their use of your SSN is specifically connected to tax considerations (such as your employer), there is often another way to satisfy their need for information controls. Of course, when dealing with private sector businesses, you always enjoy the right to do business elsewhere.

5. Avoid Phone and E-Mail Scams

Since 2013, more than 1,100 people have been robbed of approximately $5 million dollars through a telephone scam that runs throughout the nation. More than 90,000 complaints have been filed with the Treasury Inspector General for Tax Administration concerning this scam. The perpetrators obtain the name and phone number of delinquent taxpayers from tax lien information and phone records. Most of the legwork is probably done right over the Internet. The scammers then call the target pretending to be IRS personnel. The idea is to get the target to provide credit card or bank account data over the phone so that one or both of those resources can be cleaned out.

What does the caller say that might compel a person to give up his credit card or bank account data over the phone? I listened to two messages that were recorded by two different targets. The message left on Kyle's phone is as follows (pay attention to the syntax):

This message is intended to Kyle _____. Kyle the one second you receive

> this message I need you or your attorney to return the call. The issue at hand is extremely time sensitive. My name is Michelle Comma calling from the legal department of the Internal Revenue Service and my phone number is 202-809-9356. I'll repeat it - 202-809-9356. Do not disregard this message and do return the call. Now if you do not return the call and I don't hear from your attorney either then the only thing I can do is wish you a good luck as the situation unfolds on you.

The second call was to Tracey. Her call went like this (again, note the syntax):

> Good morning, this is Frank Jefferson, and I am calling you from the Internal Revenue Service Tax Audit Department. I have very important information for you, so please listen to me VERY CAREFULLY. We have received a legal petition notice against your name and your SSN regarding a tax form. A lawsuit is going to be filed against you today in federal claims courthouse. So remember to call back 202-568-6936. Now, if you do not respond to this message, we will be forced to issue a non-bailable arrest warrant against you. Thank you and good luck.

The first clue this is a scam this that the IRS will never leave any voice mail with this kind of threat. I have seen plenty of IRS abuse and intimidation over the years, but leaving a voice mail such as this is beyond the pale. If the IRS does make a phone call to contact a taxpayer (which is common), the message left is limited to the caller's name, title and phone number with a "call me back" encouragement.

Secondly, the syntax is horrible. "This message is intended to Kyle." Really? I think the caller meant it is intended FOR Kyle. And how about the "good luck" wishes? Such a statement is unprofessional, at best.

Next, both phone numbers are from the Washington, D.C. area code. No revenue officer in Washington, D.C. would make phone calls to another state to collect delinquent taxes. Anytime a revenue officer is assigned to contact a taxpayer directly, that revenue officer is located in the region where the taxpayer lives.

The person who phoned Kyle said she was from the "legal department" of the IRS. The IRS has no group identified as the "legal department." IRS attorneys are known as Area Counsel attorneys and they operate out of the Office of Chief Counsel. If a "counsel attorney" calls someone, the attorney will leave a message that says some thing like, "I'm _____ from IRS counsel's office. Call me as soon as possible," with a phone number.

A counsel attorney from Washington, D.C. would most likely be with the national office. Under no circumstances would a national office attorney work on an individual collection case. For that matter, no counsel attorney—in the national office or otherwise— ever works on individual collection cases unless the matter is already in Tax Court, as may occur in a Collection Due Process case. And a taxpayer would certainly know that his case is in Tax Court because the only way a Tax Court case is commenced is by the *taxpayer*—not the IRS. Moreover, a counsel attorney working any kind of Tax Court case would never leave a message demanding money as counsel attorneys are not tax collectors under any circumstances.

The message left for Tracey is almost comedic. For example, the caller said he was from the "tax audit department." There is no tax audit department. Auditors work in the IRS's Examination function. An auditor would say, "I'm with Exam" or "the exam function." Moreover, tax auditors are never tax collectors. Under no circumstances would a tax auditor call a taxpayer, no matter how delinquent, and put the squeeze on for money. They may (and do) put the squeeze on to sign audit papers, provide information and accept exam determinations, but they do not collect money. Only revenue officers do that.

The caller also threatened to issue a "non-bailable arrest warrant" if Tracey did not call back right away. What is a "non-bailable arrest warrant," and since when does the IRS have the legal authority to issue any kind of arrest warrant, "non-bailable" or otherwise? Of course, a warrant can only come from a court and you would never be notified of its potential issuance by a phone call.

I called both the phone numbers provided and after just a few minutes of conversation, it was painfully obvious that the people I talked with knew nothing about IRS procedure or much of the lingo. When I pressed them, they just hung up the phone. Clearly, they were simply trying to steal my clients' credit card information.

Keep mind the following when it comes to tax collection:

- The IRS will never pressure you to give credit card or bank account information over the phone to pay taxes,

- The IRS does not require you to pay using any specific payment method, such as a credit card or bank draft,

- You will never be contacted by a Washington, D.C. IRS office unless you happen to live in Washington, D.C.,

- They will never threaten to arrest you if you do not pay the amount demanded,

- Local law enforcement, such as the police or sheriff, will never be involved with federal tax collection matters,

- The IRS will never attempt to collect taxes through e-mail contacts, and

- If you have an authorized Power of Attorney in effect, the IRS must deal directly with your POA. At the very least, if you receive a call like this and you are represented by counsel, simply tell the caller to contact your representative and hang up the phone.

In any event, report the call to the Treasury Inspector General for Tax Administration. If a voice mail message is left be sure to save it and make a transcript of it. File the report at TIGTA's web site, which is here:

www.treasury.gov/tigta/contact_report_scam.shtml

6. How to Handle Undisclosed Offshore Income and Assets

U.S. citizens are taxed on their worldwide income. It makes no difference where you earn your income. You have a duty to report it and factor it into computing your U.S. tax liability. However, because of bank secrecy laws in some foreign nations such those in the Caribbean and Switzerland, and the IRS's lack of jurisdiction in foreign nations, some people have been able to squirrel money away in foreign bank or investment accounts and illegally avoid U.S. taxes on the gains realized from the investments.

But even if a person did not have any income from his foreign financial assets, he probably had a duty to report the assets. If the total value of a person's offshore financial holdings exceeds $10,000 (U.S.) at any point during the year, he must file Treasury Form TD 90-22.1, *Report of Foreign Bank and Financial Accounts,* (the so-called FBAR Form) with the U.S. Treasury. Failure to file that form not only carries an egregious civil penalty of up to 50 percent of the total value of the financial assets for each year they are unreported, but the failure is a potential criminal offense. And this is true even if there is no income tax liability attributable to the holdings.

Through a series of moves involving pressure from the State Department and U.S. courts in cases where foreign banks have a U.S. presence, the IRS has successfully breached the formerly secret enclaves of foreign banks. And owing to legislation passed in 2010, the risks to U.S. citizens of not reporting their foreign financial holdings and the income derived from those holdings have increased exponentially. Because of that, anyone who has not reported either his holdings in foreign countries or the income from those holdings must consider using the IRS's Offshore Voluntary Disclosure Program (OVDP) to come in from the cold.

The OVDP allows one to make a voluntary disclosure to the IRS regarding offshore activities, then pay the tax and a reduced FBAR penalty, and avoid criminal prosecution for either tax evasion, filing false tax returns, or failure to file the FBAR form. Since the IRS began its first OVDP in 2009, more than 39,000 people have participated. In the process, the agency has mined a mountain of data from the participants, which has led to numerous new leads on banks, promoters, attorneys and advisors around the world who helped U.S. citizens hide assets offshore.

There are still an untold number of citizens on the sidelines wondering whether to step forward or keep quiet and take their chances. Many people believe that if the IRS has not honed in on their particular bank or their particular advisor or promoter, they may fall through the cracks. While that is certainly possible, the likelihood of such an outcome grows more faint every day.

The key reason for this is the data mining the IRS engaged in with each of the 39,000-plus people who have thus far stepped forward. To participate in the OVDP, it is not enough to simply file your amended tax returns and pay the taxes. The IRS requires you to also make a lengthy disclosure about the history of your offshore activities. That disclosure includes, at a minimum:

- The names of all financial institutions where you held accounts,

- The dates on which the accounts were opened and closed,

- The names and contact information for all your points of contact,

- The circumstances of all face-to-face meetings with your points of contact,

- A description of all communications (face-to-face or otherwise) with your points of contact,

- Copies of all written communications with your points of contact,

- All of the above information relative to any independent, non-banking advisors, such as attorneys or financial advisors and finally,

- A personal interview with IRS and Department of Justice personnel regarding all of the above.

As the IRS gathers and assimilates the above information, it becomes increasingly likely that the agency will stumble upon those who have yet to step forward. Using what they found thus far, the IRS already expanded its dragnet well beyond Caribbean nations and Switzerland. The sweep now includes such nations as Israel, India, China, Hong Kong, Liechtenstein and others throughout Europe. The IRS continues to be *very* aggressive in pursuing those responsible for tax evasion using offshore bank and investment accounts. By participating in the OVDP, you can potentially avoid criminal prosecution and the egregious civil penalties associated with not disclosing the assets. Moreover, you can put the matter behind you, without fear of being blindsided later.

As of this writing, there is no calendar deadline for participating in the OVDP. However, a key element of the program is that your disclosure must be "truthful, timely, and complete." IRM section 9.5.11.9(3). A disclosure is considered "timely" only if the IRS has *no information* about your account from the bank itself or from some other source. Given the IRS's aggressiveness, there is no way to know whether or when it might come into possession of information revealing your account. Frankly, as the IRS puts more pressure on offshore banking centers to disgorge the names of U.S. citizens, it is becoming increasingly difficult to defend a decision to ignore the issue.

If the IRS does have the information prior to your disclosure, your disclosure is not considered "timely" and in turn, it is not considered "voluntary." Thus, failing to disclose offshore assets under this program carries a risk of criminal prosecution, which in turn carries the possibility of jail time and further financial penalties.

The carrot the IRS uses to induce participation in the program is a substantially reduced civil penalty for failure to file the FBAR form. The reduced penalty is tiered based upon certain facts and circumstances, which break down as follows:

The 27.5 percent penalty. The maximum penalty under the program is 27.5 percent of the dollar amount of offshore assets—for just one year. Recall that the full penalty is up to 50 percent per year.

The 12.5 percent penalty. The penalty falls to 12.5 percent for citizens with offshore financial assets that never exceeded $75,000 in value during the eight years prior to the year of submitting the OVDP application.

The 5 percent penalty. The 5 percent penalty is even more limited. It applies when one of two situations exist. The first situation applies when all four of the following conditions are met:

a. The citizen did not open or cause the opening of the account (i.e., he inherited it),

b. The citizen had only minimal contact with the account (i.e., he infrequently checked the account balance and did not direct any of the investments),

c. He did not withdraw more than $1,000 from the account for the entire eight-year period prior to submitting the application, and

d. Only the account earnings escaped U.S. taxation. That is, the funds deposited were already taxed in the U.S. or were not taxable in the U.S. (such as an inheritance).

The second situation applies in even more limited cases. In this situation, the individual must be a foreign resident and unaware that he is a U.S. citizen. For example, suppose you were born in the U.S. to parents of foreign citizenship. You grew up in a foreign jurisdiction, unaware that you were a U.S. citizen. You have an account in the foreign jurisdiction. You never filed U.S. tax returns or FBAR forms. In this case, you are entitled to the reduced 5 percent penalty.

In addition to conceding the penalty as outlined above, you also have to file amended tax returns and report the income that was avoided on the offshore assets. The next step: pay the tax and the penalty in full or arrange an installment agreement to pay in full.

If you have unreported overseas assets, you should consider coming forward under the OVDP. The sooner you act, the less likely it is that the IRS already has your information due to a bank disclosure. In that case, you could be in jeopardy of potential criminal prosecution.

It is also true that given the severity of the situation and the potential risk, it is vital that you get counsel before proceeding. You need to evaluate all your options before making decisions that could have a profound affect on your life. For help with this, contact the Tax Freedom Institute at www.taxhelponline.com for a complete list of our TFI members.

7. Be Cautious with Tax Preparation Software

At present, more than 82 percent of the approximately 146 million tax return filers seek outside help to comply with their tax return preparation and filing requirements. This includes the use of commercially available tax prep software, which is used by millions of citizens annually. People regularly ask me whether using such software imparts some level of audit security. The idea is that since a computer prepared the return, the IRS will be less likely to examine it for mistakes. While the suggestion is not devoid of logic, it is nevertheless not true.

Mechanical mistakes in the preparation process, that is, math errors, and carrying entries from one line to another, etc., are just a small part of what the IRS looks for in the audit process. The bigger picture is whether your records support the underlying claims of income and deductions. The IRS recognizes that tax pros (and certainly tax prep software) are not auditors and are not asked to police the claims that citizens make.

Thus, when the IRS audits a tax return, it is mostly looking to see whether the citizen has the documents to prove he is entitled to a given deduction or whether he underreported his income. The use of tax preparation software provides no reasonable measure of insulation from such an inquiry.

So now the question is whether the use of tax prep software provides insulation from penalties in the event an audit reveals a mistake. To answer this question, recall my earlier discussion of the basic premise of penalties.

The accuracy penalty under section 6662 is assessed when there is an error in the tax return leading to an assessment of additional tax. The tax code contains a good faith, reasonable cause provision allowing for an abatement of the penalty. This means if you acted in good faith and based upon a reasonable cause for your actions, the penalty does not apply. Code section 6664(c)(1).

On the other hand, the penalty applies if the citizen was "negligent" in connection with his tax obligations. As we learned earlier, the term negligence is defined as the failure to make a reasonable attempt to comply with the tax code. Code section 6662(c). The courts have said that negligence is a lack of "due care" or "the failure to do what a reasonable and ordinarily prudent person would do under the circumstances." *Marcello v. Commissioner*, 380 F.2d 499 (5th Cir. 1967).

Now to our threshold question: does tax prep software build in a level of "due care" or "prudence" sufficient to defeat a penalty? That depends upon the nature of the error. Suppose the error arises in a mechanical function associated with preparing the tax return. That is, the software calculates your tax based upon x percentage of your income rather than y percentage. In that case, I would argue that reliance upon the software was reasonable and that you acted in good faith. As such, the penalty does not apply.

The fact is, however, that there are few mechanical errors associated with the tax prep software available today. In the vast majority of cases, errors leading to increased taxes are attributable to substantive claims made in the return, not a flaw in the software. As the Tax Court stated in *Lam v. Commissioner*, T.C. Memo. 2010-82, "tax preparation software is only as good as the information one inputs into it." See also *Bunney v. Commissioner*, 114 T.C. 259 (2000).

Consider this example. Suppose you claim you are entitled to a $10,000 itemized deduction for mortgage interest. You use tax prep software and when prompted, you input $10,000 for that deduction. The fact is, however, you did not pay $10,000 in mortgage interest. The software correctly computes your tax liability based upon that deduction and all other information you provide. You are later audited and the deduction is disallowed. Your tax is increased and you are charged with a penalty. In this case, the fact that you used tax prep software is not a defense to the penalty. The tax prep software did only what you told it to do: figure a deduction for $10,000 of mortgage interest that you did not have.

In order to defeat a penalty, you must show that you acted in good faith and based upon a reasonable cause for your actions. Your burden is to establish that you were not negligent in handling your tax affairs. As stated above, negligence exists when you did not act as a reasonable and ordinarily prudent person would act under the circumstances.

So the six million dollar question is what would a reasonable and ordinarily prudent person do when faced with questions about complying with the tax code? At a minimum, any one for more of the following things:

a. *Read the instructions for the form you are filing out.* In the case of the mortgage interest example above, the instructions for Schedule A explain the nature of the mortgage interest deduction, its limits, and the level of proof needed to establish the deduction if it is challenged.

b. *Read IRS publications relative to your issue.* IRS publications provide more detail regarding specific issues, going well beyond the information provided in the instructions to a form.

c. *Read IRS notices, statements or other public declarations, all of which are on its web site, relative to your issue.* The IRS's web site is searchable and provides an archive of its public statements, rulings and declarations on a particular issue.

d. *Phone the IRS or visit a walk-in center for personal help.* Tens of millions of people seek personal help with their questions each year by calling the IRS or walking in to a help center. Personally, I am not a fan of this approach simply because the IRS is wrong so often in the answers that it gives to people. Moreover, it is very difficult just to get through to the IRS on the phone for any help, correct or not. But if you do opt for personal help from the IRS, make sure you record, 1) the name and ID number of the employee you spoke with, 2) the date of the call or visit, 3) the phone number you called or location you visited, 4) the question you asked, and 5) the answer you received. See my book, *The IRS Problem Solver* for more details on this.

e. *Read the tax code and regulations.* The Internet makes this easier than ever, as explained in chapter 6.

f. *Consult a tax professional.* Ultimately, when you have questions about the tax treatment of an item or transaction, carefully consider consulting a tax professional. While the law does not allow you to delegate to a third party the responsibility to *file a return*, you have every right to rely in good faith on the advice of a third party in the *preparation* of your return as I explained in chapter 16. *United States v. Boyle*, 469 U.S. 241 (1985). To win penalty relief, you must show that you provided the tax pro with all the relevant facts and that the advice was reasonable under the circumstances. See chapter 16.

8. Stop Lending Money to the IRS

In 2012, the IRS handed out refund checks to nearly 112 million people. The average refund was $2,807. If you received a refund from the IRS, no doubt you were a happy person. I can tell you, however, that getting a tax refund is not a good idea. You get a tax refund only because you overpaid your taxes. To get a refund of $2,807, for example, you must pay $234 per month in taxes you *do not owe*. What is worse, you loaned your money to the IRS for over a year—without interest! You would never allow your bank to hold your money interest free. Why allow the IRS to do it?

There is widespread misconception about income tax withholding obligations, which is why so many people subject themselves to the over-withholding that leads to refunds. Form W-4, *Employee's Withholding Allowance Certificate*, controls wage withholding. You submit this form to your employer to declare the number of "allowances" you are entitled to claim for purposes of computing withholding. If you receive a substantial tax refund, it is because you failed to claim sufficient allowances on Form W-4. You may respond by saying, "Wait. I have four kids. I claimed four allowances. What else can I do?"

That is exactly what the misunderstanding is all about. Your children, in fact all of your dependents including yourself and your spouse, are considered "dependent exemptions" for income tax purposes. You may claim all of your dependent exemptions on Form W-4. But the W-4 is an "allowance" certificate, not an "exemption" certificate. Allowances *include* exemptions, but are not *limited* to exemptions.

The term allowance is defined as *any tax return item* that operates to lower your taxes. That not only includes exemptions, but itemized deductions, the standard deduction, business losses, retirement plan contributions, capital loses, etc. Any one or a combination of these things entitles you to claim allowances on the W-4 in relative proportion.

The rules regarding the W-4 specifically allow citizens to adjust their withholding to match their tax bills. If you have over-withholding, leading to a refund, you may increase allowances to strike a balance. On the other hand, if you are under-withheld, leading to a tax debt, you should decrease your allowances, causing more withholding. The goal is to adjust your withholding to match your tax liability. The ideal scenario is that you neither have a tax refund nor a tax debt as of the time of filing your return.

In my book, *How to Double Your Tax Refund*, I have two chapters that take you by the hand through the code sections permitting this adjustment process. I show you the formula and steps needed to meet your legal obligations without lending money to the IRS interest free.

9. Pay the Taxes You Owe on Time

While this seems obvious enough, many people fall into a hidden trap. Each year, millions of citizens who cannot pay on time file Form 4868, *Automatic Extension of Time to File Form 1040*. That form gives you six additional months to file your tax return. However, that extension *does not* apply to paying the tax.

Even though Form 4868 pushes your filing deadline to October 15, you still have to pay what you owe by April 15. If you do not pay by April 15, the IRS charges the late payment penalty and interest, regardless of the filing extension. That penalty can be up to 25 percent of the delinquent tax, plus interest on both the tax and penalty. If you cannot pay on time, do not use Form 4868. There are two alternatives to help you. Use either or both, depending on your situation. In any event, file your tax return on time to avoid the additional failure to file penalty.

The first alternative is Form 1127, *Application for Extension of Time Pay Income Taxes*. This is one of the IRS's best-kept secrets. This is not a filing extension. It is a payment extension. However, *it is not automatic*. To have it approved, you must show that you took reasonably prudent steps to provide for the payment of your taxes but due to circumstances beyond your control, you cannot pay on time. Once approved, you can get up to six additional months to pay the tax—*without penalties* (but interest continues).

The second alternative is IRS Form 9465, *Installment Agreement Request*. Use it if you cannot pay within six months or your payment extension application is denied. Form 9465 asks for the monthly installment payment you propose. This process is not automatic either. However, if you, a) owe less than $50,000, b) can pay the bill in full within seventy-two months, and c) had no prior installment agreements, you qualify for the streamlined installment agreement rules. This means the IRS accepts just about any terms that will full-pay within seventy-two months. For more details on this process, please review chapters five and eleven of my *Tax Amnesty Package*.

By using either strategy, you can avoid the horrors of enforced collection. By doing nothing, you invite liens, levies and seizures of property.

10. Generally, Be Aware

Keep up with tax law and IRS procedural changes that can affect you. That does not mean you have to become a watchdog, keeping track of every move Congress and the IRS make. You just need a reliable source of information gleaned by somebody who does watch every move. That is my job. My newsletter *Pilla Talks Taxes* is the vehicle through which I report important law changes affecting your taxes and rights as a taxpayer. Go to www.taxhelponline.com for more details.

About the Author

FOR OVER THREE DECADES, DAN PILLA has been the nation's leader in taxpayers' rights defense and IRS abuse prevention and cure. Regarded as one of the country's premiere experts in IRS procedures and general financial problems resolution techniques, he has helped hundreds of thousands of citizens solve personal and business tax and financial problems they thought might never be solved.

As the author of fourteen books, dozens of research reports and hundreds of articles, Dan's work is regularly featured on radio and television as well as in major newspapers, leading magazines and trade publications nationwide. Dan is a frequent guest on numerous talk radio programs where he is heard by millions of people each year. His fast-paced interviews provide hard-hitting answers to even the toughest questions. His many media appearances include CNN, CBS, CBN, CNBC, Fox News, C-SPAN, the CBS Radio Network, the USA Radio Network and many others. His books have been recommended by prominent magazines and financial publications such as Money, Family Circle, Investor's Business Daily and more. Dan has written or contributed to major articles for Reader's Digest, National Review, Reason, USA Today Magazine and others. The Associated Press once commented that "Dan Pilla probably knows more about the IRS than the commissioner." The Wall Street Journal ranked his book, The IRS Problem Solver, as the number one tax book in America.

Dan was a consultant to the National Commission on Restructuring the IRS. He works with numerous public policy research institutes and presented testimony to Congress on several occasions. His testimony to the Senate Finance Committee blew the lid off IRS abuse and led to many new taxpayers' rights and protections. Dan is admitted to practice before the United States Tax Court and is enrolled to practice before the IRS.

Other Dan Pilla Books and Services

A Complete Package of Defense Materials

The following materials by Daniel J. Pilla comprise the most complete and effective package of IRS defense materials available in America.

The Tax Amnesty Package – How to Get Tax Amnesty is Dan's all-time best-selling book with more than 220,000 copies in print. This package consists of Dan's book, plus his all-new Tax Amnesty Supplement, a Forms Kit and Special Report – indispensable for anyone facing tax debts. Learn to stop wage and bank levies, remove tax liens, prevent property seizures and how to negotiate with the IRS for pennies on the dollar.

The IRS Problem Solver Package – Use this material to cancel penalties and interest—even bogus IRS notices. Plus, Dan helps with dozens of other notices and letters that are wrong, incomplete or incomprehensible. Keep a small IRS problem from growing. Ranked by the Wall Street Journal as the number 1 tax book in America, the package comes with the Problem Solver book, a 26-page workbook and five 1-hour CDs.

How to Eliminate Taxes on Debt Forgiveness – This book deals head-on with America's financial crisis. Since 2008, there've been millions of bankruptcies, home foreclosures, failed businesses and lost jobs. Things get worse when the IRS claims you had "income" from debt forgiveness. Learn how to solve all tax problems related to debt forgiveness. Midwest Book Review says the book is "informed, informative, soundly based on current tax law, and featuring an accompanying CD, is highly recommended…"

How to Double Your Tax Refund – Cut your taxes to their lowest legal level. Learn how to get your tax refund in every paycheck and keep from overpaying. Bonus materials include commonly overlooked deductions and how to set up a solid record-keeping system.

Taxpayers' Ultimate Defense Manual – Featuring nine devastating weapons against IRS abuse. This massive manual shows you how to use the United States Tax Court and how to get a refund of overpaid taxes. Special material includes innocent spouse issues and recovering wrongfully seized property.

Tax Solutions Network – If you suffer with taxes you can't pay become a member of Dan's Tax Solutions Network. Dan does a personal evaluation, creates a step-by-step plan to solve your problem and provides personal consultation to lead you to the solution. Get professional help without the high cost of direct representation.

Free Special Reports – As a part of Dan's continuing commitment to provide the best information on tax compliance and problems resolution, he offers a number of free special reports to help you understand your obligations and avoid problems. From our web site home page, click on "resources and publications," then click on "research reports."

"There's no such thing as a hopeless tax case."

-- Daniel J. Pilla

1-800-346-6829

www.taxhelponline.com

Index